ASTRIDE
TWO
WORLDS

Teodor Gloerabui

ASTRIDE
TWO
WORLDS

Autobiography

Teodor Gherasim M. Sc. Ph.D.

L.D. Press
16470 S.W. Wood Pl.
Tigard, OR 97224
United States of America
First Edition
Cover by Alden Graphics

ASTRIDE TWO WORLDS

Autobiography

Teodor Gherasim M. Sc. Ph.D.

L.D. Press
16470 S.W. Wood Pl.
Tigard, OR 97224
United States of America
First Edition
Cover by Alden Graphics

Dedicated

To the indomitable spirit of
Romania

and

To its warm, generous,
hardworking,
long suffering people.

Teodor Gherasim, 1960's;

Introduction

It is not easy to write about a man who literally changed one's whole life overnight. He came when the time was right, with a winning smile, a warm embrace, and a heart full of love. He told me of his past life in far-off Romania and how he came to be in America. I was fascinated by his extraordinary background, his courage, his determination and above all his unfailing optimism. In spite of extreme hardships, cruel injustices, and a life of continual struggle against fear and almost insurmountable obstacles, this indomitable human being conquered, and never lost his boyish laughter and happy disposition.

I asked myself from whence came such a man. There are not too many like him and I have traveled the world over. Eventually I found out that this unique and truly superb character hailed from a tiny village far away on the eastern side of the majestic Carpathians. It was only fitting that such an enchanting region should produce this outstanding person. And, I was, at once, reminded of another unique and glorious man who, like my beloved husband, was born of and nurtured by the people of the soil in a quiet out of the way place 'far from the deafening crowds' - Michael Collins, the greatest leader Ireland ever knew.

I liken Teodor Gherasim to my favorite Irish hero because although he never led a nation out of bondage, or fired a shot even in self-defense, yet, he did, in his own determined way, fight against evil and slavery in the form of the Communist doctrine and an oppressive regime. During his darkest hours in the dungeons of Romania's horrific prisons, he never lost his courage or faith in God. And never in the thirty years of his working life in that country did he follow the dictates or subscribe to that Atheistic ideology.

He walked shoulder to shoulder with men like himself - men of character, fortitude, intelligence, and for the most part men of learning. Educated men or those aspiring to knowledge and all that is noble in this life. And although many of his companions did not survive the hellish ordeal of the Communist prison, Teodor emerged stronger, even more determined to achieve, to reach his highest potential despite the danger and the hardships that were inevitable.

"The truest joy comes from seriousness," words written on the walls of Leipzig's Gewandhaus, could well be attributed to Teodor, for certainly he was and is a serious man and has always found his greatest pleasure in study, in learning. But his aspirations were never mundane; on the contrary he reached for the stars. Seeking the best, the loftiest in art, music, literature, and philosophy. He would fill his mind and soul with the finest this world has to offer.

A man of moral character and integrity. Honest, upright, and outspoken, I often wonder how he managed to survive in Communist Romania. A man of extreme sensitivity, gentle; his tears flow freely and his laughter erupts in spontaneous outbursts. He delights, with a child's glee, in playing a joke and recoils in deep pain over a sharp word. He is a religious man, committed to his faith, sincere, unwavering in his belief and trust in God.

I am, indeed, fortunate to have met and married this great man and it is with humility that I have tried to record and help translate some of the events that make up his life's story. May those who read this sketch - for it is not by any means a full portrait - be moved to strive for the best, to do and dare all while they have life and strength.

Louise Gherasim
February 2000

Dr. Teodore Gherasim officially nominated as International Man of the Year 2000-2001

Dear Dr. Gherasim
YOUR NOMINATION AS INTERNATIONAL MAN OF THE YEAR

The International Biographical Center of Cambridge, England is delighted to confirm your nomination as an **International Man of the Year** for 2000/2001. This prestigious award - issued by way of a **warrant of Proclamation** - will be made available to only a few illustrious individuals whose achievements and leadership stand out in the Internation Community.

Nominaton as an **International Man of the Year** is made by the Editorial and Advisory Boards of the International Biographical Center and this year I have had the pleasure of chairing the selection committees. Tens of thousands of biographies are reviewed each year by the Boards and from these only a handful are selected for this unique honour. Congratulations on being one of these so nominated.

The International Biographical Center prides itself as being one of the leading biographical reference book publishers in the world with more than 20 Who's Who titles in 132 separate editions. Among these titles, some of which have been established for more thatn 50 years, are **International Who's Who in Music, International Authors and Writers Who's Who, Dictionary of International Biography** and more recently **2000 Outstanding Scientist of the 20th Century** and **Who's Who in Asia and the Pacific Nations.**

This award - as an **International Man of the Year** - is described on the accompanying application form. You will see that not only are recipients eligible for an appealing **Warrant of Proclamation** but can also obtain an attractive **Medal of Honor** so that you may, with justifiable pride, proclaim your nomination as **International Man of the Year**. I am sure you will be excited to accept this honour.

Sincerely

NISHOLAS LAW
Director General

International Biographical Center is an imprint of Melrose Press Ltd. whose offices are at St Thomas Place, Ely, Cambridgeshire CB7 4CG, England. Registered in England number 965274

V

Chapter 1

Bucovina Sanctuary of Romanian Culture and History

"Sweet Bucovina,
Joyful garden,
Of fruitful groves
And noble youth." [1]

The word Bucovina means Beech Forest and describes a triangle of land in northeast Romania. The name was first used in 1392 by Musat Roman I and confined to the area around Baia, Siret, and Suceava.[2] Before this time, however, that same area was called Arboroasa - arbor of fruit trees.

Bucovina today stretches from the Dniester River in the north to Vatra Dornei in the southwest. From there it sweeps southeastward to Suceava and then north through Siret, Cernauti, and Cernauca back to the Dniester. It was known in ancient times as Upper Moldavia.

It is a land of great beauty. Greens: soft and varied, from the lush meadows and rich fields of the valleys to the dark hues of the lofty pines in the Carpathians.

As Mihai Eminescu writes: "Bucovina is the heaven of Moldavia." [3] And Ion Petrovici describes its richness as "a golden font." [4]

It is a place of great natural beauty, that is quite obvious, but it is also a land which is rich historically and culturally.

Historically, Bucovina has always been one of the frontier areas defending Romania and, in fact, central Europe from invading hordes from the East. As far back as Dragos 1339-1354, the kings of the region fought off the invaders. First came the Tartars whom Bogdan Voda I, 1359-1364 vanquished. He, it was who erected what today is the oldest church in the area, the Bogdana Church of Radauti.

Each succeeding generation had its own enemy with which to cope. The Turks plagued Latcu Voda I 1364-1372 and those who came after him until the indomitable King Stefan the Great, 1457-1504 whose extraordinary exploits gained for him the title of "Athlete of Christ".

Each monarch fought in turn, Tartars, Turks, Mongols, Poles and Slaves. But it was Stefan the Great's destiny to have struck at several of these attackers during his long reign.

However, he and the Romanian people knew that the final battle had not been won. It would be an ongoing war. Thus, Delavrancea in his play entitled *Sunrise* attributes the following words to the great monarch. "It is not up to us alone but to those who succeed us as well, to retain the land of Romania." [5]

Culturally, Bucovina benefited during the years 1457-1504 because, each time Stefan won a battle, he erected a church which invariably meant a monastery. Thus the towns of Baia, Radauti and Siret which existed even before the feudal Moldavian state was set up in the latter part of the 13th century, gained treasures which exist to this day.

Of these monasteries, those of Putna, Sucevita, Arbore, Voronet, Dragomirna, and Moldovita are probably the most famous.

Putna, founded in 1466, was to become the most important religious, cultural, and artistic center in Mediaeval Bucovina.

"As early as 1467, scribes, calligraphers, and miniature painters who had learned their craft under Gavril Urie came from Neamt, to work at the Putna Monastery." [6]

These artists, as well as embroiderers, icon makers, weavers, silversmiths, sculptors in wood and bookbinders worked in the quiet atmosphere leaving priceless treasures which are Romania's pride in our time.

"Attached to the monastery was a residence for the king. Outer walls and a defense tower were also built making it one of the strongest defense outposts of central Europe as well as a bastion of learning and culture."

Perhaps the most outstanding features of these and the other monasteries built about the time of King Stefan the Great, are the murals both inside and outside the churches.

Andre Graber, a brilliant researcher, wrote in 1962 concerning these marvels. "Seen from the outside, each church is a delightful decor item which should be admired in its setting of green and white - the green of the lawn on which the church stands, the white of the building and of the monastery annexes that form a rectangular enclosure around it. At the same time these painted facades, with their personages and scenes, make up an illustrated book open at all its pages." [7]

King Stefan the Great, was succeeded by his brilliant son, Petru Rares, in 1527. He was an energetic ruler as well as a lover of art and a scholar. He travelled widely in western Europe and with his training contributed greatly to the building of new monasteries in Probota, Humor, and Moldovita.

His age was remarkable for its cultural dynamism. New decorative elements in architecture were added to those of the previous age, but it was in painting that Petru Rares' age was to excel, producing "an important chapter of Romanian art of outstanding originality." [8]

Despite the harsh climate, they remain, to this day, a multicolored testament to the artists who executed these marvels. Depicting, for the most part, biblical scenes, they represent the beliefs and teachings of the Christian church and are a proud reminder of Bucovina's long Christian tradition.

In the 15th Century, the monastery in Putna had also a famous school where grammar, rhetoric, and logic were taught. One of its greatest teachers was Eustatie. Others noted for their excellence down through the centuries were: Iacob Putneanu (1717-1778), Vartolomeu Mazareanu (1720-1790) and Clipa Gherasim (1760-1826).

Iacob Putneanu whose innovative teachings on promoting the Romanian language and preserving the traditions of the principality of Bucovina were exemplified in philosophical statements such as: "The beginning of wisdom is knowledge; the value of learning is the cornerstone of life." And in times of invasion and moral decay, his words were even more pregnant. "No one will offer you redress in these decadent times, learning alone will afford you the sweet smelling flower which will soothe your wounds." Finally, his words "A man without learning is like a dried and withered tree," hold true for all time and all people.

Clipa Gherasim, who studied in Putna University, Iasi and Leipzig was responsible for translating the works of Voltaire and animated by the same principles as Putneanu, made copious copies of German school books to be used in Bucovina. [9]

During the following centuries, Bucovina passed from one invader to another but none succeeded in conquering the native population. A popular Romanian proverb describes this phenomonen: "The water passes, but the stones remain."

The Turks tried for two centuries to establish a stronghold on Bucovinan soil but were unsuccessful.

In 1774, the forces of the Austrian Empire occupied the entire area and remained until 1918.

This occupation was a dastardly affair set up between Turkey, Russia, and Austria. The Austrians maintained that a corridor between Poland and Hungary was "necessary" because these countries were, at the time, under Austrian rule.

The population of Bucovina was then more than 90% Romanian. But, with the coming of the Austrians, the situation was gradually and systematically changed. Lavish grants of land and privileges [10] were offered to those of the Jewish, Polish, Austrian, Hungarian and Ukrainian races to settle in that part of the country. The plantation of Bucovina was to be "a model" of interracial integration. But, as is usual in such cases, the native Romanian population was constantly pressured and subjugated.

In 1775, the Romanians in Bucovina numbered 90.8% of the population. After only 135 years, the number had decreased to 34.3% while during this same period, the intrusive peoples such as the Ukrainians had increased from 2.6% to 37.9 and those of the Jewish race grew from 0.6% to 12.8%. [11]

It is now known that the Austrian Empire set up a historical process whereby the Ukrainian and Bucovinian peoples would be subjected and governed by the Austrians and later by the Russians. [12]

Despite the oppression of the native people under the Austrian regime, an elite circle of intellectuals who had their center in Cernauti emerged at the beginning of the 19th century. Among them were the historians, philosophers, and writers such as: Eudoxiu Hurmuzachi and his family of four sons, Aron Pumnul, I.G. Sbiera, Iancu Flondor, Ion Nistor, and Vasile Gherasim. In the arts, the names of Mihai Eminescu, poet, Ciprian Porumbescu, composer, and George Enescu, composer, virtuoso violinist and conductor of world wide renown, as well as others, appear.

On November 28, 1918 after W.W. I, Bucovina was reunited with the motherland, Romania. For twenty-two years the province enjoyed peace and prosperity under the Monarchy.

In 1940, following the Treaty between Molotov and Ribbentrop, Bucovina was divided into two parts. The northern section was occupied by the Red Army under the pretext that a corridor was "necessary" to gain access to central Europe. In reality, it was to open a door for Communist activities and influence in neighboring areas.

So the process begun by Austria was, in fact, realized and brought to completion. The Ukrainians were now in possession of Northern Bucovina.

Doina

From Tisa to the Nistru's tide
All Roumania's people cried
That they could no longer stir
For the rabbled foreigner.
From Hotin down to the sea
Rides the Muscal cavalry;
From the sea back to Hotin
Nothing but their host is seen;
While from Dorna to Boian
Seems the plague has spread its ban;
Leaving on our land a scar
That you scarcely know it more.
Up the mountains down the dale,
Have our foes flung far their trail.

From Sacele to Satmar
Only foreign lords there are;
While Roumanians one and all
Like the crab must backward crawl.
And reversed is everything:
Spring for them is no more spring,
Summer is no longer summer,
They, at home, the foreign comer.
From Turnu up to Dorohoi
Does the alien horde deploy
And our fertile fields enjoy.
With their rumbling trains they come
Making all our voices dumb,
And our birds so much affray
That in haste they fly away.
Nothing now but withered thorn
Does the Christian's hearth adorn.
And the smiling earth they smother;
Forest - good Roumanian brother -
You too bend before their tide,
And the very springs they've dried.
Sad is this our countryside... [13]

In 1941, the Romanian army under the command of General Ion Antonescu reconquered Northern Bucovina and once more united it with Romania. For four years the province remained under Romanian administration. Then after the fall of Stalingrad, the battlefront was pushed back to a new position to the east bank of the Dneister. In 1944, the Russian Foreign Minister, Mr. Molotov, declared that if Romania ceased fighting against the U.S.S.R., he would guarantee that no land would be occupied by Russian troops and there would be no involvement in Romanian affairs. Once more Romania was deceived - lied to, and eventually sacrificed.

Shortly after this declaration, Russian troops crossed the Dneister and occupied the same territory they had vacated in 1941.

After the defeat of Hitler, the Red Army took over the whole country of Romania and installed a Communist Regime in Bucharest. For 50 years the country was ravaged, plundered, and raped by these foreign intruders.

Communist Atrocities in Romania

Many brave men and women lost their lives fighting against the injustices and intolerable conditions brought about by the Communist takeover.

In Northern Bucovina, thousands of men, women, and children, whole families, were deported to Siberia, to the Urals, or to the far off borders of China. Those from Southern Bucovina were sent to the Black Sea area to be worked to death building useless canals.

Anita Nandris-Cudla writes of her experiences in Omsc from '41 to '61. She was aroused in the middle of the night from sleep, separated from her husband and with her three small children was rudely herded into a wagon and carried to the railway station. After a day's delay during which neither she nor her children were given food or water, they were transported on the long weary journey of thousands of miles to the tiny hamlet of Omsc above the Artic circle.

In order to survive unbearable conditions, she was obliged to clean the skins of the wild Tundra animals. There was no privacy in the underground make-shift lodge in which they were forced to live. The space was limited and of necessity unsanitary - fleas and lice were their constant companions; many occupants had T.B. or typhus while others had hepatitis or a variety of the many other contagious diseases.

In order to protect her children and to ensure their survival, Anita went into the forest nearby and collected whatever wild berries or roots she could find thus nourishing their young bodies with the only vitamin-rich foods available.

Twice, she, herself, was found unconscious, her life despaired of, but by sheer will-power and determination to see that her children would grow to manhood, she overcame typhus and tuberculosis.

She wove yarn from the hair of animals and made clothes during her few free moments after the communal work. By this means she was able to barter for extra food or other necessities.

Through her devotion to her children and her strong belief in God, Anita was able to endure unspeakable hardships and privations for almost twenty years.

With the take-over of Krutchev some relaxing of political tensions occurred and some injustices righted. Anita sent her three boys to Moscow to try to reverse the decision of their unjust deportation. After months of appealing to one court after another, they eventually were able to plead their case and were given permission to return to their home in Romania - but at what a price! Her husband had died in a concentration camp, her home was occupied by strangers of Russian origin. But Anita had survived; she had overcome all obstacles, and, though an illiterate peasant woman, at the end of her life set down in writing her story so that the world and posterity would know what the Romanian people, those like herself, - honest, hardworking and innocent of any wrongdoing, had endured at the hands of the Communists.

Another account given by Ion Posteuca who, when only thirteen years old, was among the hundreds transported by train during the night from Tereblecea, in north eastern Romania.

"While my family and those others marked for deportation waited in the train station, we were surrounded by soldiers. A train of cattle carts pulled alongside. We were roughly and savagely ushered on board. The wagon into which we were packed had only one barred window.

"I don't remember how many were finally forced into the space but I know there wasn't enough room for all to sit down on the floor. Eventually, people took turns, some stood while others sat. The situation was bad enough during the night and early morning but when the sun was hot towards the middle of the day and into the afternoon, we believed we would all suffocate. But worst of all was the thirst that overcame everyone. So intense was this suffering that when the train stopped we beat on the sides of the wagon and pleaded for water. In response to our cries the soldiers cursed us but did not try to alleviate our terrible distress.

"Our agonies were further multiplied when a few days later we were detained in a railway station for a whole day because another train had priority to move ahead.

"After three weeks of cruel sufferings, our train halted in a desert area. There was nothing to be seen for miles. We were ordered to evacuate the filthy wagons. It is difficult to describe the condition of the people as they descended from the cattle carts to the dusty ground below - ghosts, specters, merely skin and bones, gaunt sickly faces and bloodshot eyes.

"Our greatest joy at that moment was to discover that not too far off there appeared to be an area of marsh land. No force on earth could have stopped the onslaught in the direction of that water-sodden patch.

"Nobody knew where we were until on the horizon we saw a caravan of camels. Then we realized we were in Kazakhstan.

"For a day and a night we were forced to walk. Finally we came upon a makeshift mud hut. This was where the collective farm was set up and in this place we were expected to work from early morning until late in the evening. But first we had to clean out the pigsty that was to be our home. It was infested with bees, mice, and rats.

"After three days a ration of food arrived, but we weren't allowed to wait for it to be unloaded. We had to begin work at once, for at that time all the male inhabitants were away fighting at the front so the heavy work was allotted to us - 'the enemy of the people'."

Continuing to recount his horrific story, Mr. Posteuca then describes how those who harvested the grain received 15-30 kilograms for their own use but it was to last for one year.

"When winter came a new scourge was visited on the miserable deportees - fierce cold weather plagued them for months on end. There was no fireplace for the ten families who were crowded together in that stinking shelter. The only means they had of cooking their scant meals of cereal was to build a fire in the middle of the floor. Later a stove was improvised. As the days passed, the inhuman conditions became more unbearable - hunger, cold - blizzards, frosts and the seemingly never-ceasing, howling winds from the steppes. The unhealthy and unsanitary conditions became too much especially for the old people.

"After an extremely difficult winter, spring eventually arrived. The unfortunate families were starving. All that was left to eat were the leftover potatoes from the previous Fall."

In his own words the young boy of thirteen tells his heartbreaking story. "I was now old enough to go on the tractor brigade. This turned out to be my salvation. I was literally saved from the jaws of death by doing that kind of work, for I was given grain and a kilogram of milk. But others were not so lucky. When the time came to harvest the crops many were too weak to work. Their emaciated bodies refused to move.

"After all the hard work and when the harvest was secure, we were only allowed to keep one kilogram for every month we worked and with that small supply we began our second winter.

"During that winter of Stalinist hell our family experienced more tragedy. My oldest brother became sick with typhus. At the last moment of his life, he asked me for a small piece of bread. I would have given all the gold in the world to be able to give him his last wish but that was impossible. His dying word was 'bread'.

"I buried his beloved body like a pagan. In that terrible time, I didn't even have a bit of candle to burn at his graveside. I covered his poor skeletal frame with a few rags; there was no such thing as a coffin. Only a handful of stones marked his last resting place there on the steppes of Kazakhstan.

"From that moment on, I resolved to do all I could for the other members of my family who were still alive. Unfortunately, soon after my mother became ill. I tried to smuggle some grain to her for I knew she was starving but on the way to our hut I fell asleep and my intentions were discovered by one of the guards. I was badly beaten and returned to my work station where I remained until war was declared against Russia. In the confusion that followed my family and I escaped and found our way home to beautiful Romania once more."

After the division of Bucovina in March 1941 a rumor was circulated one night throughout the northern section of the province.

Word reached the area that families who wished to vacate their homes and be repatriated in the southern sector would be allowed to do so. This rumor was spread abroad by the Bolshevik authorities in order to find out who would avail of the so-called evacuation policy.

The little village of Fantana Alba situated in the valley carved out by the Suceava River on the Varnita Plain had been the spot chosen by the officers of the Red Army for the massacre of 10,000 innocent people. Men, women and children, the old as well as the very young, entire families desiring only freedom were mowed down in cold blood. This place was chosen because it represented the new border established by the Bolsheviks during their occupation of North Bucovina.

Thousands of people also applied for repatriation in the town of Adancata. For three days they waited, sleeping wherever they could in order to receive their papers. After the third day when nothing happened, they organized and marched to the church in Suceveni and taking the banners and icons returned to Fantana Alba which was the closest point to the border. There, soldiers with drawn guns confronted them.

The massacre took place on April 1, 1941. The people were lined up in rows facing Romania and told to await the special decision from Stalin, himself, regarding their fate. When the order finally arrived, peaceful, innocent people, men, women, and children were fired upon and thousands brutally massacred. Those who escaped were hunted down and either imprisoned or deported, while those who were wounded remained where they had fallen unattended.

"Finally, three days later some peasants were forced to bury the mangled bodies in a common grave. The dead as well as those still breathing were thrown in together.

"I alone survived," said Georghi Ursache, "when my mother who was carrying me on her back in a knapsack received a bullet through her heart. The man who saved my life was soon deported and I never saw him again."

The atrocities committed and the murder of so many innocent civilians marked the beginning of the genocide ordered by Stalin in the occupation of Northern Buvcovina. The dark night of Communist Atrocities in Romania had indeed begun. [14]

The officer in command who received and executed the order from Moscow is still alive. Each year he attends a memorial service to honor those thousands whose voices continue to cry out from their mass graves. He, as well as others who were present at the murders, talk to each other of the nightmares they have endured ever since that fateful day so many years ago.

Witnessing this ceremony, Professor Elena Bodale now living in Portland, has described the officer mentioned above as being a tormented man. "For the last fifty-six years he has had no peace. His tortured brain and his uneasy conscience have continually plagued him as he daily relives the scene." She observed that before he left the cemetery, he took a piece of wood from one of the humble crosses "hoping, no doubt, to mollify the specters who haunt him day and night as he continues to hear the cries of the dying thousands from Fantana Alba."

This crime against humanity was not an isolated incident but followed by periodic purges of the villages surrounding Fantana Alba.

In Patrautii de Jos, for example, on June 13, 1941, sixteen men were shot and twenty-one were arrested and deported. Sixty-two were taken during the night from their homes and later were also deported to Siberia and Kazakhstan. Thirty-two were forced to fight with the Red Army at the front where they were eventually killed. Later, seven more men were rounded up and sent off to Karelia.

As the years passed, this same village suffered continuous and similar injustices.

Recent statistics have revealed that the number of persons deported from Northern Bucovina in one night alone - June 13, 1941, was as many as thirteen thousand. Add to these figures the ten thousand who were killed in Fantana Alba and the population of Bucovina was drastically reduced in a short period of time. [15]

After the fall of the Communist Empire, 1989, northern Bucovina instead of being returned to the Motherland, was automatically annexed to the Ukraine, even though the Molotov-Ribbentrop Treaty was declared null and void by Russia. To this day it remains in Ukranian hands.

Meanwhile, the people of Bucovina cry out to their so-called friends in America. "Why did you sell us so cheaply? We waited. We waited for you for over 50 years. For you, the most powerful nation on earth, to reunite us with our homeland. Do we wait in vain?"

It is a paradox, even today, that a powerful country such as the U.S.A. should, at such a critical period in the history of mankind, have allowed a dying man, President Franklin Delano Roosevelt, to attend the Yalta Conference and thus play into the hands of the tyrant, Stalin.

The weak, spineless, Mr. Chamberlin may have signed away the Sudetenland, Poland, and Czechoslovakia but the moribund American President with Mr. Churchill gave away half of Europe to their erstwhile allies.

Happily for Germany, her eastern section was returned after 1989 but what of Romania's north-eastern section?

What are the ambitions of the Ukraine today? Does she wish to become an empire by stealing from her neighbors the lands that are rightfully theirs for hundreds of years. It is time she reconsider the lawful claims Romania has on Bucovina and return it to its rightful place on the map of Europe.

At the Prague Conference in 1990 under the leadership of the International Association for Democracy and Independence the question was asked by Nicolae Lupan regarding the unification of Bucovina with Romania.

"Since we have been in Bucovina for the last 2000 years and the Russians there only since 1940, why delay returning the territory?"

The answer was: "We can return the South of Bessarabia or Odessa but North Bucovina only over our dead bodies."

"Why over your dead bodies?"

"Because Bucovina is now Russianized," came the decisive answer.

This answer, as everyone knows, is not accurate. The towns and cities may have in recent years seen a large increase in the Russian speaking population but the peasants and other residents of the countryside still remain Romanian, speak the language, and follow the customs and traditions of their native country.

Romania's long history has been a continuous blood-letting. "We were born in a tempest, and we grew up in a blizzard. Frontier people," wrote Mircea Eliade, "we fought and died for all." [16]

Even today, in the late 1990's the Romanian people of North Bucovina live under constant strain. Although their Russian neighbors are a minority, they remain a thorn in the side of the native inhabitants.

And, if the living are uneasy, the dead have received no better treatment. In the cemetery of Cernauti, for instance, several famous Romanian personalities have been buried. These noted and revered persons: Aron Pumnul, Aglaei, sister of Eminescu, Professor Vasile Gherasim, Dimitrie Dan and Gh. Hurmuzache and others whose graves were, at one time, venerated are now desecrated, denegrated or have disappeared completely. In fact, there are very few tombs left that are dedicated to the great names of Romania's past. Even the works of art that once adorned these grave-sites have been pillaged, destroyed or vandalized. [17]

Finally, the exiled Romanian poet, V. Posteuca in his poem entitled, *Vesela Gradina*, speaking of Bucovina says:

> "De cand rusii te pradara
> N'avem soare nici odihna
> Fara tine n'avem tara
> Bucovina, Bucovina."
> "From the Russian plunderer
> We have neither sunrise nor rest
> Without you, we have no land,
> Bucovina, Bucovina!"

Chapter 2

Granicesti - Home Sweet Home

Over the hill the moon ascends her fiery crown
of crimson deep,
Staining the ancient forest red, and the lonely
castle keep,
And staining red the tumbling waves that from
a murmuring fountain well,
While down the sweeping valley rolls the solemn
music of a bell.

Mihai Eminescu -Calin

G ranicesti, the word means border. In the time of Alexander, the grandfather of Stefan the Great, fifty villages were under the administration of the bishop of Suceava. By the time of Stefan the Great 1457-1504 forty-four villages each with its own priest was placed under the bishop of Radauti and the remaining six were under the jurisdiction of the bishop of Cernauti. With this reorganization, the village of Granicesti, at the time known a Cranicesti was number thirty and became part of the dioceses of Radauti.

When Stefan the Great died the monastery of Solca was built on land situated between Radauti and Suceava. To guard the outlying areas against intruders, tracts of land were given by the monks to the peasants in return for their protection. Thus the modern village of Granicesti was founded.

During the reign of Stefan Tomsa the first church was erected with the help of the monks from the Solca monastery. It was dedicated on November 8, 1615, the feast of the archangels Michael and Gabriel.

Today the area boasts a population of about 6,000 inhabitants including the surrounding hamlets. The village is situated on a plain on the eastern side of the Carpathian mountains, while the main highway running north to Poland and south to Bucharest divides the village.

The face of Granicesti changes with the changing seasons. In winter it is blanketed with snow, at times as much as two meters deep. The wind, "Crivat" howls across the steppes of the Ukraine and freezes everything for at least three months. But when Spring comes the land bursts forth into a riot of color and with the warmer weather, the hearts of young and old rejoice. The brightly colored native costumes are a familiar sight in church and on festive occasions, particularly at Easter time. Summer brings long days and hot weather. Again the wind from the East blows with unfriendly storms of dust and hot air. Autumn is short, a time of haste and long hours of work. The crops must be harvested and preparations made for the coming winter.

Among the oldest families in the village are the Gherasims, the Morosans, the Tibus, Clipas, and Moldovicians. My ancestors - the Gherasims, gave a gift of land for a new church and cemetery. In 1758 Teodor Gherasim and Teodor Ungurean built this church to accommodate the growing population.

Entering the village from the north, there are six or seven houses on the right before the Mardare Gherasim home is reached. Then there are, at least, twelve houses one after another belonging to Gherasim family members.

The Gherasim name derives from the Greek meaning longlived and the family first came to the Granicesti area before 1615, from Transylvania.

Because of his wounds in a heroic stand against the Turks, my great-grandfather "Buzatu" was given all the land around the village by his grateful monarch, Stefan the Great. It was from this family that my father, Mardare, eventually descended.

My grandfather Teodor Gherasim married Domnica Clipa when she was eighteen. She was tall and proportionally well built with dark brown eyes and fair skin, a full mouth and high cheek bones. Upon their wedding day, they received twenty-five hectares of land, cattle, horses, and sheep. In those days, this meant they started their new life very well off. And, in time, ten more hectares were added to their property.

Grandfather had nine children, seven boys and two girls. Father, whose name was Mardare, was the sixth child. He was intelligent, ambitious, and hardworking. His greatest desire was to go to school to pursue a higher education. Having finished elementary school in Granicesti, he started high school in Siret. But his father and mother needed his help on the farm and he was obliged to leave. This was the first great mistake of his life and one which he would always regret. "Had I continued to go to school, I would have become a person of importance but I lost the chance," he often said to me.

During the years 1915 to 1916 the Russians occupied the entire area of Bucuvina to the Transylvanian border. It was at this time that twelve soldiers were billeted for eight months in my grandfather's house. This intrusion into and total disregard for the privacy and daily lives of the family had only one purpose, and this was to observe the enemy, the Austro-Hungarian army which was quartered not many kilometers away.

During their stay, the Russians took everything, all they could lay their hands on: animals, carts, food supplies, fuel, and clothing. My grandfather was forced to give up four horses, two cows, and several sheep. To protect and provide for his family, he had a deep trench dug near the house. In it he hid two horses and two cows for several months. Father was put in charge. It was his duty to clean and feed the animals. Each evening, under cover of darkness, he was supposed to fulfill this task. Unfortunately, he was careless one evening and the trench was discovered. For this grave deception, grandfather was to be imprisoned and fined. Father, who knew Russian, went to the Sergeant in charge and tried to explain. Meanwhile, the animals were released from the trench into the daylight. But having spent so much time in complete darkness, they were blinded by the light of day and couldn't move. The officer seeing that they were obviously blind, considered them useless for transportation and dropped the charges against my grandfather.

When he was eighteen, father was obliged, like all his peers, to serve two years in the Austro-Hungarian army. At that time, 1916, Transylvania and Bucovina were under the rule of Franz Joseph, the Emperor. Due to his bravery and native intelligence, my father soon rose in the ranks to the position of sergeant.

He describes his experiences in detail. "The recruitment office was situated in Cernauti. After five weeks of intensive training, I was sent to Dolina, Poland where I was assigned to an Artillary Unit and given warfare training. At this barracks, living conditions were extremely crude and food was scarce. So scarce, in fact, that one kilogram of bread was divided among twelve men every other day. There were 25,000 men training under these conditions.

"It was a period of intense instruction, physical and intellectual. Lessons in Russian, Polish, and German were mandatory. I was assigned to Artillary Unit #123 which was to operate in Lumbach, Austria. From there, however, I was transferred to northern Italy and after five days World War I ended. Luckily, I was able to catch a train with wounded soldiers leaving for Cernauti. But on the journey, which took four days there was absolutely nothing to eat or drink. Many did not survive. Just before the Romanian border, the train needed coal and water. When it came to a halt, the able-bodied sought food. Eventually, a man with a pig was persuaded to sell his animal. On that occasion, I ate three portions with some potatoes. This food probably saved my life."

It was late in the year 1919 when father finally arrived home to find that his two older brothers, who had also served in the Austro-Hungarian Army, had preceded him.

There was general rejoicing upon his return, not only because the family was reunited but because their beloved Bucovina, after 144 years of occupation by the Austro-Hungarian Empire, 1774-1918, had also been reunited to the Motherland. My father was scarcely home when, this time, his own country now united, demanded his services. In 1920, he was recruited and had to report to the military center, in Cernauti. For the next five years, he served in the army again gaining the rank of sergeant during that time.

Before he was recruited, he was in love with Elisabeta Morosan. They were engaged to be married. Unfortunately, for Mardare, Ion Chitan, a neighbor, had returned from America a rich man. He bought land, animals, and machinery, and built a big house. It was not difficult for him to persuade Elisabeta's father that he was the right man for his beautiful daughter.

They were married soon after. It was the year 1924.

My father, upon hearing this, immediately borrowed a horse, a revolver, and some bullets, and with a few days leave, he proceeded to gallop, posthaste, to Granicesti approximately 60 kilometers away. As night fell, a storm arose. The going was rough. Suddenly, a wild animal sprang from the ditch in front of the tired horse. It immediately took fright and reared on its hind legs tossing my father onto the side of the road. He was knocked unconscious and remained in that condition, until a farmer, who was passing by, lifted him into his cart and took him to his home.

For several days, he remained with the farmer's family who cared for him and to whom he probably owed his life. During his convalescence, the farmer's wife persuaded him to return to barracks, to forget Elisabeta, and to get on with his life. But my father was not one to forget so easily. He resolved to get even with Elisabeta's father. As it happened, Elisabeta had a younger sister. Her name was Ecaterina. She was only thirteen.

> *"Although the world would call me free*
> *Each year the more her slave am I,*
> *For in her very way to be*
> *There's I don't know what, I don't know why.*
> *Already from the day we met*
> *Was my freedom mortal shot?*
> *She's but a girl as they, and yet*
> *There's something more, I don't know what."* [1]

Mardare returned to his unit and, not long after, he was called to his superior's office.

"You have a very good record, Sergeant Gherasim. Your educational background is good and with some more training you might follow a successful military career."

My father was delighted and about to accept the offer when he received a letter from home.

For the second time in his life the intervention of his parents, in his choice of career, caused him much heartbreak. Again he was asked to come home. His father even went so far as to promise to build him a modern house if he were to return.

Mardare felt he had no other option but to accede to his parents' wish. So a few months later, in January 1925 he was released from his duties in the army. He returned home and tried to apply himself to the work on the farm. But his heart was broken. He was embittered toward Gheorghe Morosan, Elisabeta's father and now his own parents stood in his way, denying him the security of a military profession.

As Ecaterina was too young to get married, Mardare decided to bide his time.

While awaiting an opportune moment and Ecaterina's growing up, Mardare made sure to be present at all the local dances. He would keep his eye on the youthful, vivacious, young girl. He also made sure he was the one to dance with her as often as possible.

It was during these innocent moments that Ecaterina and Mardare made their plans. They would wait two years, till the day Ecaterina would be fifteen.

> *"And if the branches tap my pane*
> *And the poplars whisper nightly.*
> *It is to make me dream again*
> *I hold you to me tightly . . .*
> *And if the clouds their tresses part*
> *And does the moon outblaze*
> *It is but to remind my heart*
> *I long for you always."* [2]

Finally, the long awaited day came. Ecaterina was now a beautiful young girl of fifteen. She had blue eyes flecked with hazel, a straight slender nose, and shapely lips, high cheek bones, and her thick, dark brown hair fell well below her waist.

Although, she had only an elementary education, cut short by the war, she was no illiterate country girl. She had a solid religious foundation having spent many hours listening to the local priest, a very learned man. She liked to read and was an excellent seamstress. She had a fine singing voice and was part of the church choir. Her speaking voice was always calm and gentle.

One evening, in the late summer of 1926, Mardare, with four of his brothers, harnessed a cart and drove it close to the Morosan house. He sent a message to Ecaterina.

As soon as she came to the gate, he asked her to go for a drive with him. Walking towards the cart, he asked her to marry him.

"If you don't come with me now, I won't come back again. I've waited two years for you, Ecaterina."

Ecaterina tried to reason with him, "I'm too young and besides, I haven't my father's permission. We will both be in trouble."

But Mardare was determined to have her for his wife.

"Ecaterina, I can't wait. I can't eat, I can't sleep. I can't live without you."

Mardare didn't wait for her to answer either. He took off his cloak, wrapped her in it and gathered her up in his arms. He then carried her to the waiting cart. Immediately, his brother, Procopie, shook the reins and the horses started up suddenly. Vasile, his youngest brother, jumped behind to guard the rear, while Arhip took his place on the opposite side to Mardare. So Ecaterina was surrounded and completely concealed from the view of passersby.

In their haste to be off, the horses, on command, bolted and didn't slacken their speed even when they drew near the Gherasim home but took the gate posts by force and broke the shafts of the cart. By the goodness of God, no one was hurt, not even the animals.

It wasn't long before the local police and most of the Morosan family were knocking at the Gherasim household.

Eventually, after much shouting and some discussion, Ecaterina's voice was heard.

"I love Mardare and I want to be his wife."

In the end, a compromise was reached. Ecaterina was allowed to remain with her love for two weeks. If, at the end of that time, she should change her mind, she was to be permitted to leave. However, Ecaterina's mind was made up and the two were married but without her father's blessing. He withheld the land he had set aside for her and refused to help in the building of their new home.

As a result, Mardare and his young bride began their married life on a difficult bases.

My mother's forebears were the Morosans and were also numbered among the oldest residents of the village. The records show that they were established in the area in 1848.

Gheorghe Morosan, my mother's father, was a well respected man in the community. He was elected Mayor of the village and held the position for 10 years. He was probably the richest farmer in the area owning large tracts of land. He had a big house, which was well furnished. In front was a large courtyard or entryway with two wells supplying fresh water and behind the house, apple, pear, cherry, and plum trees, as well as various types and varieties of berries grew.

Gheorghe married Zanova Clipa in 1895 and had seven children five boys and two girls. In time the boys inherited the land and did very well.

All I can remember about my grandfather, Gheorghe, is the day of his funeral. It was 1932 and my mother, Ecaterina, took me with her to see him for the last time. The house smelled of burning candles. He was dressed in national costume as he lay in the open coffin. As each mourner approached, I noticed he/she placed money on or near the icon resting on his chest. Afterward I asked what this money was for and was told that it was to help grandfather pay the fees necessary to cross the Heavenly borders of which there were nine.

Unfortunately, my maternal grandmother died before I was born. She died during the first world war leaving a fairly young family. Mother was only a baby of three at the time. It was an extremely hard blow for Bunicul (grandfather) Gheorghe to lose his wife at a young age but his oldest daughter, Elisabeta, took charge of the household, and life for him was tolerable until she decided to get married. The household was then in the hands of twelve year old, Ecaterina, until an older brother married and brought his bride to live in the Morosan family home.

My beloved grandfather
Teodor Gherasim, 1936

Chapter 3

Childhood Days

When memory of bygone days
My spirit would detain,
Down long and often trodden ways
I travel the past again.

Mihai Eminescu
- When Memory

I was born in 1929, March 20, to be exact. The American economy hit rock bottom when the stock market crashed that year and the reverberations were felt in my country a few years later in 1933. From the beginning of my life, it seemed that what happened in America had a decided effect on my personal wellbeing.

I was baptized into the Orthodox faith and named Teodor (gift of God) after my grandfather, Teodor Gherasim. A proud man - he was proud of himself, his family, and his achievements. And he had every right to be so. He was one of the richest farmers in the area, and was respected and looked up to by everyone. A man of character, integrity - his word was sacred. He never wronged anyone and always showed respect for those less fortunate.

My first remembrances were of this tall, erect, strikingly handsome man who frequently came to our house. He would take me by the hand and together we went everywhere. From him, I learned to be strong and courageous and never to be intimidated by anyone. For example, when we entered the mayor's or the priest's house, he taught me to pay strict attention to all the questions asked that I might give accurate and precise answers. From him, I acquired a vast knowledge of the workings of nature. He was a fine farmer. *The Call of the Wild* was music to his ears. He knew how to interpret the many and varied songs of the honeybees and it was due to his lessons taught with patience and love, that I owe my lifelong passion - beekeeping. He sensed the needs of the very soil beneath our feet. These needs he explained to me in his own inimitable way, when, one evening in early spring, he took me by the hand and led me through the thick snow to a field planted with winter wheat. "Look," he said as he demonstrated, "This is how a man breaths. If he doesn't breath he dies. So, it is with the earth!" And he proceeded to dig holes in the snow exposing the dark earth to the light of the sun.

As I grew older, I realized that my grandfather had other characteristics. He was imaginative, industrious, and practical. He observed that there were approximately 100 hot days in the Bucovina summer; just sufficient time for the maturation of grapes. The only problem was to find such a grape. Nothing daunted, he travelled the country collecting several different plants. These he cultivated and eventually came up with a hybrid which in time, found its way into every household in the village of Granicesti. It produced a rose wine named "Zibre" by the locals. The word was coined from Zebra because those who imbibed this potent beverage were apt to see the world in many colors rather than in the proverbial rose.

Other crops which he tried to modify to suit the climate included watermelon and a giant corn called "maseaua calului" (Horse's molar), making him the Mendel of Bucovina - Gregor Johann Mendel the Austrian priest and botanist born in Silesia to whom we owe so much, since our modern research is based on and devoted to amplifying his original findings.

Of the six or seven horses in his stable, one was cared for in a very special way. This was Stela, a pure-blooded English mare with a red coat and a white star in the middle of her forehead. Stela had the best of everything. She was exercised daily and trained by one of his seven sons to run in the annual races in Radauti. Despite all the love and care lavished on her, she never once won a race, to my knowledge. Eventually, my grandfather got tired of pampering Stela and renegated her to the rank of the common farm horse. She was the first horse I rode as a small boy and, to this day, I remember the day she was harnessed for the very first time as a work horse. As the rough harness was placed on her shiny red back our eyes met. I detected, at once, that the mare realized, somehow, her life had drastically changed and not for the better. As we stared at each other, I'm sure I saw a tear-drop run down her intelligent face. And my heart was sad.

The only recollection I have of my grandmother, Domnica, is when I was four years old. Upon visiting her one day, I recall, she picked a big juicy golden apple from a bough laden with fruit and gave it to me. I was so happy because we didn't have such beautiful apples in our garden at home. As I bit into it, she said, "Tu esti bucatica rupta din mos-tu," (You are a chip off the old block) meaning my grandfather. I felt big and important and I understood.

In the early part of January, 1934, my grandmother, Domnica, died. That was a very hard winter. The windows were covered with snow; even the houses were buried beneath the heavy snowfall. Because of this, my grandmother's body remained four days in the coffin in a spare room. The winds, coming from Russia across the wide open plains, howled and would not stop. Eventually, the men were forced to dig a path all the way from the house to the cemetery.

I was proud of my ancestors on both sides of my family. I had heard that on the Gherasim side, my great grandfather, George, had been mayor of the village for at least ten years - a position only the most outstanding citizens held. On my mother's side, my great grandfather, Grigorie Morosan was elected three times and was responsible for buying the land in the center of the village where today the church and school stand.

One day when I was about six years old, my mother and father had to go to Radauti to do some shopping. At the time our family had grown to include three children, Veronica who was one year younger than I and Aurel, the baby who was only two.

We were warned to be good and promised candy and cookies when our parents returned. A neighbor was asked to check on us, but I was in charge. For what seemed the longest time, everything went well. We were so good the neighbor lady decided she could leave us alone for a few minutes. As soon as she was out of sight, we immediately needed to have something to drink. It was a warm day and the bucket sitting on top of the well looked inviting.

I ran for my own special cup - cana lui Doru, a gift I had received from my aunt, Elisabeta. Unfortunately, as I tried to fill my cup with cool fresh water from the bucket, it slipped from my hand and went down, down into the well. But luck had not entirely deserted me. When the cup landed on the surface of the water, it didn't sink. Instead, it bobbed about like a little boat on a lake. I watched it fascinated. But then, it occured to me that at any moment it could fill up with water and that would be the end of it. How was I going to get it? It was so far down!

I looked at the interior of the well. Its walls were made of rough stone. If I were careful I could climb down holding onto the rope that lowered the bucket into the well.

My sister, Veronica, was scared when she saw me descend into the blackness and started to cry. But I assured her that I would be all right.

There were a few scarey moments but I was determined to succeed. Having retrieved my cup, I climbed out of the well with the help of the rope none the worst for my adventure. I looked back and for a moment reconsidered the depth and the blackness and felt I really had accomplished a great feat.

However, while Veronica and I were thus occupied, my little brother, Aurel, was also actively engaged all by himself. Alone, he had wandered into the hen house. My mother had several hens which were in the family way with a nest full of eggs. It happened that one or two of these would-be-mothers had left their nests for a few minutes, just long enough for Aurel to get his chubby hands on the eggs. Before I could find him, he had disposed of most of the eggs and was covered from head to foot in yellow goo.

As soon as my parents returned home we were called to give an account of ourselves. My mother noticed at once that Aurel had on a spotlessly clean outfit.

"My goodness! What happened to the clothes I put on him this morning?" she asked.

Of course since he was only a baby it was easy to tell the story of his wrong doing. But when the question was asked by my father as to what we two older children were up to while Aurel was doing so much damage, well, that was quite another matter.

Finally, the truth was told and I received my first caning. It was a hard lesson especially since I had been so proud of myself and my achievement only a short while before.

The long winter nights of my early childhood were very special times. The women of the village gathered in groups in different houses to sew, card and spin the wool shorn the previous spring. I loved these evenings because while they worked, the women told stories, jokes, and recounted the events of history — ancient and not so old.

I remember the group of women with whom my mother associated even to this day. I was inspired by their knowledge and intelligence: Minodora Tibu, Eufrozina Gherasim, my aunt, Tania Zaharia, Margareta Morosan, Margareta Simionese, Eufrozina Tibu, and Elisabeta Chitan.

A much repeated French phrase at the time which was attributed to the illustrious politician Gambetta, 'N'en parlez jamais. Pensez toujours!" was recommended by the wise members of our community. Having been occupied by foreigners from 1775 until 1918, the people had become cautious and suspicious. They did not speak freely during the ordinary course of the day, but during these gatherings when among friends and family, their guard was let down and real feelings were released.

In this way I and my younger sister, Veronica, learned much even before we ever went to school. It was from Eufrozina Gherasim that I learned for the first time how the Romanian people settled the land around the Tisa, Nistru, and Danube rivers and the area around the Black Sea. For over 2,000 years they made great sacrifices to hold on to this land and maintain their freedom.

I learned that the areas immediately north and south of the Danube were occupied by Tracian, Ilirican, and Dacian tribes until the Dacian state was established north of the Danube. It's capital city was Sarmisagetuza. This state became too powerful for the comfort of the Roman Empire, so it was eventually destroyed. The last king of the Dacian state, Decebal, died by his own hands. When he realized that all was lost and that Traian, the Roman Emperor, in A.D. 106 had defeated his forces, he decided to end his life. He would not be subject or slave to a foreign lord.

After that, the Dacia Felix, happy Dacia, became a Roman province and was renamed Dacia Traiana. From the union of the Dacia and Roman legions, the present people of Romania were born.

After the year A.D. 250, the barbarian hordes from Asia started their invasions of Europe. During these times, Romania was Europe's most eastern outpost and bore the brunt of the attacks. These attacks lasted for a thousand years. It wasn't until the reign of Stefan the Great in 1457 - 1504, that the country was, for a time, freed from the barbarians.

Despite this constant influx of foreigners over hundreds of years, the country north of the Danube remained and still continues to this day to be a homogenous nation, maintaining its language, customs, music, and to a large extent, its religion. While the areas to the south of the Danube were swallowed up by the Slavs, Tartars, Huns, and Turks.

I was six and a half, when one beautiful summer day the young prince Michael of Romania was visiting the historic sites around our village. He was accompanied by his teacher, Nicolae Iorga and some of his classmates.

As the procession of cars drove through our village, I stood in the middle of the road dressed in native costume. With arms waving, I brought the entourage to a halt.

Immediately, I drew myself up straight and saluted army style. Then in a clear loud voice I spoke:

"Deviza noastra este credinta
Si munca pentru tara si rege."
"Our motto is fidelity
And work for country and King."

The bystanders applauded and commented proudly upon my behavior.

The prince who was now standing in the open car offered me a big box of candy. This gift, I later shared with the whole family and many of the neighbors. It was a very special day in my young life and neighbors and friends didn't allow me to forget it. I had brought honor to our village.

Another special day for me came not long after. A cousin, Gavril Tibu had returned to Granicesti to give thanks to God for his beloved parents, brothers and sisters. This thanksgiving took the form of a religious service as well as a big party to which we were all invited.

During the celebrations, I was to learn that Gavril was a very rich man. But it hadn't always been so. As a young man, he had gone off to Vienna to study for several years during which time, his parents, brothers, and sisters all made great sacrifices to keep him there. He was considered the brightest in the family and it was therefore agreed that he should get every opportunity to be a professional.

Gavril did not disappoint his family. Having graduated as a brilliant student, he returned home and was immediately rewarded with an outstanding position as Director General of all the Forestry Departments in the Bucovina area. This position also offered him a beautiful home with several servants, a car and other amenities.

A few years later, Gavril saw to it that his whole family benefited. Soon the Tibus were the most prosperous farmers in Granicesti owning tractors, reapers and binders and other machinery for their own use and for hire.

I remember my parents often spoke of the benefits of a good education and would point to the Tibu family as a very fine example. I decided there and then that when I was old enough I, too, was going to go to a university. To be even better than Gavril, was my greatest desire at that time of my life, since he was a cousin on my father's side and I wanted to prove to all the relatives that my family was the best in the whole village.

Mom &Dad 1965

Mom & I 1941

Dad & I, 1944

My High School
Graduation, 1948

My friend Nastase and I, 1946

Chapter 4

Early School Days

Days go past and days come still,
All is old and all is new,
What is well and what is ill,
You imagine and construe
Do not hope and do not fear,
Waves that leap like waves must fall;
Should they praise or should they jeer,
Look but coldly on it all.

Mihai Eminescu
- Gloss

When I was seven I started elementary school in the village. My grandfather accompanied me the first day into the large two-story building. The front door looked huge and on the marble slab decorating the floor of the entrance hall, I noticed a big 1908.

"What's the number for, Grandfather?" I asked.

"That shows the year this school was opened," answered my grandfather as he squeezed my hand. Immediately the Director, Mr. Verenca, came to greet us.

"Welcome Teodor. Mr. Sandovich will be your teacher. I hope you'll be a good student."

"I will," I answered and grandfather smiled at me.

"I expect great things from this boy. He's a sharp one; I can tell you that."

The first day was easy. Soon, however, the work of learning began in earnest and I realized that my years of freedom, my care-free life was forever over. And I was reminded of Stela, the old horse, and I knew exactly how she felt when her life changed drastically for the worst.

Mr. Sandovich was a very strict teacher. Nor did he hesitate to use the stick or strap to help improve the learning abilities of his students. He was young and full of enthusiasm ready to take on many extra activities. One such activity was the formation of a school choir.

Initially, he chose ten or twelve of the best voices. I was happy to be one of those lucky ones and I remained with the group for three years. After that, unfortunately, I had an accident during a sports competition in which I injured my vocal chords. This incident was a turning point in my childhood.

My mother had told me not to enter the sports contest but I didn't listen. As a consequence, I fell, hurt my larynx and lost my singing voice and the opportunity to participate in the Christmas concerts that year. But I learned a lesson I would never forget. I made sure, from that time forward, to listen very attentatively to what my mother said.

It wasn't long before I realized that my father and Mr. Sandovich had come to an agreement. I noticed that my teacher never allowed a day to pass without asking me some question or other. At first, it seemed, I might be mistaken, but then I observed that several pupils escaped and didn't have to answer a single question. Why was I always the one to be asked? Nor was that the only difficult thing. For if I missed, I got the stick.

About this time, my big passion was skating. Instead of doing my homework, I'd spend all my spare time on my skates. These precious skates were obtained by great sacrifice.

During my early school years, my prized possessions included eight to ten rabbits and twelve doves. In order to obtain a pair of skates, I offered to exchange two of my finest rabbits who at the time were pregnant.

The deal was made and I became the proud owner of my first pair of skates. Soon, I was the best skater in Granicesti. In fact, I practiced so long and so often that my grades and my school work suffered accordingly.

Consequently, I was forbidden to go skating. But this was another time that I didn't listen to my parent. The result was my father took my skates and split them in two just like any ordinary old piece of wood.

For two days I cried, not only for the loss of my beautiful skates but for the fact that I had given away my best rabbits, which, in time, had produced seven babies.

When finally my grades improved, my father said he would not interfer with my free time during the vacations. I immediately began to make plans. I must find a way to get another pair of skates.

We were obliged in school to take woodwork one day each week. This was my opportunity!

After some trial and error, I came up with my own invention and made a pair of wooden roller skates. I was the first and last boy in Granicesti to own such a new and wonderful way of getting around. However, there was one drawback, being made of wood, they soon wore out.

Years later, I was to see a model very similar in a store in Bucharest made from metal.

I feel I owe my creation and my creative instincts to Simion Hatciu. This man was in his mid-thirties when I was still a small boy. A natural genius, he had little schooling but was able to turn his brain and his hand to all sorts of inventions.

Among the many creations I was privileged to see and appreciate were: machines for agriculture - a reaper and binder, a tractor drawn initially by horses but which he later revised to be driven by a gasoline engine. He built a small bi-plane which, although he managed to get airborne, eventually crashed leaving him toothless.

He was the first to build a camera and set up a photo developing shop in Granicesti. He constructed his own private band consisting of a violin, drums, accordion, flute, and cymbals. All these instruments he played himself and even composed the music he produced drawing on the folk tunes of the area. Whenever a tool was broken or a household utensil was needed, Simion came to the rescue.

In 1936, the community of Granicesti outgrew the old parish church. A new tract of land was obtained and to dedicate it to the service of God, the Metropolitan Archbishop, Puiu Visarion, came to the village. For the occasion, four children were chosen to honor the distinguished guest. Arestide Palievich, George Chitan, Margareta Moldovician and Teodor Gherasim. Each had his own job, Margareta offered a bouquet of flowers, Arestide recited a poem, George read a salutation, as a representative of the student body, and I gave a historical account of the village. The bishop was so impressed that he said: "Please take a photograph of these children they look so lovely in their national costumes."

In the discourse that followed, Puiu Visarion, aware of the upheavals in Russia and Germany warned of the catastrophies that would inevitably follow the spread of Nazism and Communism. "The enemy without is bad enough but the enemy within our borders is far worse. Those who follow the Communist ways will destroy our nation in the end - church, monarchy, people. Divide and conquer." This was the first time I heard about Communism and 'the hell' that was unleased in the country that introduced that system and form of government to the world. The bishop admonished us to keep faith in God, to hold fast to our customs and language as a last resort to preserving our nation.

I remember in the winter of 1937 one of the houses in the village caught on fire. The mother of six children was burned to death. This tragic event was talked about for months. Everyone felt sorry for the family. We children collected clothes and small objects while our parents gave money, animals and other assistance to the stricken father. Eventually, all the men assisted with the rebuilding of the house. I learned from this sad occurance how closely we were tied to one another in our small village. What affected one family affected all.

Another humanitarian gesture which made an impression on my young life was the feeding of the poor. A center was set up in the city of Suceava where every day a hot meal was provided for all who were either too old or too poor to provide for themselves. The food served was donated by each household in the village and was considered a sacred duty by all.

A project which took three years to accomplish and which benefited the whole community was the work done by us students on a barren slope just outside the village. With young pine trees donated by Radauti nursery we planted 12,000 trees. To this day the area is known as the students' forest.

To honor Ion Gramada, a hero from the village who gave his life in World War I, a community cultural center was opened in 1938. Among the activities engaging the people of the village was a men's choir of forty-five members. The national and provincial costumes were made and worn on special occasions at this center. A library of around a 1,000 books was eventually set up and the young people were given instruction in elocution, the recitation of poetry and in the techniques of debating.

Thus our community strove to preserve and pass on the traditions and customs of our beautiful Bucovina and our beloved country, Romania. In the years that followed Granicesti contributed more than its share of professionals as a result of this experience - several engineers, doctors, priests, professors and lawyers were to attribute their beginnings and interest in higher education to the community efforts begun and fostered at that time. They were good times, happy times and we hoped they would continue forever. But the black clouds of war were gathering on the horizon. We all knew that sooner or later we would be plunged into another world war.

On September 1, 1939 following the Treaty between Molotov and Ribbentrop, Poland was attacked by Germany and Russia. As a consequence Russia occupied the eastern section while Germany took possession of the west.

The Polish army fought to the death to preserve its independence, but it was impossible to withstand the power of the Soviet Union as well as Germany at that time. On 7 September 1939 Romania opened its borders to the thousands of Polish men and material that sought an escape route.

A hundred thousand Polish refugees also joined the fleeing crowds. Among them were the sixty thousand soldiers and their officers. These men were considered political prisoners, but they were treated with respect and hospitality by the Romanian people. In fact, Romania was the only country to offer a refuge to so many Poles and this included members of the government and even the President of the Polish Republic. With these exiles came the treasures of Poland as well as eighty-two tons of gold which was en-route to safe keeping in America. Later a second transport of gold, two-thousand seven hundred and thirty-eight tons, as well as other valuables were deposited in the National Romanian Bank and would eventually be returned in 1947 to the Polish government. This act reflects the rectitude and honesty of the Romanian people. So unlike our Russian neighbors who on several occasions vandalized and robbed our country's treasures and never returned as much as one cent.

Not only did we open our frontiers to the Polish army but to all ethnic groups fleeing the Nazi and Communists, particularly the Jews who were desperately trying to escape Hitler's clutches, and the White Russians seeking safety from Stalin's revenge.

During those trying days only two avenues of escape remained open to refugees in Europe, the first was over the Pyrenees into Spain, the second, over the Carpathians into Romania. Most of the Jews who arrived, eventually found refuge in Palestine. But at that time they were funneled through Romania and were aided by such organizations as the Jewish Council and the World Council of Churches.

It was for this reason that Rabbi Moshe Weenberger declared: "The Romanian people have tried to keep alive humanism and faith in the human spirit, and we Jews must recognize this fact and never forget it."

I remember the stream of soldiers, the endless flow of trucks, tanks, and other vehicles that day and night passed through our village for three weeks. At night the sky was lit up by the lights from these vehicles as they came nonstop along the road while during the day the thundering heavy equipment made deep ruts in the gravel and polluted the air with clouds of dust and smelly exhaust.

Some of these weary, foot-sore men, worn out by continuous walking day and night stopped to wash-up or drink at our well. My mother often gave them some coffee.

I was struck by the fact that they were all very young men. How many of them would ever again see their native land. Most of them joined the American, English, or French armies giving their lives in heroic deeds on the battlefront.

One officer gave me a lantern with four reserve batteries as a gift for my services as I had become very friendly with them despite the handicap of language. This gift I protected for twenty years, ordering batteries from Germany. It served very well at night when I needed to control my beehives.

Within hours the whole region was in chaos and it seemed the entire population was on the move. Children were crying in the streets unable to locate their parents. Desperate parents were screaming looking for their children. Trucks, cars, carts, wagons and anything that would move jammed the streets of the cities and the roadways leading away from the soon to be occupied area.

I remember one incident when the father of a fleeing family came to my father asking him to replace a harness which had broken. The going fee for a harness was 300 lei. At such a time my father was loath to part with his harnesses. He badly needed them for his own animals. But the unfortunate refugee was in dire straights.

"I'll give you 600 lei for a harness," he offered, his eyes wide with fear and despair.

"All right, all right," my father answered and parted with his very best harness."

In a few hours he was to realize that he had not made such a good bargain. Everything not only doubled, but quadrupled in price as the Russian army advanced.

Towards the end of 1939, while I was still in elementary school, my father was called up by the armed services to prepare for war. Being the oldest, I was expected to shoulder a large portion of my father's work around the house - taking care of the animals, the poultry, and even working the land.

On June 26, 1940 an ultimatum from Stalin to the Monarchy in Romania ordered the King to withdraw his troops from Bessarabia and Northern Bucovina within 48 hours. This caused great consternation. There was little anyone could do as the Russians moved swiftly occupying all the territory as far as the Siret and Prut Rivers. At that time my father hoped that Hitler might attack Russia but his wish was not granted until a year later. On 22nd June 1941 when Germany attacked the Russian front from the Baltic to the Ukraine, Romania, under Marshal Ion Antonescu also went to war against the Russians attacking what was left of the front from the Ukraine to the Black Sea.

In 1941 I left the elementary school and applied to the high school in Siret. But before entering its hallowed halls, I had to take up the gauntlet.

When I announced my intention of attending school, my uncle, Teodor Morosan, had other ideas. He was the head of the family while my father was away and therefore such a decision had to be approved by him.

His immediate reaction to my request was that I was needed on the farm. I had fifteen days before the reopening of school to prepare for the entrance exams. While studying for these tests, my uncle came looking for me as it was time to bring in the crops.

When I refused to go with him, he applied his whip to my latter-end leaving welts that remained for several days. This was part of the pain I had to endure to follow my desire to go to school. Nevertheless, despite the pain, I made up my mind no matter how difficult the road that lay ahead I was willing to trudge forward and not change my decision.

By the first of September I was ready for the exams. It was a very trying time. My whole future depended on the results. To add to my distress there were many more students applying than could possibly be accepted.

Therefore my joy was supreme when one week later I arrived in the school with my mom to check the list for my

49

name. After an initial disappointment I, at length, found it and, then, there was no holding me back.

As we reentered the village some friends stopped us to hear the news. Amid congratulations and cheers, my mother spoke up.

"Now I have trouble. Pillows, blankets, and a quilt have to be made before this young man will be ready to go to school."

Immediately, the women standing by offered to help. I would be ready to attend high school the following week even if it meant a community effort.

The high school in Siret was built in the early 1800's. It housed about 500 students at any one time. All were selected carefully not only for their mental abilities but for their rectitude of character and family background. Several children from poor families who showed promise were given scholarships enabling them to better their conditions.

After five years of elementary education, I now faced eight years in high school as a boarder.

The school day started at 8:00 a.m. Classes required by all students were: three languages - French, German or English, and Romanian, Mathematics, History, Geography, Chemistry and Physics. Business classes, music, art, and religious classes were also included on alternate days. Sports were an after school activity and not allowed to interfere with the academic program.

The discipline was strict. There was no leaving the campus and when we did go from one place to another we were always accompanied by a teacher.

Several hours of study were obligatory each day after class. Since I had come from a village school, I found that the time allowed was not sufficient for me to compete with the students who had the advantage of city schools.

The first opportunity I got, I purchased a candle and some matches. I found a small office without windows close to the dormitory. Each evening after the lights were put off, I crept from my bed and continued my study by candle light in this room.

But even my diligence in studying hard did not always pay off. Towards the end of the first term, my geography teacher called upon me one day to answer a question. When I hesitated, he asked me to come to the front of the class and point out the position of Romania with regard to the sun during spring.

At that moment I hadn't the slightest idea of the answer. But I wasn't going to admit to my dilemma. Stretching out my hand to the globe, I gave it a swift turn, sending the world spinning on its axis for several seconds. When it finally stopped, I turned triumphantly to the professor and said, "There's the place".

Professor Mute didn't even smile. "Go to your place, Gherasim. Your mark for the lesson is 3." This was a failing grade. Needless to say, I wasn't very happy. I spent the rest of the term trying to make up for my foolish prank.

The first term was very difficult. But by the end of the second term, I had joined the first group of scholars. I was extremely proud of myself and particularly happy to show my parents my progress and grades.

When I was growing up, a teacher was a person set apart, sacred in the eyes of his or her students. Devoted to learning and the instruction of the youth of the country, a teacher was the embodiment of patriotism, ethics, morality, and a fountain of knowledge and learning. From the very beginning of my school life, I have held teachers in high regard as did all my schoolmates. It was a privilege to learn and a God-given duty to respect and look up to all those who taught.

Now, even after fifty years, I still feel a warmth and respect for the dedicated teachers I was priviliged to have. Among them the Professors Valceanu, husband and wife,

Manolache, and Mironovici were all superior teachers and especially dear to me.

It was Professor Valceanu who in giving an etiquette lesson produced a test which I consider prophetic. The test question required an essay answer of about one page.

"Romania is now at war with Russia," he began. "You get the opportunity to go to America. When your ship docks in New York, you are approached by a well- dressed lady.

'Welcome to America,' she said with a smile and extended her hand.

"The lady made you feel good. She seemed kind and was soft-spoken."

'I need a handyman. You need work, I have been told. I have a nice home, a big garden and I need someone to take care of them. You will have a place to stay, food, and a salary.'

"You think a moment before you answer." Then realizing that this lady was offering you so much, making everything so easy for you even ignoring your poor attempts at English, 'Yes,' you responded, 'I accept.'"

"The lady was happy and continued, 'But that's not all; I have the feeling that you are an honest man, that once you give your word you can be relied upon to keep it. I will draw up a contract. What do you say?'

"You accepted. You were happy. Several years pass. You have prospered. You had time to save. Eventually, your employer told you that since she had no children that you would be the one to inherit her property and anything else she owned.

"Then one day a telegram arrives from Romania. Your mother had died. What do you do? Do you go home or do you remain in America and fulfill your contract?"

The professor paused a moment to make sure everyone understood. Then he said: "Now it's your turn. You will have half an hour to answer this question."

I thought for some time. What indeed would I do in such a situation? Then the answer came distinctly and directly as if I knew all along what I had to say. I would stay until my job was completed. I would fulfill what I had promised. I had given my word, I must respect that fact.

The result of the test was surprising even to me. I got ten points which meant top grade or A. The teacher was pleased that I had used my head. It must be remembered that travel in those days was slow. There were no jet airplanes to transport people quickly and efficiently. Were I to leave America, it would have taken weeks to get to Romania. So my decision to remain and fulfill my obligations was considered the most logical. Later, this decision was to prove prophetical - was, in fact, my destiny.

CHAPTER 5

School Days Interrupted

Things you'll meet of many a kind,
Sights and sounds, and tales no end,
But to keep them all in mind
Who would bother to attend? . . .
Very little does it matter,
If you can yourself fulfil,
That with idle, empty chatter
Days go past and days come still.

Mihai Eminescu
- Gloss

On March 23, 1944 our high school in the town of Siret closed. As a result of the Stalingrad fiasco, the axis troops were continually retreating and among them were the Romanian soldiers.

My father sent a letter at the beginning of February telling us that conditions were critical and that God alone knew what would happen when the Russians occupied our country. He continued to share his anxiety about the future and his family in the following words:

"Trecu-i podul Cepanoasa,
Ma palii un dor de casa.
De sotie si copii,
Inapoi nu sti cand vii."
"I crossed Cepanoasa bridge,
Homesick and longing

For my wife and children
Not knowing when I'll return."

On March 25, father arrived home in his sergeant's uniform. We made a little party for the occasion. It would be our last time together for many months to come. The following morning, he, father, had to return to his military duties and, on this occasion, he had decided to take me with him. I was just fifteen. This was the first time I was to be so far away from my mother, my sisters, and brothers for such an extended period. But this unexpected change was not intended to be a vacation. I was entering a war zone. Anything could happen.

As the professors and students from Siret were to be relocated in a city in the southwest, Ramnicu-Valcea, my father didn't want me to miss any school, war or no war. He, himself, had lost so much because he was unable to finish his education. He would see, personally, that I arrived safely at the new location.

We set off for Solca, accompanied by an uncle, in a horse and cart. After we joined up with the military unit, I bade my uncle goodbye. It was my father's job to take care of important old military documents and he was responsible for their safe conveyance to Caracal in southern Romania. For this purpose, he was given a covered wagon in which I was able to ride and sleep.

Immediately, I was faced with some of the horrible effects of war - thousands of refugees blocked our passage; carts, wagons, and horses ploughed over the muddy roads, while the soldiers of the retreating Romanian army and German escort guards with Russian prisoners tried to carve a passage through the confused, scared, and disoriented civilians.

"Move on, move on." I heard a German shout at a sick, tired Russian prisoner.

The man couldn't muster up any more energy. He stumbled forward but it was plain to see that he would not be able to go much further.

"I'll be obliged to shoot you if you can't keep up," the soldier warned.

As we continued on our way, I heard three shots and I knew that the German guard had lost patience with the slow prisoners.

In order to relieve the congestion on the main roads, our commander decided to follow a secondary road through the Trotus Valley. This route enabled us to reach Ploiesti after four weeks.

During this journey, we met with nothing but hospitality and warmth as we passed through the villages. On one occasion when I was drenched to the skin and the weather had turned very wet and cold, we arrived at a small house on the edge of the village of Rapele. There a farmer's wife opened up her home to us. She fed us and gave me clean clothes to wear and while I was asleep she washed and dried my clothes. It was just like being at home and I felt so good.

Another person who deserves mention for his kindness and generosity to us was Mosul Jinga from Caiuti. An old veteran from the First World War, he could not do enough for us. We stayed with him for three days, resting ourselves, our animals, and, eventually, when we moved on, he supplied us with food and wine.

When we reached the outskirts of the industrial city of Ploiesti, it was about midday. Hardly had we set foot in the area when the air-raid sirens were sounded. The American air force had decided to destroy the oil fields and refineries in and around the city.

My father quickly looked for cover. He hurriedly pulled the horse and wagon into a ravine. He wished to release the horse, so while he held the reins, he gave me a knife to cut the harness. In my anxiety and haste, I cut not only the leather strap but I gouged a large gash in my father's hand. I felt so bad when I saw the blood but there was nothing I could do. Then my father told me to run away some distance from him. If the bombs hit that particular place, he didn't want both of us to be killed.

The whole area was engulfed in smoke. After about half-an-hour when some of the black clouds dissipated, the flames leaped high on the horizon. The city of Ploiesti was on fire.

The planes then returned to their base in Italy; it was time to move on. My father retrieved the horse and patched the broken harness. We were soon on the road south towards dense forest where it was easier to hide from the attacking planes.

During the following days the skies over Bucharest and many other large cities became veritable infernoes. The death toll on the citizen population was immense. In Bucharest the large train station to the north of the city, which at the time was crowded with refugees fleeing the north eastern regions, was completely demolished. Thousands of innocent people were killed.

We stayed in the forest of Saftica for about four days because it was impossible to continue on our journey by road. It was under these conditions that we tried to celebrate the Paschal Feast in 1944. During the Easter morning, General Radu Korne, the hero of the Eastern Front, came to our area and as a gift, through the charity of the Red Cross, he distributed two colored eggs and a piece of blessed bread to each one of us. My father called me to follow him to the wagon. There we prayed together for peace for the world but particularly we prayed for the safety of my mother and the family at home under the occupation of the Russian Army.

As soon as there was a lull in the bombardment of the big city, our commander ordered us to move in the direction of Bucharest. All this journeying had to take place at night during black-out. It was a very difficult time.

After about two hours we passed close to the airport of Baneasa and continued in the direction of Alexandria. I was astonished to see the Viting hospital in flames despite the fact that it was clearly marked with a Red Cross which was visible from the air.

Towards the end of April, we arrived in Caracal and joined the rest of the regiment. After twenty-four hours rest we were given orders to evacuate the city as it was not safe. My father deposited the documents he had in his keeping with the rightful authorities. That accomplished, we left for Devesel, a village eight miles away from Caracal. There a school was quickly transformed into a barrack. The unit was organized and training resumed. For my part, I was happy to be able to sleep once again in a real bed after five weeks on the road.

Ten days later, the unit got new orders and my father was put in charge of a training program. At this point, he decided it was time for me to join my schoolmates in Ramnicu-Valcea. He accompanied me to the train station. After that I was on my own.

Arriving in Ramnicu-Valcea, a journey of about 120 kilometers from Devesel, I was impressed with the atmosphere and appearance of the city. It was clean and beautifully situated in the southern Carpathian mountains, in the Olt Valley.

I had no trouble in finding the school and almost immediately met my old professors and school friends. They were all happy to see me. Soon my professors found a job for me and I was given sleeping quarters in another school as that one was full.

I learned sometime later that the Russian troops occupied the village of Granicesti on April 8th. When they entered the village at eight o'clock in the evening, the German forces who were there made a valiant attempt to defend the area but after only two hours, they were overpowered. It was during the fighting that my grandfather's house was demolished. Fortunately no one was hurt.

The mayor at the time was Lazar Flutur and the assistant was Meliton Gherasim. The Russians immediately confronted these two men and ordered them to produce the following supplies: Forty head of cattle, 5000 kilograms of grain, 300 hens, 15.000 kilograms of potatoes, large quantities of alcohol and other foods. Both men refused to carry out their orders. As a consequence they were badly beaten. Mr. Flutur died of his wounds sometime later, whereas my uncle, Meliton, died within two weeks.

After that on May 13, the entire population of the village was evacuated to Calafindesti, a forest area about ten miles away. The people had to remain there until August 18th surviving as best they could in the open air.

I remained in Ramnicu-Valcea all during the summer vacation and worked in the Cooperativa "Infratirea". While I was there, my first job was packaging books and later I was allowed to sell them.

At that time, I had a bright idea. Since my father was 47 years old, and had already spent several years fighting at the front, I decided to write a letter to King Michael asking that he be allowed to join me in Ramnicu-Valcea as I was all alone there. My mother was, at the same time, in occupied territory under the Soviet Red Army.

Ten days later my father arrived in Ramnicu-Valcea. He came to the high school where Professor Gheorghe Manea Manolache told him where I worked. He showed me his release papers as a result of my petition. Needless to say we were both very happy and my boss gave me the rest of the day to celebrate.

Eventually, the question came up about where we would be able to stay. First, we decided to go and spend some time in the park - Zavoiul. There we rented a row-boat and spent several hours on the lake listening to the singer, Maria Tanase. Her songs were so beautiful, I remember, that my father was overcome with emotion and cried all the time.

Towards evening we planned to look for an apartment suitable for the two of us. A petition to the Housing Authorities got us a small house within a week. It had a little garden, and was situated on Traian St. The next problem was to find work for my father.

In a leather factory, Simianu Brothers, I obtained a position for him. So life became regulated. We both had work and were able to save. Furthermore I had prospects that in the Fall I could be able to continue with my schooling.

During my sojourn at the bookstore, I made two good friends who were about my own age - Mircea Ticos and Bordea Gheorghe. They taught me all the tricks of the trade - to deliver goods, to sign documents, to mail certain orders, etc. All this information was very valuable because I was soon appreciated for my many talents and trusted with special jobs.

At times, the manager, who was Father Marina attached to the Church of St. George in the center of the city, would call on me to render certain services. I helped him to transport financial records for Income Tax purposes and I was present when he negotiated the amount he should pay.

One day when he came to inspect the store, he saw that I was very depressed.

"What is the matter with you?" he asked.

I told him that a student had just arrived from Bucovina. He had passed the front lines during the night and gave us a report of the situation.

"All of Southern Bucovina is being evacuated to the forests," he said.

I was extremely upset as I thought of my mother and the rest of the family.

Father Marina told me in a very convincing way that I was not to worry because in two or three months I would be at home.

This answer struck me as being strange when no one knew from one day to the next what was going to happen.

Then one day instead of going to the air-raid shelter during the bombing of the barrack, I went to the nearby forest and joined two men who were already taking shelter there. In the course of their conversation I was surprised to learn that Fr. Marina was a Communist. Others who were mentioned as being of the same persuasion were Misters Rosianu and Folescu and names I no longer remember.

This information was, to my mind, confusing. How could a priest be a Communist? Communists didn't believe in God. So I continued to ponder these questions but I didn't speak to anyone about them.

Several days later Fr. Marina arrived on a bicycle with a package of meat. He was tired and perspiring. He asked me if I knew how to ride. I told him I did. He then asked me to take the package to the priest's house across from the church.

"But be attentive," he said. "You are not to go inside. Ring the bell and remain on the step until the housekeeper answers the door."

On my way there, I considered that the amount of meat for a man whose wife was dead and who had only a servant with two children living in his house was quite a large quantity. Had this been a single occasion, I might have forgotten the incident but when I was asked to deliver a like quantity of meat again after three days under the same strict conditions, I became suspicious. How many mouths were being fed in Fr. Marina's house?

This priest later became the Patriarch of The Orthodox church in Bucharest.

We continued working during the summer months in that city. Eventually, in the beginning of August the American planes started bombing the military barrack. Then on August 22, 1944 an announcement, repeated several times during the day, stated that the King, Michael I would speak to the nation that evening at 9 o'clock. Everyone was curious to know what the King would have to say.

All were glued to the radio when the time came and saddened to hear the news:

"The war is over for us. We no longer fight against the Allies. Instead, we now join our forces with Russia against Germany. Marshal Ion Antonescu, the commander-in-chief of the armed forces, has been arrested as has Michael Antonescu, the foreign minister. We will soon have peace and the opportunity to rebuild our country after these four years of war."

The people rejoiced at the news. They began to dance in the streets and public places.

But their happiness did not last long. The cold reality of the situation soon became clear. In fact, the most difficult days were still to come.

Chapter 6

The Trials and Tribulations of War.

With faces pale as marble, as marble too as cold,
Women carrying muskets pass through the ruddy glow.
Their hair hangs o'er their shoulders and does their breasts
enfold;
Mad with lifelong suffering and with dark hatred bold,
Black their eyes, yet gleaming with the brightness of despair.

Mihae Eminescu
- Emperor and Proletaria

N o sooner had the King spoken to the nation, than the German air force retaliated. The ally of yesterday had overnight become the enemy.

Bucharest was bombed continuously for four or five days until the Romanian Army liberated it and forced the surrender of the German troops who were in and around the city.

The Russian Army arrived in the capital at the beginning of September as our new allies... I was learning something about the logic of war.

At this time, I was still in Ramnicu-Valcea. Within two weeks the Russian Army arrived in that city also. Day after day the vehicles of war and destruction passed through the streets. While I watched the tanks roll into the main thoroughfare, I was rudely awakened to the tactics and behavior of our new friends and allies.

Two expensive cars with their seemingly professional occupants pulled to the side of the street to allow the tanks to proceed. However, as the last tank drew near, it stopped. The commander, machine gun in hand, dismounted and approached the parked cars. He ordered the gentlemen drivers to get out and hand over the keys. Immediately, he directed that an officer take control and drive the vehicles away. I had my first lesson under the Communist dictatorship. Individual and personal property did not concern the Russians.

After a few days the general population was disgusted with the conduct of the Russian soldiers. Several rapes were reported and one young woman was so badly injured that she had to be hospitalized.

The difference between the Russians and the Germans was very evident. Their dress was dirty and unkept; their boots didn't fit; and they were consummate thieves, particularly at night. I came to hate every last one of them.

All the Russian prisoners of war were freed and German soldiers took their places. Our whole world was turned upside down in the space of a few days. It was pure madness, no rhyme or reason to anything anymore.

My father and I decided since there was no secure place left in the city that it was better to leave. We went to Cepari where my friend, Professor Gheorghe Manea Manolache, was living in his parents' house.

Since it was early Fall, the vineyards were ready to harvest, so my father immediately found work. For several hours each day, I helped to tutor two young boys who were preparing for high school. For this, my father and I were able to stay at that house, the home of the Oancea family and received food as well as a small allowance. I savored the warmth and companionship of family life and often thought how nice it would be to be able to return home, to be with my mother, my brothers and sisters again.

After fifteen days, my father decided to try to return to Granicesti. We left for the train but when we arrived at the station, those coming from the north informed us that it was dangerous for us to travel in that direction. The situation was catastrophic. All able-bodied men were being rounded up and deported to Russia to work in the mines. People were desperate. Fear and panic gripped the entire population.

Despite this warning, my father made up his mind to return home. He told me to remain in Cepari where I would be safe with my new friends. Since he knew Russian, he decided he would be able to avoid being exploited by the Russians and besides he felt that travelling by night, he would not be so easily detected.

I remained in the Oancea household and enjoyed the activities associated with the harvesting of the grapes, the making of wines and the distilling of alcohol, despite the loneliness I felt when my father departed.

School had begun in October. The boys whom I had tutored were now attending high school so my job was done. I wished to return to school myself but in Suceava, so I was obliged to go home no matter how difficult and dangerous it might be. I was still considered a child so I would be allowed to go to school even by the Russians.

When finally, I did get on the train, it was over-crowded. There was no room at all inside, so I was forced to ride on the catwalk near the engine. A thing unheard of in any other civilized country was commonplace in Romania then and during that period of chaos.

As soon as the train moved I had a problem; my back was against the engine and in front I was facing the elements. Consequently, one side of my body was burning while the other was slowly but surely being frozen.

I managed to hang on until we reached Ploiesti some two hundred miles away. Fortunately, a large number of people alighted from the train at the city and I made my way along the catwalk to the engineer's compartment. The man who was shoveling the coal asked me where I was going.

"To Suceava," I answered.

"Oh ho! You better stay in here, you'll never reach Suceava if you stay out there, young man."

So I thanked the man and crouched down inside the locomotive and remained there until we pulled into Suceava six hours later at 3:00 A.M.

Although I was only 30 kilometers from my home, I was obliged to wait around for three hours for the next train which would take me to Dornesti. The ground was covered with the first fall of snow and I was shivering despite my heavy jacket.

I took the first train that arrived thinking it was the right one. It was too late when I learned that I was on a non-stop express train going to Russia. This train was pulling huge tanks of petroleum commandeered from our Romanian oil fields but destined for that country.

It was my good fortune that some miles north of Darmanesti, the railway line was in disrepair and the locomotive had to slow down. I didn't hesitate for one instance to jump from that moving train into the ditch. No way was I going to find myself in Russia.

By this time it was full daylight so I continued to walk along the road parallel to the tracks. I was by now about ten kilometers from my home; there would be no difficulty walking the rest of the way.

I hadn't eaten for two days, but I was so happy I began to whistle. I met a man and saluted him but he merely looked at me in dismay and said nothing. I continued to encourage myself by singing and reciting poems by Octavian Goga.

BATRANII

"De ce m-ati dus de langa voi
De ce m-ati dus de-acasa.
Sa fii ramas fecior la plug
Sa fii ramas la coasa."

The Old Folk
Why did you send me away
Why did you send me from home
It were better I remained as the ploughboy
It were better to help with the harvest.

When I reached Granicesti, I came upon a man who was digging in his field accompanied by his son, probably foraging for the last of his vegetables before winter set in.

"Good morning," I said.

"You're Mardare's Teodor?"

"Yes," I said. "Did my father get home?"

"Yes," he replied, "but the people of Granicesti think you were killed by the Americans in the bombing of Bucharest. No one has heard of you in such a long time."

From this man I learned what happened to the people of the village while I was away. One morning the Russians came and commanded all to leave their homes and possessions. Most of the people fled to the forest. My mother, brothers and sisters were among them.

I was relieved to know that my father had arrived home. I also learned that he was lucky because many men had been forceably taken from their homes and families and sent to Russia to replenish the ranks of the German prisoner work force who had died or escaped.

Arriving at our front door, my mother threw up her arms in surprise and excitement. Then as she embraced me, she started to cry.

"Why are you crying? You see me healthy and safe and happy."

Her answer was: "The human being has a right to cry when he is very happy."

It has been thirty-six years since that moment, yet the feeling is still the same — the love, the warmth of mother's embrace and the supreme joy and happiness of being united once again with my family. What a divine moment! What supreme joy!

I had a little gift for everyone. Having worked in the stationary supply store, I was able to get a mathematical set for each of my brothers and sisters. But for my mother I had a woolen skirt and sweater which was the admiration not only of the family but of the whole village. For my father, I had purchased a hat. Needless to say, he felt proud and very moved by my generosity. The special foods my mother prepared for the evening meal reminded me of Christmas and I was the center of attention as I told my experiences and adventures to the entire family.

Slowly, the complete story of what had happened during the previous eight months was, in turn, told to me. When the Russians entered the village, the house was occupied by about fifty soldiers who lay side by side each night on the floor in our casa mare. They were rough and coarse and caused a lot of destruction. They demanded and bullied and took what they wanted.

One night as my mother was sleeping with my younger brothers and sisters a Russian soldier tried to rape her. Because of the screams of the children an officer was alerted and came to her rescue. That time was difficult for everyone; but especially so for the women without their husbands.

Soon after this, the entire village was evacuated. An order from general headquarters to establish a safe zone made it necessary to clear out the whole area. There was nowhere for the people to go except into the forest.

There they set up temporary shelters and settled in as best they could. Those who had animals were lucky. My mother had only a few hens, one cow, and an old horse left. The Russians had taken everything else.

Talking about the Russians taking everything reminds me of the story of Froky.

Froky was a small red horse with a strong chest, a short neck and an enormous head. I don't know who named him, perhaps he came with it, as we later learned, he hailed from the Calmuki Steppes.

When the Russians came, they brought a large cannon drawn by four horses. Froky was one of these horses and not only was he a bag of skin and bones but he was without shoes. His legs were cut and bleeding and his joints were swollen.

Froky lay down in our courtyard when he was released and the following morning was unable to rise. The Russians quickly replaced him from my father's stable. My mother heard the horse whinny as it was harnessed to the cannon and that was the last she saw of her fine horse.

She went to inspect Froky as soon as the Russians left and found he was near death. Perhaps a little warm milk would help, she thought.

When Froky tasted the milk, she opened her eyes and new life seemed to surge through her emaciated frame. Slowly but surely she regained her health and strength and was to live for many more years becoming a great help and never failing to work hard for us. And, I might add, for many of our neighbors as well.

Now that the family was united again, we tried to return to a normal life style. Papa went about his chores on the farm, mother turned to and took care of the household as she always did and I returned to school the following week but this time I went to Suceava for the final years of high school.

* * * *

The Communists had taken complete control of the country. It was the year 1947. The year before had seen a bad harvest; foodstuffs were scarce; many people were starving. Soon the winter set in and the cold of that year added considerably to the hardships the people had to endure.

Supplies of corn and wheat were sent from America to supplement the dwindling supplies in the country but the Communist authorities would not allow the food to enter the country. In fact, all the food supplies were diverted to the U.S.S.R. Later, some of this food was actually returned to Romania in the form of relief from our "benevolent benefactors".

It was during these tragic days that I got involved in gathering food and clothing for the starving in the city of Suceava - particularly the families of prisoners and the sick in the hospitals.

A train coming from Putna was selected to stop at all the intervening stations to pick up these supplies. In Suceava, itself, my dear friend, Traian Corinu, with the help of other students and myself, unloaded and distributed the food and clothing.

A few days later, the Securitate started rounding up all who were involved in this operation. I was taken from my classroom and with several others marched to the prison. There I was locked in a cell with about twelve other students. As it was late by that time, we were left to ourselves for the night.

In the dark and musty cell, the hours slowly crept by. We were all scared and unsure about the outcome.

Certainly, the leaders would be condemned to prison terms. I hoped I would not be sent to Siberia or some other far away place, never to see my family again. I so wanted to finish school. The very thought of being deprived of that privilege was almost too much to bear.

I didn't speak much that night, but I prayed a lot. Towards morning I dozed off and dreamed that I was in a beautiful meadow looking after sheep. A crystal stream ran nearby and the birds filled the air with sweet song. I was so happy, I started to sing also.

When I awoke, I remembered my dream and took it to be a good omen. My spirits revived and I felt courageous. I even encouraged my companions who were unable to sleep.

Later that morning we were taken, one by one, before the officer in charge. Prior to my turn, my friend, Traian passed by my cell. He took the opportunity and risk to gain my attention. Then quickly he whispered: "Tell the Securitate that you collected food for the hospital - nothing else."

It was this statement, which I stoutly affirmed, that led, eventually, to my release. But prior to that I was beaten and interrogated for three days by a brute of a man named Manole Botnaras. This giant savagely kicked me with his boots as I lay helpless on the ground. There wasn't a sound spot left on my body, particularly my head which was troubled with buzzing and ringing sounds for many days after.

Looking back on that traumatic ordeal, I wonder and marvel that I wasn't seriously injured by such brutality, since I was still a young boy. God and my mother's prayers certainly saved me on that and many other horrific occasions.

Eventually, I was allowed to go. But, to this day, I know I owe my speedy release to Traian. For had I mentioned helping the prisoner's families, I would, undoubtedly, have been sentenced to several years in prison. Traian, my dear friend, who was about five or six years older than I, received a ten year sentence.

I returned to school to the astonishment and applause of my classmates. No questions were asked at that moment, but later, in private, each wanted to know the details of my ordeal. All, including myself, considered my release a miracle.

I was treated as a hero by my classmates and this gave me a sense of pride and satisfaction despite the pain I had suffered and still bore for quite some time. I recalled the wound my great-great grandfather, (Buzatu - scarred lip) had received while fighting for his king and country and was pleased that I, too, was following in his footsteps. Perhaps one day people would speak with pride of the brave Teodor Gherasim, who when only a teenager, championed a humanitarian cause for which he paid dearly with beatings and imprisonment.

I finished the final year of high school and graduated with good marks enabling me to apply for entrance to the University in Bucharest. My father and mother were delighted and strove by every means in their power to see that I lacked for nothing in my quest for a higher education.

Part II

Arrested

Chapter 7

Arrested

I little thought that I would learn to die;
Forever young, enveloped in my cloak,
My dreaming eyes I lifted to the star
O solitude.

Mihai Eminescu
- Ode

On November 19, 1946 there was an election in Romania. At the same time my father was elected Mayor of Granicesti.

When the votes were tabulated in the big cities, the Communists Party named B.P.D. had only 11%. The P.N.T. (Peasants National Party) had 89%. The next day the result was completely reversed. The P.N.T. received 11% and the B.P.D. 89%. Those who objected were arrested, deported, disappeared, or were killed. As the Securitate operated mostly during the night, it was easy for people to be taken. My father lost his office as Mayor. For fear of arrest he was obliged to sleep in different places each night for the next four months. Thus did the Communists take power in Romania and the greatest deception perpetrated on our country over its entire history was launched.

In December of the following year, a thousand university students were arrested. King Michael was summoned to Bucharest and forced to sign his abdication. If he had refused, the arrested students were slated for execution. So the last opponent of Communism, the Monarchy, was removed.

77

On December 30th, 1947, while the Parliament was on vacation, a small group of Communist deputies who didn't represent the vast majority of the people, declared that the state be henceforth called the Romanian Peoples' Republic.

These devious acts opened my eyes to what could happen in my country.

In May of '48 another round-up of students took place. Thousands were arrested, mostly legionnaires and those who were members of the P.N.T. and P.N.L (National Liberal Party). The cream of Romania's youth - vibrant, intelligent, enthusiastic. These young men and women were then thrown into prison and thus began Romania's Calvary.

It was a glorious morning when I left Granicesti, my childhood home, and all that I had known and loved until then. My father took me to the train. He didn't say much; neither did I. My heart was a whirlwind of contrary emotions. I was sad to bid goodbye to the past; joyous to be on my way to the big city and to a life of learning in the exhalted halls of the University of Bucharest. What did life have in store for me, I asked myself. I was also so grateful to both my parents who had sacrificed so much and encouraged me to pursue my fondest dreams. Where did they acquire such insight and appreciation of the higher things of life. I had seen so many other young men from my village whose parents had, it seemed, more resources than my parents, yet, they were denied the privilege of a higher education - their help was needed on the farm, or so they were told.

The journey by train from quiet Bucovina in the north to the bustling noisy metropolis that was the capital of the country, was in reality a 'right of passage' for me. I had to discard my local costume and don a suit and tie. This in itself was a breaking away from the past, my childhood, my family. For the clothes I had worn up to that time were those made by my mother's hands. Now I wore garments fashioned in a factory - impersonal clothing with no identifying mark except the name of an unknown manufacturer. My native dialect had to be abandoned; in essence, I was forced to adopt the idioms and nuances of the big city in order to fit in. I thought on these differences and the changes that were about to occur in other facets of my life. I would live in the university for the first four years so that would not cause me too much stress or concern since I had been a boarder in Suceava during high school. But there would be little or no supervision. I was now a man and on my own. I made up my mind to lead a sober, restrained life-style and never give my parents any reason to regret their decision to allow me to fulfill my dreams. I would work hard and make them proud of my achievements. In fact, I would, I told myself, be a model student and an upright and decent man.

I arrived in the "Crumbling City" in September 1948. The title it had been given suited it well. Already the signs of neglect and deterioration were plain to see. And besides the physical drabness of the buildings, the streets, the stores, a spiritual and moral apathy was palpable - one had only to look on the somber, grim faces of the populace. No one smiled, people hardly saluted each other. Bucharest was a dying, cold unwelcoming place. In this hostile atmosphere I began my new life. I embarked on the road to higher learning, my lifelong ambition to fulfill.

Upon entering the university each new student had to present an I.D. card, a High School Diploma, and a land owner's certificate - the latter was to identify those whose parents were landlords and thus were not eligible to attend the university.

My cousin, Filon Tibu, who was also starting his university career, and I spent many an anxious day thinking over our predicament. We were very determined to go to school and secure for ourselves a good position in life.

Were we to tell the truth about our parents' resources we would not have that opportunity.

Eventually, we decided to falsify a public document. Instead of 10.45 hectares which our fathers owned, we eliminated the one leaving the 0.45. This small acreage allowed us to attend school but it gave us many sleepless nights. For, had the authorities found out about our deception we would most certainly never have been admitted to the university and might have spent several years in prison instead.

The university building was a very beautiful structure enrolling approximately ten thousand students. The architectural style was a combination of Roman and Baroque. Inside the School of Economics, the wall of the central hall portrayed a mural depicting the story of the development of Romanian Economics. This left a deep impression on me and I was proud and happy to be a student in such a fine establishment.

Soon, however, my hopes and dreams were dashed. I was devastated. The entire system seemed to be disorganized. The long standing, experienced, and qualified professors were fired from their jobs: Demetrescu, Mladenatz, Leonte, and others and in their places Mata and Barladeanu, who had been staunch Communists without academic recognition, were installed. In fact, Mr. Mata didn't even know the Romanian language correctly. This was a big disappointment to me and the other students. Nevertheless, I was determined to follow the courses and to graduate. The Communist authorities decided to reform the curriculum also and during the latter part of my first year '48 - '49, this change was implemented.

Instead of Market Economy, Marxist methods were introduced. In place of the History of Commerce, Dialectic Materialism and International Economics Relations plus the Economics of Labor were substituted. The standards of the university very shortly fell and even the Russian Educational Commission which was well aware of Romania's high educational standards in the days prior to the Russian takeover, declared a few years later: "Why had such a system to be destroyed and be replaced by an inferior one?"

The same tactics were used in many of the other colleges of the university. The History, Literature and Fine Arts departments all suffered tremendous changes in their curriculums and consequently mediocracy ensued.

I came to the conclusion that what I learned in high school was worthless. Our new courses proclaimed the mighty achievements of Russia and only Russia. Nothing had been invented, discovered, or conceived except by the Russians. For example the modern advancement of beekeeping was introduced by P.I. Prokopovici who invented the framed hive in 1814. The truth of the matter is that Dadant, Root, and many others came long before the Russian, Prokopovici. They declared that the Wright Brothers were not the first inventors of the airplane but the Russians. These outlandish claims were so preposterous as to discredit people like: Morse, Edison, Watt and others. In their places, men like Alexander Graur and Agitrop Mihail Roller were acclaimed. Thus, without any shame, were the courses in literature, and the history of the country altered and falsified information regarding the inventors and scientists of the West propagated.

In Romania we were obliged to forget our historic past, only what was 'good' was to be taught and that began with the Communist Revolution of 1917. The foundation of the old society was considered corrupt, bourgeois, and therefore, must be destroyed and forgotten. At this time the words of Orwell were constantly in my mind: "The first step to eradicate a people is to erase their memory."

In literature our greatest poets and writers were banned or censored: Eminescu, Alexandri, Cuza, Goga, Crainic, Blaga, Radu Gyr, Voiculescu, Cosbuc, Petrovici as well as many lesser known names. In the fine arts: Brancusi, Enescu, Lipati, all world renowned artists, were in exile unable to work or produce in their own country.

In such a situation, the generation of 1948 could not stand by and allow lies, deceit, and fabrications to continue to be propageted, so an underground organization was formed. This group obtained their leaders from the universities throughout the country. Their main objectives were to keep the history and culture of past ages in Romania alive - in essence to preserve and tell the truth.

The shock of what had occured in the capital had taken its toll on my intelligence but I was soon to learn that changes were taking place in the country towns and villages also. Upon my returning home for the summer vacation, I found that the whole economy of the area had undergone a radical transformation. The entire population was visibly depressed. Each farm had been given a quota which had to be met regardless of its ability to produce.

My father called me to witness one such transaction. He was forced to part with a kilogram of wool for 5 lei. Had he not been able to give the wool at that time, he would have been forced to buy the same quantity in the nearest town for 50 lei in order to fulfill his obligation to the State. As if this state of affairs weren't bad enough, the police had the authority to arrest all who failed to meet their quotas.

At this time, three young men from the village, exasperated by the injustice, took the law into their own hands. They awaited the Chief of Police one evening and having disarmed him, beat him unconscious. Later, they paid the price, for they were arrested and each was sentenced to seven years in prison.

The four years of undergraduate work went by quickly. I worked part-time while attending school during the last three years, thus helping with my own expenses and aiding my sister, Veronica, who had started her course of studies.

Summers were spent at home where I helped with the farm work and, in my free time, went fishing in the lake not too far away.

I was almost finished with my final exams, only three days remained and I would emerge with my Diploma in Economics. During this time I had also followed courses to gain a law degree and had just finished my second year in that field.

At 3:00 a.m. on May 21, 1952, I was awakened in the student dormitory by three armed Securitate officers. In that dormitory there were twelve students.

"Nobody move. Where is Gherasim's bed?" cried one of the officers.

But there was no need for him to ask as they immediately surrounded my bed.

"Get up. Put on your clothes. You are under arrest."

As I got out of bed, they checked my nightstand and took all my books and class notes.

Immediately, my friend Gabriel Bogheanu jumped up. "What's going on?"

"If you want to help, help. Prepare his bag," shouted an officer.

Bogheanu grabbed two bags. He looked around at the coats and jackets that were hanging nearby. Those which appeared to be wool and were the warmest, he quickly stuffed into the bags. One coat was his own, and one was belonging to Ion Bulborea. These, with my own clothes gave me three sets.

Looking at me, Gabriel signaled that I was to take all. He realized no one knew when I might be released. I was then blindfolded before I was allowed to exit the building.

As I entered the street, I was able to see over the blindfold that there were two large black cars parked close to the curb; their windows were draped in black. I was told to get into the second car and while I was doing so, I saw Professor Cornea Dionizie being pushed into the first.

Inside, I was flanked by Securitate. Immediately, the cars started up. I tried to look around. The guard on my right gave me a blow and said: "Stay quiet Bandit, you will be free when you see the back of your head."

And on the other side the officer said: "The worker class will destroy every resistance against Communism."

So, I realized I was being charged with something to do with anti Communist activities.

Having traversed many streets, turned several corners, obviously in an attempt to confuse and disorient me, we, finally, came to a stop about twenty minutes later. My destination was a cell in the prison on Rahova; this I was able to ascertain by the chiming of the bells in the nearby church

I was, at once, stripped of my belt, my shoe laces, and tie. I was asked my name, birthdate, place of birth and name of parents by one set of officers. Then as soon as I had given the information, they transferred me to another set. I was again blindfolded and was led down a number of steps. Unable to see, I was allowed to bang into the walls as I proceeded. At this the guards only laughed and made fun of me. At that moment I felt I was descending into hell.

Arriving in the basement, I realized there was sand under my feet; then I found I was in a corridor. After about 15 meters, I heard a key unlock a door. Then I was pushed into a small cell about 3 x 6 feet with only an iron bunkbed with three tiers. There were two other prisoners there already. Since I was the last to enter I was obliged to take the top bunk. At my feet there was a small window. The glass panes were broken and the chill air blew in freely. I heard the rain falling on the pavement above.

Soon, I found out I was only one among many hundreds who had been arrested and placed in that prison on that particular night.

Later that morning, the church bells rang announcing the celebration for the Feast of Sts. Constantine and Helen and I verified, in my mind, that I was near the Patriarch's Palace.

For three months I was retained in that prison under the most severe conditions. Daily, I was taken out to be interrogated. These sessions lasted anywhere from three hours to twelve hours. At times I was beaten; at other times intimidated. They threatened by telling me that my family would be destroyed; my sister, Veronica, would be expelled from her classes at the university if I did not confess to their outlandish accusations. I was tortured by bright lights and kicked with iron tipped boots; the scars and nodules I carry to this day.

During the interrogation I was accused of having attended meetings of the Student Movement. I was told I had read literature banned by the Communist system and I had helped poor students with food and money.

It was about this time that the two other students in my cell were removed, and a new prisoner became my cell-mate. He was a young man about my own age named Iustin Morarescu. He had been a brilliant student following courses in the humanities when he was arrested. By some miracle this man had retained his sanity although he had been through the 'hell' that was Pitesti, Aiud, and Gherla, three of the most brutal prisons.

When he entered my cell he was no more than a mere skeleton: dark circles under his eyes which were sunk deeply into their sockets; his skin was sallow and barely covered his bones; he was devoid of all energy. He sat

85

down beside me and sighed deeply. Then he spoke in faltering whispers.

"I have been placed here to spy on you. The Securitate are having a hard time convincing you that you're a 'bandit,' a criminal, a traitor. I will be free in three weeks if I can tell them something about you."

He sighed again. It was difficult for him to muster enough energy to talk.

There was fear in his dark eyes, and he became aggitated.

"I must know something," he continued.

There was pleading in his voice and expression. He looked at my shirt. It was not of any great value but it was nice. I saw by his eyes that he really liked it, so I offered to give it to him in exchange for his long tunic. This gesture touched him and he became more friendly.

"Pitesti was a 'hell' on earth." And he placed his head in his hands as a sob from deep within his chest escaped. I did not interrupt but waited for him to continue. "The Securitate run that prison and their experiments are modeled on the principles of Pavlov. In order to apply the Pavlovian techniques to humans, they must first reduce their victims to the condition of animals."

In the course of the next several hours, I learned of the atrocities that hundreds endured in that diabolic place and prayed that I would be spared that experience.

Beginning with prisoners from the "correction" group, the "re-educators" set about training a number of students who would in turn train others. They infiltrated the cells and through their Pavlovian techniques day and night reduced the unfortunate occupants to zombies.

Some examples of the methods used were so revolting that my stomach soured and I tried to vomit but nothing came up. He spoke of the four phases of "re-education" - the "external unmasking" - the tortured inmate had to divulge the names of his accomplices - innocent neighbors, family members, and the imaginary crimes he, himself, had committed. During the "internal unmasking" he was obliged to name the prison guard(s) who treated him humanely. There was no escape from his tormentors, sleeping, eating, in the most intimate moments, he was never alone. In the third phase, the "public moral unmasking" the prisoner was forced to officially renounce his family, religion, and national values. Some of these "unmaskings" took place in mock religious services. Instead of an altar and a crucifix, there was an animal's penis. The bread and wine were replaced with human fecal matter and urine which had to be consumed by the prisoners. The fourth phase occured when the human robot was ready to torture his fellow inmates thus giving proof of his "re-education."

During the three days of his stay in my cell, Iustin described the horrors of the meal times in Pitesti, Aiud, and Gherla. A "bandit" was not allowed to use his hands to eat his piece of bread. Often his hands were tied behind his back and the bread was thrown on the floor in front of him, thus he was forced to kneel and use his mouth, like a dog, to eat it. The smallest crumb had to be picked up with his tongue or lips. Other scraps of information wrung tears, agonizing tears, from the depths of Iustin's soul.

"Even our sleep was controlled," he continued. "After thirteen hours of continuous torture, the prisoners were allowed to 'sleep', but only in certain positions. Stretched on their backs with bodies rigid, hands outside the blankets, the students were not permitted to change their positions in any way whatsoever. Other students - those who had been 're-educated' stood watch at their feet with bludgeons ready to strike at the ankle-bones if even the slightest movement was observed. These students were also tormented by lack of sleep so were therefore easily provoked by any resistance of their charges. No pity was shown for it would revert to the condemnation of the striker. For once a man's resistance was broken, he would talk about everything; so if his watcher did not strike him hard enough, he would eventually tell, thus exposing the actions of his watcher who was in turn considered to have made an incomplete "unmasking" and therefore would have to return for a routine course of "unmasking" a second time.

"After hours of wakefulness, a man would fall asleep only to be brutally awakened for some involuntary movement. The result of this act had a shocking psychological effect on the victim."

For many hours I pondered the situation. What could I tell this man to save myself and him. I finally remembered that during the last free elections, I had helped my father with the counting of the ballots in our district where the National Party gained most of those votes. This Party was opposed to the Communists and was disbanded soon after. I also told him that I collected food and clothing to help the starving families of those men who were in hospitals or sent to prison. And, finally, I mentioned that I had three cousins Ion, Petru, and Gheorghe Hutulean from Miliseuti, who had been deported to Dobrogea because they were active members of the National Party and had been financially well-off - thus they belonged to the class known as Bourgeois.

This information satisfied Iustin and after three days, he was removed from my cell and I never saw him again.

After three months of torture and interrogation, my file was complete, they had compiled enough paper work to have me condemned for a lifetime. I was then transported to Jilava - "the Tomb without a Cross". There was no hope of escape from that dungeon. My spirits sank; all my dreams, my vision for a professional career, my hopes for the future - a wife and family - were all dashed to pieces.

"Oh God!" I cried, "What have I done to deserve this?" I castigated myself; I questioned my motives, my ambitions. Had I been too presumptuous, too conceited. Why should I, in my pride, think that I could do and dare all. Had I remained at home, I would have had a living, albeit a poor one, but I would not have been transported to this 'hell', this infernal existence.

For several days I sat and stared into space ignoring the miserable specters around me. I did not touch the rotten cabbage slop or miserable bean mush that was served twice a day. The very odor caused my stomach to retch. My tired, aching body would not, or could not avail of the few hours sleep we were permitted. My head throbbed from the cruel blows and from my tormented brain. Every bone in my body, it seemed, screamed for attention and salve. "My God, my God why have you abandoned me?" Christ's prayer in the Garden of Gethsemani became mine.

It was my cry in the darkness, my utter dejection, my degradation - I could fall no further - eventually this realization gave me the courage to throw myself completely on God's Mercy and also allowed 'the light' to reenter my soul.

Jilava is a fortress on the outskirts of Bucharest, built in 1870, it was one of thirteen fortresses around the city protecting it against the many invasions from the East, particularly the Turks. All these fortresses extended about fourteen meters underground for added protection. These buildings were, consequently, very old and badly needed repair. They had suffered not only the ravages of war, and time, but had endured natural disasters such as earthquakes. Consequently, the structures were unsound, leaking, allowing moisture to penetrate, and being underground, the light of day never entered those murky chambers. They were therefore dark and dank and the floors and walls perpetually wept. The air was foul, musty, in places putrid.

They had been, at times, used for the cultivation of mushrooms - All, with the exception of Number 13, which was set aside as a prison.

Before I was transported to this hell-hole, I had a dream which clearly showed me my destination and thus I recognized the place immediately when I was led into the underground caverns to Section #1, Cell #6.

Prior to my entering the cell, I was ordered to strip naked. Thus were all prisoners presented to their cellmates - the ultimate humiliation, degrading of the human being. I went inside crouching, my hands covering my private parts, trying to retain some semblance of dignity and modesty. I found a seat on the side of a bunk-bed and remained thus until the guard had completed his 'duties' with several other prisoners who were being admitted and subjected to the same treatment. After about twenty minutes of shivering in the cold, my clothes were returned to me.

When first I entered the cell despite my humiliation and shame, I could hardly believe my eyes. In a space of about ten to twenty feet there were forty-five to fifty people crowded like sardines in a can. These men were ranging in ages from sixteen to seventy plus. They were all starving. I had entered a cemetery - a sepulcher of ghosts with hollow gaunt faces and yellow-grey skin. The conditions in which they existed were unimaginable and indescribable to those who have not experienced them.

In one corner a large metal container called 'Tinette' after the French General who invented the object which was carried thereafter for the convenience of his army, stood full to the brim with human waste. The only privacy was given by a dirty rag strung in the corner from jutting or broken stones in the walls. With no ventilation, no windows of any kind, the air, what there was of it, was putrid. At first I was overcome by nausea and felt faint. "Merciful God deliver me from this insanity," my heart cried out. But the stark reality of my situation dawned on me a few days later and brought me to my senses. I had to survive in this graveyard. I would live to tell of these atrocities. I summoned up my courage. I was young. I would not be broken, I refused to be broken by the Communists. I was proud of my country, my home, my parents and I would survive. I would carry on the traditions and culture that had been handed down for two thousand years. I would sire children and teach them about the real Romania and its brave and noble people.

Needless to mention, there was no such thing as toilet paper. In such close and cramped quarters, devoid of any sanitary or hygienic conditions, it would have been impossible to live free of fleas, lice, roaches, and other vermin had it not been for D.D.T. Why they bothered to give us this lifesaving disinfectant, of course is another question. Probably Amnesty International had something to do with it, or perhaps they wanted us to die a slow tortuous death from starvation. Whatever the reason, it most certainly was not humanitarian.

Each prisoner was given a packet. That was a God given gift which probably saved more lives than we will ever know, since there was no medical treatment, whatsoever, given to the prisoners. If a man got sick he either looked after himself as best he could or his neighbor would take pitty on him and would try to administer to his wants.

In another corner of the cell, there was a second container of drinking water. This water, however, was rationed. Each man was allowed only so much three times a day. This he used not only for drinking but to wash his face, hands, and private parts. A shower was a luxury. It was permitted with irregularity from once a month to once in three months. If one hoped to get hot water on those occasions, then one was expecting miracles. The shower heads were old and corroded and the water came in spurts according as the guard gave the command to central control. The entire population of one cell was marched to the shower room for this event. Those who were lucky crowded around the showerheads that worked. When the guard shouted, "Hot," men ran under the faucet as quickly as possible to try to get wet, then backed off and applied the acrid lye soap to their bodies. When this procedure was accomplished, the guard would shout, "Cold." Those who didn't like icy water or who couldn't bear the shock often returned to the cell covered with soap and had to clean it off as best they could.

In the three years I spent in Jilava, I can say with great satisfaction, that I had two good showers. This feat was accomplished because of the extraordinary talent of my good friend, Ion Glavan. Ion was a tenor whose natural ability to charm the birds was soon recognized. Although forbidden to speak or sing, Ion managed, at times, to sing sotto voce. It happened that one of the guards, who had less of the brute beast about him than his companions, heard Ion and stood to listen. Noticing that he had attracted the guard's attention, Ion said: "Officer you like? I have another." So it was that Ion managed to hold the guard's interest on several occasions. Having achieved this feat, Ion decided to use his skill for the benefit of as many of his cellmates as possible. On one such occasion when I was in the shower, Ion serenaded the guard so well that he forgot to give the order to turn off the 'hot' water. There was great rejoicing in Cell #6 that day.

We were awakened each morning at 5:00 a.m. by the tolling of a bell. Having washed our faces in whatever water was left from the night before, we each prayed for God's protection during the coming day. At 6:00 a.m. the cell door was opened and the prison commander came in.

"What is the number of prisoners here?"

"Forty-five," was the answer given by the cell leader.

Then we had to line up to be counted. When all was satisfactorily concluded, the door was closed until our morning meal was served. This sumptuous repast consisted of a cup of sloppy watery cereal. Its one redeeming feature - it was usually fairly warm.

After things quieted down again, we used our free time to study and learn from each other - all done in silence. In the cell in which I found myself, #6, most of the prisoners were from the intellectual class. Some were university professors, others were doctors, lawyers, diplomats, judges, and men of letters, writers, poets, and literary critics as well as priests and clerics of various churches and denominations.

Some of these men, like myself, lived to remember and recount the horrors. To mention a few of whom I'm proud to be numbered: Ovidiu Cotrus, Marcel Petrisor, Demostene Andronescu, the Boila brothers, Ion Zamfirescu, Paul Constantinescu, General Popescu Corbu, and General Arbore.

Our cell was transformed into a university. We had our own special way of transferring information and recording it. After we had finished the food in our tin can containers, we turned them upside down and covered the bottom with a damp soap film over which we sprinkled some D.D.T. When this mixture dried the excess was blown off, leaving a surface on which we were able to write. A crude pen was designed from a piece of wood stripped from the side of a bunkbed or the wooden planks on which we slept. Or a nail might be found which would do the job. In this way I enriched my French vocabulary and aided by my good friend, Paul Constantinescu, who now lives in Chicago, we transferred the words to the cell wall, where, no doubt, they still can be seen today. This list was compiled to help others who also wanted to learn. Our teacher during these lessons was General Popescu Corbu who had studied in France.

On occasion when the guards were busy either supervising other prisoners or engaged with additional activities, we availed of these opportunities to learn from the other professors, improving our math skills, and learning the laws of physics. In this way we had lessons in engineering, law, history, medicine, and literature. I thanked God for this gift which, no doubt, helped preserve my sanity as well as furthering my education.

The appetite for knowledge and learning was so great among the prisoners in that cell that it was impossible to satisfy all our demands. Even in that environment the days were not long enough for our active minds and eager hearts - there was so much to learn!

At 11:00 a.m. our daily supply of bread was delivered. The sight of this activity still remains clearly in my mind - a nightmarish experience. The loaf was cut into eight sections. Each man was allotted 120 grams of bread, not enough to keep a small child alive. In order to ascertain whether or not each person had his correct amount, a make-shift weighing scales was improvised. Three pieces of wood and a length of yarn from someone's sweater were all that were required. In this way each piece was weighed before it was handed out. Not a crumb was wasted, but, like the scene in the Bible after the feeding of the Five Thousand, all scraps and crumbs were carefully gathered up and, in turn, all in the cell benefited by these extra morsels. After this process, a great silence ensued. Each man according to his beliefs and customs offered a prayer or a sigh of gratitude having carried his precious treasure to his own special corner or space. Some, however, too ravenous to wait any longer, crammed a portion into their mouths. I watched as they devoured the dry hard bread unable to wait to masticate it; the unchewed portion would form a lump bulging in their emaciated gullets as they tried to swallow. It was an undignified and debasing scene, in my estimation, lowering man to the level of the animal. At that moment, General Arbore, who had been a minister in the Antonescu Government, looked at me. I had not eaten all my bread as yet. He beckoned to me to draw close to him. Then, in a whisper, he advised: "I'm here for life. I'm sure I won't survive this ordeal; I'm an old man. I want to give you a suggestion that will protect your health. Do not eat the whole portion of bread at one time. Divide it in three parts. Eat one part in the morning, one at noon, and one at night, because in the stomach the gastric juices must have some work to do; they must have some food on which to work. If you eat all at one time, the juices will work on an empty stomach and destroy the lining eventually. You will end up with ulcers and probably cancer."

This was very good advice. I received it gratefully and afterwards followed it faithfully. The general had already spent over seven years in prison at the time of our meeting. He was frail and in poor health. He died in the prison of Aiud around 1960, as he had predicted.

At 12:00 noon a bowl of 'soup' was distributed. This concoction was made from rotten cabbage, usually, but at times beans, peas, and compressed scraps of discarded gristle were used. The rotation of cabbage and beans was about every three months - all calculated to destroy the stomach. One day we found a nest of mice in this 'sumptuous repast'. A portion of mashed potatoes, beans or barley followed - "Arpacas in Valuri," (barley water) as the prisoners called it.

Between 1:00 and 6:00 p.m. we were again left to our own devices if the Securitate didn't decide to haul one of us out for interrogation.

Our 6:00 p.m. meal was a repetition of the midday one except we were not honored with the first course of rancid soup. These three contaminated, dirty meals were the only food we received during those long days and even longer nights.

A single forty-watt bulb suspended from the cold, damp, brick ceiling high above our heads, burnt night and day. I was interned in this hellish place to await my trial. Of course there was no knowing when that might take place. As it turned out, I was obliged to wait almost two years to appear before a judge. Often I asked myself during that period, is it possible that I'm forgotten, completely? When the Minister of Internal Affairs came on inspection, I asked him when I might expect a trial. He handed me a piece of paper and a pencil. "Write down all the particulars regarding your arrest."

Having given the basic information I concluded with the following statement: "I have been here two years. I am not guilty and have not been given a trial. The conditions here are worse than at Auschwetz and Buchenwald concentration camps during the Nazi regime. With no medical help, insufficient food, brutal treatment, inhuman living conditions, three or four prisoners die every night."

An example of the desperation felt by most of my cellmates is illustrated in the death of Teodor Samoila, a lawyer. One afternoon we were taken out for ten minutes to get a little air and exercise. This was such a rare affair that everyone was eager to avail of the opportunity. However, Teodor refused to go. Locked in the cell alone, he managed, with the aid of his long underwear, to hang himself. I was first into the cell when we returned and found him. Immediately, I checked his pulse only to discover he was dead.

The evening before, I remembered talking to him about Goethe's Doctor Faust. He told me, after he had heard the story: "I would gladly avail of the devil's bargain if I could visit my home and see my wife for just a few days."

During the night, after 9:00 p.m. when the guards had completed their rounds and had settled down for the night, we contrived to hold discussions or lectures. These talks were conducted not only to further our education but to enable us to forget for an hour or so the intolerable conditions in which we now found ourselves. Many of the prisoners in Cell #6, as I have said, were highly intelligent and extremely well educated men. One such personality was Ovidiu Cotrus. He was a writer, an essayist and literary critic.

His forte was universal literature with a special emphasis on Russian. His first lecture was about Tolstoy's *War and Peace*. He analyzed the Napoleonic epoch and the Russian influence with regard to expansion. Russia, he declared, does not remain impassive for long. So his explanation concluded by drawing a parallel between what was going on at the present time between Moscow and Berlin. To convince us that his explanation was authentic he quoted the exact phrases and sentences, even mentioning page numbers from the masterpiece. These conferences were more exciting to us who listened because he was so fearless of censorship or of being found out by the authorities that he completely disregarded their admonitions and their ideas of what should be taught and what omitted. For three weeks we listened to this amazing man expound on the merits of not only Tolstoy, but Dostoyevski and Pushkin. I look back on those moments as some of the most exhilarating of my life and wish with all my heart to inspire the youth of the world but particularly of America to take advantage of the abundance of knowledge and learning available to them. Seek out and assimilate the good, the best in art, music and literature. Fill your minds with the glorious fruits of brilliant men and women of the past and the present, and you will not be tempted to eat the dross and filth that is corrupting and killing so many.

I was so deeply impressed by those lectures that I asked the professor: "How is it possible for you to know so much? How can you remember in such great detail all these works, even to the page from which you quote?"

"Todirica, my mother died when I was young and my father never remarried. He was a writer, a professor, and a poet. He took me everywhere he went. He had many meetings and conferences with other writers, artists, professors, poets, etc. When we sat down in a cafe or restaurant, my father was usually recognized. Immediately, he would be joined by several friends or admirers and a discussion invariably ensued. I could not escape. I was intoxicated with the wealth of knowledge that was displayed before me. I grew to maturity fast, surrounded by mature adults at all times."

I looked at him closely. I was convinced at that moment that this great man, this giant of knowledge and learning didn't have long to live because he had been arrested from the street without sufficient clothes or bodily protection. He could not possibly resist the cold damp atmosphere and conditions of that infernal place. Eventually, my feelings proved correct. He contracted T.B. and after three years of imprisonment was set free. Unfortunately, he died soon after.

Doctor Balmus was another person endowed with great intellectual gifts. He studied four or five years in France working in the field of Infra-microbiology at the Pasteur Institute. His only guilt was that he married a colleague - a French lady. Upon his return to Bucharest he was employed as Director of The Institute of Balneology. His brother was Rector of the University of Bucharest.

He was arrested on the trumped-up charges of being a spy for France. His contribution to our education came in the form of talks about germs and microbes and how we might avoid being contaminated, which, in such an existance, was almost ironic. He suggested we use our physical strength as little as possible in order to subsist on such a low calorie diet. A normal man needs 3,000 - 4,000 calories, a pilot needs 7,000. What we had to do in order to preserve our health on 1,200 or less was therefore very important. Everyone, he realized, had contracted rheumatism in those damp cold dungeons. In order to recover from some of these ill effects, he recommended trips to the baths at Felix, Herculane, Slanic Prahova, or Slanic Moldova when we would be released. This recommendation I faithfully carried out several times during my working years in Romania.

After three years Dr. Balmus was freed and was exonerated receiving back his old position at the university because the Securitate could not prove anything against him. His brother, however, lost his position as Rector during the time that he was in prison and never regained it. Such were some of the flagrant injustices committed during the Communist reign of terror in my beloved country.

Several members of the original group into which I was first introduced were moved to other cells - #9 through #12, - Reduit - The Respite. When the prisoners were transferred to this area it meant that their interrogation period was ended and they were ready for trial.

A group of Catholic priests took their places. Immediately they joined in friendship with the Orthodox clergy and other ministers of various denominations. With this change, the topics of discussion automatically changed to religious subjects, the life of Christ and the miracles of the Bible. Among the members of the clergy there were several who made a deep impression on me. The very old Orthodox priest, Father Nichita, was continually praying, only ceasing to answer a question or two during the day or night. Other names, I remember, were Fathers Neacsu and Herder, the latter a Catholic priest.

During the month of November 1952, a special consignment of soldiers from the Minister of Internal Affairs made a detailed search of all the cells and each individual prisoner was bodily searched - a strategy to intimidate, especially since it was carried out in the middle of the night. All prisoners were ordered to stand erect with hands behind their backs and faces to the walls while the wooden structures with their miserable coverings were examined. The dust created on this occasion was such that it was impossible to see further than a few inches. The result of this search was that the soldiers confiscated a handkerchief on which someone had drawn the spaces necessary to play chess and a few crumbs of stale bread in the form of chess pieces and also a game of dice created in a similiar fashion. A small iron tip from a shoe which was used for cutting and three needles were also confiscated, as well as a crude knitting needle. After many years of imprisonment, clothing wore out, so it was necessary to improvise by making new clothes from old ones. Other articles made by my cellmates from small pieces of bone were miniature figures of Christ or the Blessed Virgin. I managed to save three of these icons and even took them with me when I was eventually freed.

Those who were accused of being in possession of these contraband objects were transferred to the "Black Cell" for several days. In the lowest part of the fortress, in bitter cold, they were further deprived of food and drink - only a piece of bread and a cup of watery coffee a day was their fare.

December came with its usual bitter cold weather. My parents, always anxious about my health, wanted to help me fight the winter. My mother sent a cojoc, a sheepskin coat with a large collar. She knitted two pair of woolen stockings and an inner under pants for me. This package also contained a loaf of bread, sugar cubes, garlic, some bacon, a bar of soap, toothpaste, and a brush.

The whole cell was astonished when I came back with my new clothes. However, it was the lump of sugar, the small piece of bread, and the bar of soap which I took while the guard was making inventory that really delighted them. The rest of the food had been conficated by the guards. Each man fondled the soap and inhaled its sweet fresh scent. "First contact with civilization," someone murmured and passed the bar to his neighbor. The priests conversed quietly a moment, then Father Nichita approached me.

"Todirica, you have brought a great gift to our cell today. You realize that with that piece of bread and that lump of sugar we can celebrate the Holy Sacrifice?"

I was delighted to share my small gifts. That Christmas evening was really a joyous celebration although it took place in our dungeon cell below the frozen earth, in a dirty little corner of the great bustling city of Bucharest.

During the service, my small piece of bread was changed into the Body of Christ by the hands and hearts of the united clergy - Orthodox, Catholic and Lutheran. And another miracle immediately followed when each man irrespective of his creed, Jew, Protestant, even the skeptic, came forward and with outstretched hand carefully and reverently gathered up a tiny particle and received into his heart the Sacred Body of Christ.

Only those who were privileged to witness this scene can comprehend the impact, the effect this service had on those present. With tear-stained faces and bowed heads kneeling on the icy stone floor, some with scarcely enough to cover their boney frames, these men knew the joy of being completely united to their Eternal Father. They realized the injustices of this world are nothing compared with the joys of the world to come and they received the strength they needed to support their sufferings and even gave thanks to God that He had chosen them to be partners and participators in the sufferings of His Divine Son.

* * * * *

'Tis sweet to climb the mountain's crest,
And run, like deer-hound, down its breast;
'Tis sweet to snuff the taintless air,
And sweep the sea with haughty stare:
And sad it is when iron bars
Keep watch between you and the stars;
And sad to find your footstep stayed
By prison-wall and palisade;
But 'twere better to be
A prisoner forever with no destiny
To do, or to endeavor;
Better life to spend
A martyr or confessor,
Than in silence bend
To alien and oppressor

T. Davis - Irish poet

Chapter 8

Jilava - An unmarked grave.

By my own dreams consumed, I endless wail;
At my own pyre I am consumed in flame,
Shall I then luminous one day return
As does the Phoenix.

Mihai Eminescu
- Ode

The beginning of the year 1953 brought the usual winter weather. We suffered through the cold and harsh conditions, the nightly deaths, the interrogations, the cruel, brutal treatment by the guards.

About this time, I developed a cough. All those who came to the prisons were initially given the worst place in which to sleep. They had to lie down on the floor under the wooden plank beds. This space was called Serparie - snake's nest. As one can imagine, there was nothing to equal this hole in the cell. One was forced to lie on the damp cold stone where no air penetrated, with only about twenty-five centimeters between one's face and the dirty boards of the bed above.

Shortly before I was placed in cell #6, a group of Jewish Zionists had preceded me there. These people were anti-Communists and were staunch supporters of the Israeli State. They were also well educated, many of them having studied abroad, particularly in France and Germany. One of these men was an important and well-known scientist. Soon after his internment, he developed a serious case of T.B. and started to vomit. His place was next to mine, so I often helped him in his infirmity. I even allowed him to eat from the same plate since he had nothing from which to eat at the time.

My cough got worse and my friend, Dr. Balmus, suggested that I report my situation to the prison commander. The following morning at inspection time, I stepped from the ranks and said: "I am sick. I have a headache, a temperature and I am dizzy. I don't know what is wrong with me. Please, allow me to be transported to Vacaresti." I knew there was an X-ray facility there.

"Put his name on the list," he said to his assistant.

A week passed before anything happened. Then one day, I was called and ordered to take my coat and follow the guard.

In the yard, a large truck awaited us. On the outside the word "Paine", - bread - was written in bold letters. Inside, the space was divided into eight cubicles - four on either side. The partitions did not reach to the roof of the truck. In the front there was a driver and a guard while behind two officers with drawn weapons stood alert. Into this truck six men and two women prisoners were escorted. The two women were taken in first, one on each side of the truck. I was then ordered to get in, and was placed in the section next to one of the women.

When the other prisoners were seated, the officer in charge gave the order to start the engine. As soon as the engine was reved-up, there was a knock on the partition to my left - the woman's side. I put my ear to a slit in the plywood.

"What cell are you from?" she asked.

"Six," I answered.

"My husband is in your cell. His name is Daniel Gherthler."

"I know your husband," I answered.

"God has helped me. I have some pills for him. Will you take them to him?"

"Yes, but be careful. Don't tell anyone anything. I can be severely punished," I responded.

The next thing I knew was that a handkerchief full of pills had landed in my lap. I now realized I was in a very serious situation. Immediately, I tried to figure out what I was going to do.

I had on me, at the time, two pairs of long socks. At once, I took off one pair and made it look like a scarf. I put the pills into the area where I had joined the two socks and placed them around my neck. When that was done, I became calm and awaited the outcome.

When we arrived at our destination we were ordered out of the truck and into the building. When it came to my turn, the officer shouted at me: "Bandit, what did you receive from that prostitute?"

"Nothing," I answered.

Then he turned to the woman and asked her what she had given to me.

"Nothing," she answered.

"When you two return to Jilava I will show you," he threatened. "I saw with my own eyes, a letter or something else flying across the partition between you two."

It was my turn to be X-rayed. After I heard the doctors consulting, one said he saw three holes, one in the left and two in the right under the shoulder. They went on to say that since I was young, I would probably survive given more food. What a joke! All those who had accompanied me that day were given nothing to eat from the time we left Jilava till we returned late in the afternoon, and all were extremely sick people.

When the X-rays were taken, we were again ordered back into the truck. This time our places were changed. So I was prepared for something to happen when we reached the prison.

Upon our arrival, I was taken to a small room near the entrance and the woman was taken to another. I was ordered to strip naked. I placed my clothes separately on the floor, my pants, then my jacket, etc., and finally the socks I had made into a scarf. When the guard returned he examined each piece of clothing very carefully.

"Tell me what you received from this woman."

"Nothing," I repeated with determination.

The guard continued to search believing he would find something, concentrating on my pants and coat.

"Where is your handkerchief?"

I stooped down to take it from the pocket of my pant. When I presented it, he was visibly shaken and forgot to check the socks which resembled, at the time, a scarf.

"You don't want to tell what she gave you?"

"She gave me nothing."

"I'll report you. You'll be punished," he again threatened.

He ordered me to dress and I was returned to the cell. Upon entering it, I made the sign of the cross and fell on the floor.

Immediately my cellmates came to my assistance.

"What has happened to you, Todirica?" they asked.

"It was better for me to stay in this cell than go for medical control." At once I realized, I must not say anything about my adventure. I answered "The doctors found three holes in my lungs." At once the group was silent and moved away.

Slowly, I got to my own place.

The evening slop was sloshed into dirty bowls and soon each man was busy, absorbed with his own needs, forgetting me completely for a while.

I used this opportunity to quietly make contact with Mr. Daniel Gherthler briefly telling him I had spoken to his wife and that she had sent the pills, which I slipped into his hand. I warned him to hide them carefully in different places and never to mention that he had received them. These pills eventually saved his life.

Ten days later, the cell door was thrown open and I was called out. A report had been filed by Lieutenant Stefan, nicknamed by the prisoners 'Square head', and the decision to punish me was made by Colonel Ciaky, who was the commander-in-chief of Jilava prison at the time.

Luckily, I had my coat and all my clothes on. Before I left the cell, my legs were shackled and I was forced to drag a heavy iron ball after me as I groped my way along the icy halls. The rings around my ankles were fitted too tightly. They bit into my flesh and since they were never removed night or day for the next two weeks, the blood congealed in my legs and to this day I bear the marks and the discoloration on my shins and ankles. Sick though I was, they took me to the 'Neagra' - the Black Hole, the lowest, darkest part of the fortress where those who had disobeyed orders or violated the rules were lodged in solitary confinement. I could barely see my way. The ground beneath my feet was slick. The cold was chilling, pervasive. My body revolted. I was shaking with fever. My head ached. I was sure I would never again see the light of day.

For fourteen days I had to endure the darkness, the filth; for the foul cell into which I was shoved was strewn with excrement, and the noxious odor of stale urine filled the air. I could not see what horrid insects infested the place but I could hear the rats, and when my eyes grew accustomed to the dark, I could see their glassy eyes watching me from odd places about the cell. "My God, my God, why have you forsaken me?" I cried as the tears ran uncontrolably down my cheeks.

107

There was nowhere to lie down except on the slimy hard cement floor. For fourteen days I existed in that infernal place on a ration of bread and a cup of greasy 'coffee' or some other unpalatable beverage. When, finally, I was released from that hell-hole, I could barely walk.

Somehow, I managed to reach Cell #6. When the door was flung open, I was pushed in. I stumbled, hunched over and was saved by some of my cellmates from crumbling onto the ground. They got me to my old space where I lay gasping and weak.

Immediately, Alexandru Ionescu proposed that all the prisoners in the cell sacrifice one meal so that I could receive an extra portion of food. No one objected. It was in this way that after a month I was able to feel my body gain strength and some vitality. I was only twenty three at the time and had a strong healthy body before I was imprisoned, so the extra food was quickly assimilated.

It was later discovered that Mr. Daniel Gherthler's wife had talked. In a delirious state, she had boasted to other prisoners in her cell of her accomplishments.

Near me in the cell were two Italian Embassy employees, Misters Olivotto and Cenei, who had been arrested by the Securitate as they were leaving the country. Despite their privileges under International Law, they were searched before boarding the plane. In their luggage were found gold coins (Cocosei) and some gold jewelery. These items were confiscated and the two were thrown into prison - their crime being that any gold objects were not allowed to leave the country.

With these men, I made a deal. In return for some of my old clothes, I asked them to teach me Italian. As a result, I soon had a good command of the most common words and phrases used in everyday conversation. Was God preparing me or was it all coincidence?

I noticed a peculiarity about Cenei, who was a Jew. Everyday he saved a small piece of his daily allowance of bread, which he kept wrapped in an old rag. Soon he had quite a store. Being an older man, his strength was not equal to some of the chores that were daily assigned to his cellmates. Emptying the 'tinette' was particularly difficult for him. When his turn came for this task, Cenei offered his crumbs to whomever would take his place. This method of self-preservation seemed odd to me and opened my eyes to the ingenuity of the Jewish mind; for I never saw another prisoner barter his food for favors.

About this time, February '53, five members of a spiritualist group were added to our number. There was great excitement among our group when they joined us. One of their members - a clairvoyant had predicted that the Communists would be defeated, and a personality of the first rank would be struck as if by lightning. We didn't really believe what they told us. But, when Stalin died a month later we began to think otherwise. On that occasion there was great rejoicing in our cell. A ray of light began to shine upon our poor miserable existance. Surely now there would be a change, a chance to be free, to be released from this infernal world.

Sure enough, after that, there were small signs of relaxation in the prison conditions. Word spread among us. "Summer, we will be outside. In Autumn we'll be free! The Russians will be going home." Everyone had his opinion. There was an air of optimism. Each man in his heart believed that freedom was within his grasp. It was a period of great hope. Our spirits rose. With God's help we would live to see the light of day, our loved ones, our homes.

During the summer of '53, a Mr. Luka, who was the General Consul in the Romanian Embassy in Berne, received a phone call from Emil Bodnaras, the Vice-Prime Minister. In the telephone conversation he was told he had been given a promotion to a post in Paris. This seemed an excellent opportunity for him since he had a daughter married and living in that city.

He was told to pack everything for his move to Paris immediately. But before he actually left Berne, he received another call asking him to come first to Bucharest to receive his papers and official orders. A special limousine would await him and his wife at the airport.

Upon their arrival in Bucharest, he was met by the Securitate. He was at once taken to Jilava, while his wife was escorted to their old apartment in the city.

When the door of our cell was opened, he stood naked for a moment like all the others who were introduced to us, and then was shoved in. A very tall imposing figure, I saw he was in complete shock. Unable to speak at first, he eventually realized his situation and protested loudly to anyone who would listen. Slowly, the fact that he had been trapped, lied to, and innocently become another victim of the corrupt regime dawned on him.

Soon I began to converse with him. How was it possible, I asked myself, for a man like Luka to have believed the likes of Emil Bodnaras, one of the chief architects of Romanian Communism. Luka was a highly intelligent, well educated man having studied in Germany and been awarded prizes for literature. His chief contribution was *Tataroaica*, a novel about a Tartar woman living in the Danube Delta.

He had been selected for the Diplomatic Corp twenty years before by Nicolae Titulescu who was the first president of the League of Nations. He was fluent in six languages and had a great gift of oratory. With such a brilliant mind and blessed with so many gifts, I could never understand how such a man could make a pact with the devil. Was he another Mihai Sadoveanu, I.C. Paron, Atanasi Joya, or Cisec Oscar Luka! All those of us who were students at that time could not comprehend this paradox. Eventually, we decided that Cisec, like others, sought his own glory and forgot Romania and the Romanian people. We called him 'prajitura' - 'The Cake'.

After a few days when stark reality finally dawned on Luka, those of us who were students wanted to benefit from this highly educated, widely travelled, and scholarly man's knowledge and experiences. We gathered around him when it was possible and asked him to tell us about the far-away and exotic places he had visited but which we had only read about. He proposed several different subjects for discussion but our first choice was Goethe and this for two reasons. First, because he was Germany's greatest philosopher, and secondly because he was a political personality of such dimensions in the 18th century.

For three months we were spell-bound as we listened to the life-story and then the accounts of Goethe's writings. He was not only a philosopher but one of the greatest poets, mathematicians, and writers the world has ever known. From Mr. Luka we gathered details not too often found in books.

We learned by walking in the great man's footsteps. Born in Frankfurt-on-Main in 1749, he was a very sensitive child. At the age of six, he awoke one night and walked out onto the balcony of his home. His mother found him there some time later and asked him why he wasn't in bed. "I hear crying and screaming in the big city," he replied. Thinking it was a nightmare, she told him not to worry. She soon found out, however, that there had been a horrific earthquake in a section of Lisbon at the time of her son's reaction.

Goethe came from a good family. He received a fine education, attending the University of Leipzig to study law. During that period of his life he lived in a rented room in the home of a forester whose wife Lotte Buf was very

111

pretty. Soon a relationship developed resulting in the famous book, *The Sorrows of Young Werther*, 1774. He gave up law and turned to literature reading Homer, Shakespeare, Ossian, and also studied folk-song. His affair with Lotte lasted two years and produced a child - Lotte.

In 1775 in the midst of his literary triumph, he was invited to Weimar by Duke Karl August. There, he remained for the rest of his life. He became so involved with state affairs that for ten years he spent very little time writing. He was appointed to the post as councillor of legation. He had charge of the war and finance commissions as well as being the administrator of roads, mines, and forests. In 1782 he was raised to the status of nobility by the Emperor and some time later became President of the Chamber. In the short period of twenty years, he had become one of the most powerful men in Europe.

He became interested in science and wrote his Metamorphoses of Plants and also began his work on optics. However Goethe regretted the time he spent on these works and duties calling them "a terrible disease", which kept him from creative writing. In 1786 he left for Italy, incognito. He remained there for almost two years and again "found himself as an artist."

Upon his return to Weimar in 1788, he separated from Charlotte - Lotte Von Stein whom he had loved for twelve years and took Christine Vulpius, a young factory worker, into his house, finally marrying her in 1806.

He became friends with Schiller and both of them worked on *Wilhelm Meister*. In 1809 he began his autobiography under the title of *Poetry and Truth*. In 1832, he completed *Faust* having worked on it for almost sixty years. He died shortly after and was buried beside Karl August in the ducal vault in Weimar.

For me the stories about Goethe's life and loves were of paramount importance. At that time when the Communists were in power in Romania, we had no means of gaining any information from the West, no recourse to Western culture or ideas. This man, Mr. Luka, was a means of opening up our minds. It was like a breath of fresh air. We came to realize that our generation was frustrated and deprived of the vast knowledge of Western Europe and America. All I had heard was criticism of the West. The Capitalists had exploited the workers and created the slavery of the masses. And, as I thought of the irony of my position, I laughed aloud. We were imprisoned because we were a threat to Communism. We, the intellectual class would be forced to give up our studies and follow the menial ways of the vast majority. We would be kept ignorant of all that might improve our minds by placing us in overcrowded stinking dungeons, while in reality we were being educated by some of the greatest minds in Europe. Our whole waking hours were spent in the company of the most renowned professors, the most spiritual and bravest of the clergy, the finest leaders and devoted nationalists. What fools, what utter numbskulls the Communists really were. I would have the last laugh and I would be more than recompensed when, I would be able to tell the whole world one day about the 'Utopia' that was Communism.

Chapter 9

From Jilava to Alba Julia

Tormenting eyes but vanish from my way,
Come to my breast again sad unconcern;
That I may die in peace at last, myself
Give back to me.

Mihai Eminescu
- Ode

After the period of our interrogation was completed we were all moved to a section in the prison known as Reduit - 'Respite,' the stronghold of final resistance deep within the fortress. There we awaited trial.

Approximately three months later, the cell doors were thrown open and the entire group was moved secretly to the Military Tribunal situated on Nicolae Iorga Street in the city of Bucharest.

For three days and nights we were put on trial. The presiding general, Petrescu, was aided by two other officers, one military prosecutor, named Ciungu, and all were surrounded by a large group numbering more than thirty armed soldiers. Among the audience attending these trials were some civilians - a few were relatives of the prisoners but most were informers for the Securitate.

General Petrescu was a man of little or no character. He had presided over innumerable trials during the reign of the dictators, Carol II, Antonescu, and the Communists Dej and Ceausescu regimes and consequently he was responsible for condemning thousands of innocent men and women to intolerable sentences under inhumane prison conditions.

This general was the instrument used by each individual dictator to further his own political aspirations. He, Petrescu, had no patriotic sentiments whatsoever, only personal ambition and a selfish motivation to maintain his position in society.

When I first entered the hall, I immediately sensed the hostility. It was palpable, permeating that vast arena. Hanging from the walls were banners: "Death to the enemies of the people; Severe sentences for the enemies of the Class; Down with the supporters of Anglo-American exploitation; No sympathy for anti-Soviet elements". I got tired of this hypocracy and refused to read anymore.

The roll was called, each man answering 'present' to his name. One inmate entered supported by two soldiers... He was unable to walk having been so badly beaten that he lost a kidney. This same man, Nicolae Zarna, had also lost the use of his feet, but his mind and heart were strong. I was impressed by the fortitude of his character, his will and determination. Years later, I heard he became a chemical engineer. Unfortunately, he was one of so many young students who was to spend the best years of his life in the dungeons of Romania.

Two university professors, Dionizie Cornea and Virgil Croitoru were next on the list for interrogation. As they entered the hall the prosecutor declared: "What type of men do we have here? They call themselves professors, yet they betray the country that gave them this title!"

With that, a loud and boisterous response came from the audience: "Death, death to the traitors." I was reminded of Christ's trial before Pilate. We haven't changed, I thought.

As soon as silence was restored, the list of horrible crimes that each detainee had supposedly committed was read. In response to these accusations, the respective lawyers argued their cases. From among the many lawyers present, one, Ionel Teodoreanu, a prominent and well respected man in Romania stood out. He announced in a loud clear voice that all the accusations were unfounded as they ignored the basic principle - witnesses, added to that, all the prisoners had been tortured and forced under pressure to sign false statements regarding their activities. "Where are the witnesses to all these crimes?" he asked. When none were forthcoming, he concluded, "Therefore General Petrescu, this process must be concluded immediately. These professors and students should be returned to their respective schools and allowed to continue with their studies and duties."

After the lawyer, Teodoreanu had spoken, General Petrescu called for a recess for half an hour - time to consult with the Securitate and the Secretary of the Communist Party, who then dictated what punishment not justice should be meted out.

In the meantime, we, the detainees, remained shackled, handcuffed, and silent, some in prayer, others no doubt, absorbed with thoughts of their loved ones, awaiting the outcome of this farce.

The court reconvened. General Petrescu took his position standing on a raised platform so all could see him, and in a loud voice declared: "This process will continue. We have one witness, Paul Caravia, who is in prison and therefore we have justification for this trial and the decisions which will henceforth be made here."

So it was that on the flimsy suppositions of a false witness that the Securitate and the Party Secretary condemned the entire group. Each man received a sentence ranging from twenty-five to five years. I received twelve years hard labor and was returned a second time to Jilava.

Before I left the courtroom, I had the happiness of seeing my father. He stood erect and determined and as I passed he struck a pose of defiance and encouragement. I could read the message in his eyes – "Don't give up. Don't let them beat you."

He had journeyed all the way from Granicesti to Bucharest to attend the trial. He had sold a bull, a great sacrifice for him, hoping with the money to expedite my release. While in discussion with some of the students near the university, an administrator from the Economic department joined in the conversation. He immediately offered to help my poor father gain my release if he gave him some money. My father was so happy; he trusted this man, especially since he was the administrator and had assured him that he was a friend of mine, even calling me 'Todirica' - a form of my name denoting familiarity and warmth. My father gave him all the money he had.

"Await me here," he said. "I will return in an hour."

It was a bitterly cold day. My father had not eaten. In his haste to do some good for me, he had gone straight to the university. Having waited all evening, standing about in the miserable raw weather, he finally, knew he had been duped. It was after nine o'clock and the 'good Samaritan' had not returned. He was crushed, devastated. He had accomplished nothing. There was only one thing to do; take the train home.

Upon reaching his destination, he was so distraught, so overcome, he became sick and had to remain in bed for two weeks.

Meanwhile, at the prison in Jilava, I and the other students were confined to different cells instead of being returned to 'Reduit'. I was placed in cell #12 section 2.

Our consternation was great when we realized our position. The fact that we were not returned to 'Reduit' meant, in our minds, that our sentences were not final. We had much discussion on the matter, but no one could come up with a good explanation.

Number 12 cell was big enough to house fifteen men but we were forty in number. The floor was cement, the walls were made of brick; the brick ceiling was vaulted, and all was damp. The air was putrid and the cold penetrating, almost unbearable. Yet, in the midst of all this misery, I was happy. I had seen my father! Again the image was plain in my mind. As I left the court, he was standing erect with head held high, dressed in the costume of his native Bucovina; he smiled at me and signalled with a jerk of his head for me to be strong. Thus did I receive the courage and determination to withstand the tortures and extreme conditions of the long hard days that lay ahead.

As soon as my eyes became accustomed to the semi-darkness of the room, I realized I had around me a completely new group of people. I remember well two police officers, Teodor Samoila and Andrei Butnic who were from Bucovina. They were arrested because they had been observing the Communist Activists before the war. Eventually, Teodor, unable to withstand the conditions: torture, starvation, and continual interrogations, took his own life.

After a few days another group of prisoners arrived. Two were placed in our cell. These men, it turned out, had been officers in the Danube Delta region. They had been in charge of prisoners working to build a canal in that area. Their conduct, and treatment of the prisoners was so brutal that they were accused by Amnesty International and immediately relieved of their positions. One was the notorious Colonel Albon. Later, he, himself, was seriously beaten by the prisoners who had worked under him.

I stayed in that cell for three more months, after which time another series of interrogations were introduced. The new interrogators, in the employ of the Securitate, were young and had recently graduated from Law school. They were, at least, a step above the older generation. Although they cursed and swore at me, I was spared, that time from any physical punishment.

Having been questioned for three days, during which time I consistantly negated all and every accusation that was hurled at me, the officer in charge finally closed my file with a bang and dismissed me.

After that I and the entire group from Cell #12 were again returned to 'Reduit.' We were now informed that we would eventually have a new trial.

While awaiting this trial, I had the honor to become acquainted with the saintly Monsignor Ghica. Here was a man who gave himself completely to God's service. Monsignor Ghica, as we knew him, was in reality Prince Vladimir Ghica. He was born in Constantinople on December 25, 1873, the son of Prince Ion Ghica who was a General in the Romanian army and the highest ranking military attache representing Romania in the Diplomatic Corp in Constantinople.

Vladimir was baptized into the Orthodox Church and educated in its religious observances. His parents recognized early his sensitive and sympathetic nature and sent him to Toulouse, France, to complete his high school education. After, he continued his studies in political science, law, and philosophy.

He met and became very friendly with Cardinal Mathieu; this man had an extraordinary influence on him. In time, he felt called to the religious life and as soon as he had received his Doctorate in Theology he made up his mind to become a priest in the Roman Catholic Church.

The great love of his life was to do good for suffering humanity. In 1904 he served the sick in Salonica, Greece in the hospital run by the Sisters of St. Vincent de Paul.

In Bucharest, he founded a charitable institution which, in time, became an outstanding medical center. With the help of Queen Maria of Romania, he later set up a hospital for victims of cholera. Because of his indefatiguable work many people survived that dreaded disease and in recognition of his services, King Carol I gave him a special award.

Monsignor Ghica was an extraordinary man. Born in a palace, it was not beneath him to spend his time and energy taking care of and working for the suffering poor. He had very little time for himself; any free moments were spent in prayer and meditation.

In 1923 his lifetime dream came true. He was ordained to the priesthood in Paris.

Pope Pius XI, himself, granted Vlademir's request to live with the poor in the center of Paris. Renouncing all creature comforts, he led a life of sacrifice, devotion and mortification that was heroic. Sometimes he could hardly open his eyes in the morning because they were frozen shut during the severe winter nights.

In 1931 the Pope gave him a special mission. He was to attend the International Eucharistic Congress in Japan, Buenos-Aires, Manila, and Budapest.

When I first saw the man, I asked myself why such a person was in prison. What danger did he pose to anyone? What could he do to cause trouble for the Communist regime?

I found out that he had been arrested together with eight other priests. The only reason I could conjecture for this arrest was that he had been in communication with the Papal Nuntio in Bucharest. I realized I was in the presence of a saint. He spent his whole day in prayer and most of the night. When he was placed in our cell, the first words he directed to me were: "You are from Bucovina." I was dressed in my native costume and he recognized the identifying patterns. He continued "My great-grandfather, who was King of Moldavia, lost his head in 1775 for Bucovina when the Austrian Empire occupied that land."

He went on to invite me to come to sit near him to pray. He said he had a special love for Bucovina and his life had been greatly affected by the actions of his great-grandfather.

I accepted his offer immediately; this made him very happy and I was also delighted. His talents and devotion were henceforth focused on encouraging and helping, in every way he could, all those men who, like himself, were barely existing under horrific conditions. His knowledge of the Bible was remarkable; he could recite any passage by heart. He led me on a path of spiritual exercises and meditations which gave meaning and brought peace into my life. I will never forget this extraordinary man, and I thank God for the privilege he granted me in allowing our paths to meet even if it had to be under such dire circumstances.

He was sentenced to a long term but I realized, looking at him, frail, of a delicate constitution, that it would be impossible for him to survive the inhuman conditions for more than a few months. My predictions were, in fact, realized sooner than I expected, because he died in his sleep at the age of eighty on January 16, 1953. This blessed man gave up his soul to God on the cold damp stone floor, in a stinking cell, in the hellish prison called Jilava.

After Monsignor Ghica died, the conditions in 'Reduit' became even worse. The food served was incredible, not fit for animals. Old peas were ground into a coarse paste along with the gandaci - cockroach which had infested them; to this mixture was added some water. This was our daily fare for three months and was well calculated to destroy our stomachs. At that point, we decided to take no more so we all went on a hunger strike. We numbered approximately two hundred people.

The first day each man's portion was placed on the cement floor in front of the cell door. The following day the same thing happened. But after three days since they had no more tin plates and the food had not been touched, they brought the horrid mess in a barrel. The officer shouted: "Do you want this or not?" We answered: "No." But he left it at the entrance anyway. After three more days, some of the men were so weak they could no longer move from their places. When this was reported, several guards with litters came and took them away. We did not see them again.

The stale food which had not been removed for more than six days was not touched. The stench so bad that the director, Colonel Ciaki, himself, came to try to convince us to give up the strike because we were only hurting ourselves. "If you continue this, you'll all die like flies. Remember the Americans or English will not come to save you." Then before he left, he shouted: "This is the only food you will receive, take it or leave it."

The next day, when we did not end our strike, the Minister of Internal Affairs, General Pavel Stefan, came. Upon entering the cell, the foul air assailed him. He drew back exclaiming in French "Oh, what miserable conditions and what insupportable noxious air." An inmate, General Popescu Corbu, immediately responded in the same language: "You have created these miserable conditions and insupportable noxious air. You are the Minister for Internal Affairs for this prison. These conditions are worse than those in Dachau or Buchenwald. If the Nazi were accused of crimes against humanity how do you think your crimes compare?"

After this encounter, we found that our daily gruel had some bits, and pieces of 'meat' in it - a cow's lip, including the hair, a hoof, a scrap of tail, an ear or an eye, and instead of peas, the mixture was made basically from rancid cabbage. But for this privilege twelve men, whom the establishment considered were the ring-leaders, were taken away and never seen again.

Things did not improve and those of us who were strong enough to survive this diet were given another trial three or four months later.

This hearing was attended by those arrested from our group and was conducted by army officers behind closed doors in the Negru Voda Military Tribunal Building.

During the proceedings we were again accused of anti-Communist activities, of collaborating with the Americans, of reading banned literature, and of helping the enemies of the working class.

Traian Turtureanu and Traian Anderca spoke up in defense of all present denying the accusations. "Your accusations are lies and you know it. We were here on trial before. We believed that this second trial would be just but we are, in fact, forced to hear the same accusations, to cover up for the outlandish conduct of the Securitate."

Immediately, the two Traians were conducted from the room and their sentences remained at twenty-five years.

When my turn came, I arose and with courage spoke loudly and clearly. "This group of students is not Facist, nor Nazi, but Democratic and is composed of multi-ethnic members who are anti-Communist and are good Romanians. I know a student named Nubar Hambartunian who is Armenian, Richard Hendewich who is a Pole, and Ioan Hudcic who has been Ukranianised." The presiding officers looked at each other and were obviously perplexed. My statement had opened up a new 'can of worms' for their arguments.

"Sit down." I was told in no uncertain terms. And the fear that I, too, would be removed from the courtroom made me perspire perfusely.

Following me was Professor Cornea, who had been condemned to a ten year sentence because the Securitate found a notebook of his which contained a poem entitled *Stefan the Great*. This poem had been written while he was on vacation in Putna. At the time, the true history of Romania was not accepted, only the International Brotherhood of the Prolateriat and the USSR was considered to be the foundation of all history. Since Stefan the Great was a Christian and had built thirty-seven churches to the honor of God, he had no place in Communist Romania.

Professor Cornea explained the circumstances of his arrest and conviction. While staying in Putna, he climbed a mountain in order to see the village of his childhood not too far off. It was at that time occupied by the Russians. Upon contemplating the situation, he was moved to write the poem. His explanation was rejected and he was told to be seated also.

The next prisoner to speak was my dear friend, Filaret Toma. His words were few: "I refuse to accept the decision of the Court." Then he sat down of his own volition.

Dumitru Caratas immediately stood up. Courageously, he invited the President of the Tribunal to visit cell #12 to see for himself the conditions the Romanian Communists had imposed on the prisoners detained there. "There is little difference between those outside the walls of Jilava and those inside. Tomorrow your turn will come, even if you now parade with ribbons and medals on your chests."

To this outburst, the President replied: "Be quiet, Bandit and resume your seat."

When all present had had their say, the Court announced that the sentences would be reduced somewhat. My sentence was reduced from twelve to five years. At that moment we didn't understand what to make of this sudden change in policy towards us. A question remained in the minds of all of us. Finally, the only satisfactory answer we could come up with was that the International Political situation had necessitated this change in the policies of the prison system. Eventually, we were to find out that

Amnesty International and The United Nations had intervened on our behalf. Romania, it seemed, was considered to have far too many political prisoners and far too many men and women doing hard labor in the mines and in the canals of the Danube Delta.

Jilava was, in fact, a place of transition. From it prisoners were moved and relocated in many parts of the country. Because of the constant flow of men and women from all the other areas through Jilava, news of the outside world managed to trickle into our cells. In this way, we learned that Ana Pauker, the Foreign Minister, had proposed the Black Sea canals be built "as a gigantic Communist-Socialist operation" after the example of Stalin's giant works in Russia. In reality, the construction of these canals was a means of exterminating thousands of those who, in anyway, opposed the Communist's policies.

The years 1945-1955 witnessed over a million people either arrested or deported, of whom 200,000 were never again heard-of.

After another three months in 'Reduit', we were awakened in the early hours one morning and told to prepare to move. Chained and in groups of about sixty, we were loaded into covered trucks and driven to the railway station in Bucharest. There, in the darkness we were transferred to cattle carts and had to remain confined until the next morning when the train from Transylvania arrived and our wagons were then hitched onto the tail-end of that train.

Having been locked-up for so long underground, seeing the city, the countryside, and the light of day on the feast of St. George, we were certain we had returned from the grave. Our spirits were elated, new strength surged through our emaciated bodies and our thoughts soared heavenward. God, in His Might and Mercy had rescued us from certain death.

I had been thinking for some time how I might communicate with my parents. I wanted to let them know that I was still alive. Eventually, I came up with the idea of writing a note! I had found a pencil one day, a small piece of purple lead from an old pencil, while I was out for a little exercise and I had hidden it in the lining of my jacket near the shoulder. On another occasion, while going to the toilet, Turkish style, a step up from the tin container we had to use in our old cells, I found a piece of newspaper hidden between two loose bricks in the wall. A part of this paper had a large margin without any writing. I quickly tore it off and secreted it away with my precious piece of lead. Now, all I had to do was await the right moment to send my missive.

It came on the train ride from Bucharest to Aiud. I went to the toilet which was really only a hold in the floor. Fortunately, I always wore two pairs of socks. I took off one sock, wrote a few lines: "I am alive and in good health." I placed the scrap of paper into that sock, tied it with a piece of thread from my jacket and attached another piece of paper with my parents' address to the outside. I then dropped it onto the tracks through the toilet hole. This process I repeated again on that particular journey. Eventually, one of these socks arrived at my home to the great joy and comfort of my father and mother.

Conditions in Aiud were no better than Jilava. In fact, they were worse because in that prison the policy of re-education was applied. This process of re-education was conceived by 'General Alexandru Nicolski' – Boris Grumberg, and employed the monstrous experiment suggested by Makarenko (1888-1939). He proposed forced labor in the Soviet Gulag under dire conditions. But Alexandru Nicolski was not satisfied with Makarenko's techniques and instead introduced hunger, continual terrorization, daily torture and beatings as well as forced denunciation of family and faith by degrading practices - obscene gestures, belittling of Christ and the Virgin and other sacriligious insults.

Eventually, these happenings in Auid, Pitesti, and Gherla as well as other prisons in Romania were reported to Amnesty International and the United Nations. The result was that Romania was placed on the top of the 'Pyramid of Terror'. No other country in the world could compare to it in the subtleties and cruelties of its tortures of prisoners. Those who were subjected to this treatment and who lived were never again able to be rehabilitated; they remained insane for the rest of their lives.

Finally, the experiment was discontinued when those in charge were removed from their posts - Ana Pauker, Vasile Luca, Finance Minister, Teohari Georgescu, Minister of Internal Affairs, and Colonel Czeller, Director of Prisons who soon after committed suicide.

The morning after we arrived, we were told that we were going to work in the lead mines. I had made up my mind that under no condition was I going to do so. I had heard too much about the results of such hard labor - men who had lost eyes, who had suffered from broken limbs, lost fingers from explosions, which very frequently occurred because of the primitive conditions which existed there. Others had contracted lead poisoning affecting lungs, liver, kidney and gall bladder and thus were impaired for life.

So eleven other students and I stoutly refused to go to work in the mines. For this stance we were immediately locked in isolation cells. For three days the guards, and in particular the director, Craciun, tried to persuade us to work, threatening us with immediate death if we refused. But refuse, we did. Finally, a solution was found when a detail of men, who had been working for a year in the mines, arrived back in Aiud - broken, sick, barely able to stand, these men were to be transferred to Alba Iulia and with them the Director decided to send us.

The prison in Alba Iulia was a step above the others. We actually got some greens, the tops of radishes, in our gruel. The inclusion of this one vegetable probably saved my health. I could actually feel my body gaining from it.

We students were housed on the top floor of this maximum security prison. It was a good location, as far as we were concerned, for it afforded us the enviable position of being able to see out into the city that surrounded us and particularly into the garden of a house which was close by. Every day a beautiful young woman came into the garden to collect vegetables. We young men watched her intently. As she arose from her work, she lifted her head and her hand and waved in our general direction. Of course we thought she was waving at us, and were overjoyed by her gesture of friendliness. Someone was actually civil to us. It had been years since any of us had experienced any kindness. Each man in his heart vowed to call on this young woman when he was freed. I, myself, thought I might even ask her to marry me. She, it was, who gave meaning to our day.

In the summer of 1955 while in a cell on the first floor, I happened to notice that a series of trains were passing through on their way east, the wagons of which were loaded with Russian soldiers and weapons. This sight gave me intense pleasure as I realized that here were the first indications that the Communists were leaving Central Europe - Vienna, and that the death of Stalin 1953, was, at last, being felt outside of Russia.

It had now been almost four years since my arrest. I was innocent of the charges brought against me, so I decided to do what I could to speed up the process of my release, if that were, at all, possible. Therefore I asked for a paper and pencil and wrote a note to the Director stating that my sentence was unjust and that I would declare a hunger strike unless I were allowed to go free.

The next day I was removed from the company of my school-mates and confined in an isolation cell. For six days I refused all food. Then in the evening, the Director came to my cell. I was in a very weakened condition. Accompanying the Director was a defense attorney from Bucharest who asked why I was trying to kill myself. I told him I was protesting my imprisonment as I was innocent of the charges they had brought against me.

The next morning, two guards accompanied by Doctor Oswald, the doctor assigned to this particular prison as there were so many sick and injured men and it was necessary to give the impression that they were being cared for, came to my cell. Again I was asked why I had refused the food. When my answer, the same as the evening before, did not suit the 'good' doctor, I was forceably restrained by the guards as the doctor attempted to force a tube down my throat. When I resisted, keeping my mouth firmly closed, they again applied pressure, this time to my jaws forcing my mouth open. Then the doctor pushed a spoon between my teeth breaking the two upper front. I shouted at the doctor. "For this you study for seven years to be a doctor in the service of the Securitate to break my teeth. For this you became a doctor, to earn a double salary for your services in this prison." At this point, he became very angry. I could no longer resist, so the tube was forced down my throat and into my stomach. They poured a quantity of liquid into it. The shock to my stomach was such that I felt as if I was being cut in two by a sharp knife. I still tried to shout, screaming with pain. The Director struck me in the face and he and the doctor turned and left, cursing me as they did.

After three days, I was placed in another cell with older men. I no longer had the companionship of my friends. I had a feeling of insecurity and feared each day that something more serious would happen to me.

For the next six months I existed under indescribable conditions. I was now considered a dangerous prisoner because I had declared a strike; I had accused them of being worse than the Nazi and of crimes against humanity. I felt I was being ignored at times, at other times excessively harsh treatment was meted out to me. Psychologically, they were wearing me down. I felt I was being torn apart. Fear was my constant companion. I would not be able to continue long under such treatment.

Then one day towards the end of October, a guard from the Judicial Administration came to the cell door. "Who is Gherasim?" he shouted.

"I am," I answered.

"Gather up your belongings and come with me," he ordered.

At once my heart quickened. What was going to happen to me now? Another prison? Forced labor? Or maybe… perhaps they would shoot me this time!

As I was walking to a waiting room one of the guards whispered: "You're going free." Again my heart gave a leap. But I could not bring myself to believe him. This news was too good to be true. Why was he lying to me. Did he want to enjoy my reaction when I found out that he was playing with my emotions.

When I eventually saw my old suitcases and the moldy clothes inside, I began to think that maybe the news of my imminent release was, indeed, correct. How I wished I could put on that stinking old suit and leave that very moment, but the prison authorities, ever considerate as they were, wouldn't hear of it. So my clothes were sent to be laundered and I had to wait another night.

But what was one more night. Tomorrow I would be going home. I couldn't believe it. "Oh God, how great is your mercy!"

That night I spent in a separate cell near the exit of the prison. I couldn't sleep for excitement. I heard the clock in the Cathedral chime the hours away. My mind was occupied with a thousand thoughts about my future. What would I do? I wanted to help my family, my father, my mother, my younger brother. I had lost so much time; how could I make up for those wasted years. I wanted to get married. I wished to have a family. My mind was a whirlwind of plans and ideas. After all, I was only twenty two when I was arrested, now four years later, I had matured through suffering and long days and nights of serious thinking. I wanted to make sure every moment of my future life would be put to good use. I would have no time to squander. Life would be very serious from now on for me.

Finally, I fell asleep. At five o'clock I awoke as usual; I ate my meager meal and awaited the arrival of my cleaned suit. At seven, my two suitcases were delivered bright and shiny as if they had never seen the inside of the damp prisons of Romania. I changed into my clean clothes and again waited.

Since I had some money in my pocket, money which I had been saving as a student, I was told that the price of my ticket would have to be paid out of it.

Before I left the prison, I was again obliged to make a declaration regarding my treatment over the past four years, and at the same time I was ordered to sign a document forbidding me to talk about my experiences. Nothing I had seen or heard was to be repeated in the outside world. This was the final act of intimidation by the Securitate who were desperately trying to cover up their diabolical deeds, their cruel exploitation, the unjust punishment of thousands of their innocent victims.

To terminate this session, I was given a temporary I.D. card with three conditions. 1. I was to present myself within twenty-four hours at the police station in Granicesti. 2. I was to establish permanent residence in Granicesti. 3. I was allowed to work in any state facility or private company. All sounded fine but the reality was far different. This I would soon learn.

At eight o'clock a guard came to accompany me to the railway station. We had to walk the three kilometers along the side of the road. As I passed, I realized that people were looking at me. They knew of the release of political prisoners because every family in the country had at least one member who was incarcerated for so-called political reasons. At the slightest opportunity these passers-by gave me the victory sign and other signs of encouragement. After so many years of hatred and brutal treatment, these gestures of sympathy and friendship were most heartening. My countrymen were aware of what was really going on.

When we arrived at the train station, the guard checked for the express train that would take me directly to my home town. As I had not received anything for the journey which would take at least ten hours, I asked the guard to allow me to get some food in the nearby restaurant. He replied that we could go together. I ordered a steak with potatoes and a salad. When it arrived I found it was a fat piece of pork. After the starvation diet of the prison I could not stomach such a portion of meat, so I took a small piece of lean meat with the potatoes and some of the salad.

When the guard's attention was diverted, those near my table asked what was the reason I was imprisoned. They knew immediately that I had been an inmate of some prison or other because of my physical condition. My answers were short. I was a student, a political prisoner. I had been in prison for four years.

Finally, the train arrived. The officer led me to the carriage door. When I was safely inside, he turned his back and walked away. His job was finished!

I looked for my seat number six near the window. This was a good place for me, because I could look out and admire the countryside as we passed. Also, it afforded me relative privacy, for, had I been wedged in between two other travellers, I would have had to keep up a conversation for those around me readily realized I had just been released from prison. They had only to look at my pale emaciated face, my crew-cropped head and ill kept hands and finger-nails. Everyone wanted to have a word with me. But I was only too well aware of the document I had just signed and, consequently, my answers were short and evasive. I didn't know who among the passengers might be another Securitate.

The first important stopping point was Cluj-Napoca where the engine was changed. This took about thirty minutes giving me the opportunity to observe the comings and goings of everyday people, especially the young. I was fascinated seeing, as if for the first time, the civilities of normal life. In one instance a young couple exchanged fervant kisses, another, a mother with several young children in tow was eagerly searching for someone in the crowd - perhaps her husband, and again, an old man and woman clung to each other as they tried to negotiate the unaccustomed intricacies of modern travel. About one hour after we left Cluj, the city of Aiud was reached and with it came the memories of the 'Hell' I had just vacated. It was here in this very city I had experienced the horrors of not knowing whether I was to live or die for refusing to work in the lead mines. I was sure happy and relieved when the train pulled out of that station.

Another reminder of days passed came to mind when we stopped at Gherla. Here, as a high school student, I had helped my former science teacher, Professor Gheorghe Manea Manolache, who had been arrested for anti-Communist sentiments. At the request of his wife I had taken food to him and from a distance was able to wave goodbye to him. Before I left the prison, however, I was asked to show my identification as well as my relationship to the prisoner. I said he was my uncle. The Securitate officer was suspicious. He did not believe me and when I left to go home by train, I was followed. Realizing this, I got into the train just as it was pulling out and banged the door so forcefully that I broke the window - the glass fell on the Securitate agent and forced him to draw back from the train. I was sure my action had secured my escape from arrest at that precise moment. But I didn't escape completely, for I had to pay 600 lei for the damage I had caused. But I was happy to do so under the circumstances.

At Vatra-Dornei my excitement mounted. Bucovina, my country! I had finally reached my beloved home. It would not take long now for the train to arrive close to my village of Granicesti. It was about seven o'clock in the evening, cold, foggy and very dark. But my heart was bright and warm with happiness and anticipation. Two hours more! Two short hours and I would see my mother and father, all my loved ones.

Finally, I arrived in Suceava. There, I had to remain for forty minutes. I had had nothing to eat since early morning, so I decided to buy a few pancakes to stop the hunger gnawing at my stomach. I also purchased a large bag of candies with a special objective. I had been thinking during my journey of what I should do when I came face to face with my mother. The shock of seeing me without any warning might be too much. Therefore, I decided to go first to a neighbor's house and send someone to present the candy to her.

I arrived later than I had expected in Granicesti. I knocked on a neighbor's door and was immediately welcomed with open arms. Explaining my predicament, the oldest son volunteered to approach my mother with the good news. He went to our front door and offering the candy to my mother said: 'This is from your son, Todirica."

"Where have you seen my son?" she asked incredulously.

"I saw him at the Tibeni train station on the way to Radauti," came the response.

But my mother sensed that our neighbor was lying and answered: "My son is near our house. Tell the truth, for my heart tells me it is so." She started to cry.

Everyone else began to laugh. It was then that the news was given that I was indeed in the neighbor's house.

As I approached the house, every light was lit. All the gates and doors were thrown open and my mother was standing at the front door waiting, her arms extended. I immediately ran to her, kissed her hand and threw my arms around her. My God! My God! You have saved me from death, my heart cried within me.

Her first words were "God has brought you home! My prayers have been answered," and the tears ran freely down her joyous cheeks.

"Yes, Mom, my prayers, also," I responded.

I then kissed my father's hand and embraced him. At that moment I was so overcome with emotion I had no power to speak. The tears rolled down my face and all in the house wept audibly. I likened myself to Lazarus or the Prodigal Son. I was alive! I had returned from the Dead! I had come home at last.

Part III

'Freedom'

Chapter 10

'Freedom'

Midst the dense old forest stout
All the merry birds fly out,
Quit the hazel thicket there
Out into the sunny air.

Mihai Eminescu
- Old Forest Stout.

Not long after my arrival home, my father took me aside and showed me several articles from the local newspapers. "Thieves gunned down in our nation's cities - Bucharest, Constanta, Cluj, Timisoara, Iasi, and Brasov." He didn't want to alarm my mother but he warned me. "Be very careful. These are not ordinary thieves and robbers. How many thousand prisoners were released from the nation's gaols when you were set free? Do you understand me?"

I listened to what he had to say. He continued: "The Securitate have ways of getting rid of many of these men who happened to escape with their lives a few weeks ago. Strange as it may seem, they escaped with their lives while in prison, now they are fair game."

So began my days of 'Freedom.' I stayed at home helping my father for about a month. Then, when I had regained some of my strength, I began to feel the need to return to my studies. I realized my release document stated that I could work in private plants, of which there were none, or a State Institution, which did not exist in the small village of Granicesti. In order to make a living at my profession, for I was qualified as an Economist, I would have to return to Bucharest for the last three days of Finals. I studied the release document further and found that since I had been arrested in the capital, it would be necessary to receive an I.D. card from the city of Bucharest.

Preparations for the Christmas season were in full swing. Mother had started to decorate. The special dishes: sausage, caltabosh, cozonac, etc., were being prepared and the house was full of the odors of my favorite foods. How long it had been since I spent Christmas at home. I thought of the miserable Christmases of the last four years. I thought of my friends still incarcerated in those horrible underground dungeons unable to see the light of day. I looked across the fields covered with snow, the fields where I had played as a child, the apple orchard, and then down the road to my grandfather's house. The old man was no longer there, but his spirit lived on and not a day passed that I didn't hear his voice sounding in the depths of my soul. "Try again, Todirica, try again." How often these words gave me courage and goaded me on over the years, only God, and perhaps my grandfather knew.

I wanted so much to spend the holy season with my family but it wasn't to be. I discussed these matters with my father. He encouraged me to finish my degree and follow my destiny. And he agreed, despite the disappointment of not having me at home for yet another Christmas, it was the best time to leave in order to escape the attention of the authorities.

So in mid-December 1955, I departed once more. I availed of the Christmas season to leave unnoticed and avoid, especially, the local police. Also I wished to enroll in the university - the Economic School - for the beginning of the New Year in order to finish my degree as quickly as possible.

Arriving in the city of Bucharest for the first time since my arrest, I was crushed to see the change that had taken place. What had been a beautiful city, 'the Paris of the East' was tranformed into a maze of concrete blocks, having no architectural design or structure whatsoever except a monotonous sameness which seemed to rise up from the sidewalks and obliterate the light of day. Small shops and businesses which once had given character and color to our beautiful metropolis had vanished and in their place nationalized stores with cheap merchandise. The street cars, the trams and buses, once privately owned and operated were now government property and reflected that distinction. They were never on time and always crowded. People had to line up for everything from food to transportation.

Thus was the middle-class destroyed and Lenin's theory of a world 'Utopia' established in a relatively short period of time. Everyone was now at the same level - the bottom of the ladder - all except the Communist 'elite'.

At the university, I was fortunate to be received by Professor Ilie Murgulescu who granted me permission to enroll in the required classes.

Before I could actually sign-up, I had to present myself to the Rector, Professor Haseganu who promptly placed another obstacle in my path. "You have been arrested, imprisoned as an enemy of the people. You have been in the company of politicians, military personnel and other undesirables, anti-Communists, therefore you will not be allowed to join the regular classes but you may continue your schooling by studying at home for the public examinations. You will present yourself at certain times during the year for these exams. Since you were in prison, the academic program has been revised. I see you have completed your fourth year except for the final examinations but, taking into consideration the new discipline, you will have to retake the entire prior four year course by way of year-end exams. For the first year, two exams, for the second year, two exams, for the third year, three exams. The fourth year, all the examinations must be taken. And since the program has been extended for a fifth year, you will have to pass the four examinations for that period also. In total, you will have to pass sixteen examinations in order to finish your degree."

At that moment, I had a strange feeling that the authorities were not in favor of my continuing with my studies. This man had done everything in his power to discourage me.

He concluded by saying that he would allow me three years to complete all his requirements. If I were unable to do that, I would not receive my degree.

What a fool he was. How little he understood my character. Hellfire would not have held me back at that time. Yes, despite all these unjust and time-consuming set-backs, I was determined to achieve my goal. So I immediately registered for the program and, undaunted, borrowed all the necessary books from the library. My course of studies started that very evening.

Needless to say, from that day on, I barely had time to sleep or eat. I would show that... Dean how many months, not years, it would take me to finish.

During this period I got a temporary job working with the Census Bureau. This position lasted for a year and a half and was ideal under the circumstances.

Each year, at the beginning of March, June, and September the examinations were held. When March came around, I sat for the two tests required of me to pass my first year of university and by June, I had finished both tests for my second year of school. And, when September came,

I was ready for the three examinations required for the third year. This was a very difficult time for me; I barely slept - studying night and day to fulfill all the requirements. During the next six months, I regularly took the exams necessary to pass the fourth year of school - five in all. For the fifth year, I studied more often at the University Library. For one thing, it was much warmer than my poor apartment in winter and secondly, I had become acquainted with a very nice young woman who was also a student. Her field of study was Finance and Banking.

The lady's name was Octavia. I was introduced to her by a friend who was married to a lawyer. Octavia had a boyfriend, who like myself had been arrested and imprisoned. At the time of our meeting, I did not realize that my friend in Jilava, Ion Zamfirescu, was this same boyfriend. My relationship with Octavia grew to the point where I wished to marry her and I actually went to meet her parents. They had been merchants in the city of Bucharest until the Communists took over; then they lost everything. Her father at once put an obstacle in my way. He would not allow his daughter to marry a man who didn't have a place of his own into which he could take his wife.

"But," I argued, "I'll get a place." As soon as I could I wrote to my father telling him about my situation and that I needed his help. He was happy to hear that I intended to get married and, to that end, he sold some land and sent me five thousand lei which I put in the bank.

For three weeks I waited in line all day long at the Bureau of Housing. When I finally realized I was getting nowhere and that a man in my position, - unmarried, no children, and without a permanent job, was at the bottom of the list for space in an overcrowded city with a shortage of housing and apartments, I studied the five people - four men and one woman, who were in charge of allotting the apartments. I waited until the office closed and then I followed the woman to her home. I was desperate! After twenty-one days I had achieved nothing.

When the woman got to her apartment building, she stopped as she sensed I was following her, but then she continued inside and towards the elevator. As the door was closing, I entered.

"Begging your pardon, Madam," I said, "I must talk to you. My name is Teodor Gherasim. I have waited patiently in line at the Housing Authorities for over three weeks without any success. I'm in love; my first love! I want to get married but I have nowhere to live. Can you help me? I have five thousand lei. It is all I have."

"Are you from the police?" she asked.

"No," I answered. "All I want is not to lose my girlfriend whose parents have laid down the condition that I find an apartment before they will even consider our marriage." I then showed her my check and continued: "If you have ever been in love in your life, help me."

"If this is really the situation," she said, "you go immediately and cash that cheque in the bank. Come back here without a word to anyone."

I ran all the way to the bank and back. When I presented her with the cash, she said: "In thirty days, you'll receive a letter from the Bureau announcing the place and date of your meeting with Inspector Saba. He will give you a key and show you the apartment."

For the next two weeks, I heard nothing. Eventually, I wrote to my father, letting him know my entire story. He came with great speed to Bucharest.

I met him at the train station in the bitter cold of a snowy February evening. He looked tired - even old. What had I done. Caused this poor man so much unnecessary trouble and worry, as well as a long tedious journey in the middle of winter. He greeted me as he always did with a warm embrace and a pleasant smile. "How are you? I came as soon as I got your letter. Mama sends her love. It's been a hard winter. But with God's help we'll pull through."

"Are you hungry, Father?" I asked.

"Sure," he answered.

I took him to a good restaurant and was happy to see him enjoying himself.

"It must be nice to be a rich city boy," he commented with a twinkle in his eye. "By the way, what have you done with the money - the five thousand lei? It's a lot of money, you know. Did you get a receipt for whatever amount you gave that woman from the Housing Authorities?"

I answered, "No."

Then my father looked at me with disgust. "I have supported you in school for twenty-five years for nothing. This is elementary! Anyone with half a brain would have demanded a receipt."

In that moment, I realized my mistake. How could I have been such a fool.

My poor father returned home very disappointed in me and I remained with empty pockets. Then after three more interminable weeks of waiting, I received a letter from the Housing Authorities, telling me to await Inspector Saba at Balta Alba at 10:00 a.m. where I would receive the key to a little apartment, on Zavideni Str. nr. 6, Bloc 1.

I was so excited I could hardly contain myself. When I was, finally, in possession of my new home, I closed the door, sat on the floor trembling, cried a moment, and then started to make my plans. First, I would inform my father so he wouldn't worry anymore. Then I would tell Octavia, and eventually, my colleagues of my good fortune.

That evening I presented myself, flowers in hand, at the home of Octavia's parents. With great anticipation, I awaited her father's permission to marry her. In a previous discussion, he had promised to give me some furniture as soon as I got the apartment. So, not doubting his word, I had hired a horse and cart which now awaited outside the front door.

I was deeply disappointed when I received only a very small table and four chairs. The horse and cart cost me more than they were worth. But despite all this, I was determined not to give up. I would overcome all obstacles. However, my initial disappointment was small in comparison with what was to come.

I had to return to my apartment without the consent of Octavia's father to our marriage.

I still remained good friends with Octavia, but when she kept putting me off, telling me to wait, I decided I couldn't wait forever for I had a great desire to have children of my own. I also had the feeling that her father would never allow me to marry his precious daughter. I was, after all, a 'boy' from a small country village, whereas Octavia's family were and had been 'city merchants' for sometime.

Nevertheless, I still loved her and wanted so much to have a good future with her as my wife, a family, and a nice home. So while studying and working, I saved what I could and started to furnish and decorate my little apartment. I bought a new carpet, drapes, and some household articles - dishes, silver-ware, pictures, etc. Eventually, I had a comfortable nicely furnished place in which to live.

I had almost finished my studies and had passed all my exams so far for my degree in Economics. I didn't have much free time but still I continued to see Octavia, hesitating to say good-bye to her.

About this time, my social and economic situation took a turn for the better. This began when I was invited by the General Director of the Census Bureau, Mr. Gheorghe Sfetcu, to dine with him and another friend, Ion Smedescu, at the "Carul cu Bere" Restaurant in downtown Bucharest. Both these men had been classmates of mine at the university. They were aware that I had been arrested and were curious to know what had happened to me while I was in prison.

"Teodor," the Director said, "By virtue of our friendship, I would like to help you. But I can only do this by rewriting your Resumé. My friend, Doamna Winersan, who is in charge of personnel will see to it and make sure that you have the 'correct' papers. Otherwise, you'll never be able to have a decent job."

Accordingly, over the next three months, I had to obtain many different documents, references, etc. from various persons in authority in and around Granicesti. Eventually, my new Resumé was completed and with a warning from Doamna Winersan: "You must take great care not to get into any kind of trouble. If your record shows the slightest mishap you will lose the opportunity to have a good job for the rest of your life. And again, I warn you never to mention my name, or the name of the General Director to anyone, not even your best friend. Finally, you must leave this job at once and seek other employment." Within the hour I left her and the Census Bureau and never returned.

The following day, I was fortunate to obtain a position as Inspector of Technical Equipment in the Department of Agriculture and Forestry. It was November 15, 1957. My salary increased from 600 to 1250 lei, so I felt very well off. There was only one draw-back, at least it appeared so initially, I would have to spend twenty-six days out of every month on the road in different parts of the country. In the long run this arrangement was really beneficial for me. I was away from the center of activity - the Capital and the prying, all seeing eyes of the Securitate. And there was an added bonus, the long evenings alone after work afforded me ample opportunity to study.

After obtaining such a fine position, I again approached Octavia with the question of our marriage. This time she seemed more agreeable despite the continued disapproval of her father. But she suggested, never-the-less, to wait at least another two years.

Undaunted, I waited and when after almost two years I broached the subject once more and was told to wait further, I decided she wasn't serious. It was the end of the year 1959. I turned in on myself and gave my full attention to obtaining another degree: Masters in Engineering at the University of Cluj. One evening when I was at home in Bucharest, cooking my supper of sausages and eggs, I heard a knock on my door. My neighbor, Ion Vornicu, came in and introduced himself. I asked him to sit down and offered him a drink. During the course of our conversation, he confronted me with what he considered a serious matter.

"You're not very happy, why?" he asked,

"I'm probably tired," I said not wishing to tell a stranger my innermost thoughts.

After we talked some more, he informed me that there was a young woman in the apartment complex who was interested in meeting me. I was surprised and asked her name.

"Why don't you come to dinner at my place the next time you're home and I'll introduce you," he said.

"Why not," I answered.

So it was that I met Florica Ion, a very serious and beautiful young woman who, I came to find out, lived just below me and who had watched me coming and going for at least, five years.

She held a responsible position at the Meterological Department and had been a graduate of the University of Cluj. At the time, she was living with a retired aunt.

Our friendship, of necessity grew slowly since I was away from the city for such long periods. I asked her to accompany me to the theatre for our first date. She was, indeed, a very fine young woman and over the next year and a half I grew to appreciate her wonderful qualities -

cooperative, hardworking, peace-loving, rather retiring by nature.

I, finally, realized I had wasted many years chasing Octavia, so now I concentrated instead on winning the hand of Florica.

In March '63, I was called to the office of Marin Tiganu, personnel services. He addressed me: "I have information regarding your past. You were arrested and imprisoned."

"You understand that ten years ago the Communist regime made many mistakes in arresting and punishing thousands of good people. I was one of them," I answered directly.

"My position from the Director is to take the proper measures when I receive this kind of information," he said.

"A man can't be punished twice for a presumed offense," I answered. "So I suggest you wait until tomorrow when we both can think about this matter and I assure you I'll have a solution." To say that this man liked to drink would be putting it mildly. So, I knew where my priorities lay. No matter how difficult it might be to obtain two bottles of Scotch or how expensive, I just had to do it.

The next morning, I arrived bright and early at Mr. Tiganu's office. Discretely concealing my expensive Four Star Scotch Whiskey in my brief case, I entered and shook hands.

"Good morning, sir," I said and immediately presented him with the whiskey.

Without a word, he snatched up the bottles and quickly hid them in a desk drawer under lock and key. Then he withdrew his I.D. party card and showing it to me said: "This Red Card obliges me to take a firm stand and make a correct decision regarding your future in this Bureau."

"Yes, I answered. "If this is your decision, I agree. Fire me, say I was an undisciplined worker, anything you like, but don't touch my Resumé." I could feel the skin tightening over my jaws and my whole body perspire, for I hated to beg.

He was agreeable to this solution, and obliged by saying that I had broken my contract and therefore had to be let go. But before I left, he strongly advised me not to return again to his office or that plant.

It was March 23, 1963. I walked out into the snow and the bitter cold. Alone again, without a single friend on whom I could count, and with no one to talk to, I walked the streets of Bucharest for several hours. "Oh God!" I said to myself, "is there any justice in this world?" All I asked for myself was to be left alone to live my life, to have a good job and to work hard. Was that asking too much. The questions hammered at my brain as I walked aimlessly along the bleak streets of the cold heartless city, but no answers were forthcoming.

At length, my grandfather's voice clear and resolute sounded in the deep recesses of my heart, "Todirica, try, try again." I braced myself. I had much to offer. Of course I would find a job. My Resumé wasn't altered. I had nothing to fear. I stopped by a coffee shop; I needed something warm.

As I sipped the beverage, my mind covered the period of time I had been working at the Department of Agriculture and Forestry. What could have happened? How could my years of imprisonment have been made known to Mr. Tiganu? The only answer was that the Securitate were on my trail. Would I never be free of those infernal scoundrels. I must be more vigilant in future, avoid all possible indiscretions.

Two days later, I found a far better position which allowed me to remain in Bucharest - Chief Economist for Planning and Organization of Workers in a manufacturing plant for wood products.

I had over the years made it a habit to wear dark glasses summer and winter. This enabled me to observe without appearing to do so. The Securitate were everywhere and I had to be extremely alert. I had learned a hard lesson - trust no one, speak to no one, have eye contact with none. How often on my way home from or going to work had I noticed a certain man following me, watching my every move. To confuse and allude this menace, I had changed my patterns of behavior - my work hours, the routes I took, and even though it caused considerable inconvenience, from time to time, my means of transportation in order to shake off this tenacious leach, but all seemed to no avail.

Finally, I stopped paying him any attention and I woke up one morning to find he was gone. I never saw him again . . . I felt I could breath. My spirits soared, life seemed good. But I knew I could not let down my guard, no, not for one moment.

Although I had obtained a good job, my mind and heart were not quiet. The fact that I had been, at a moment's notice, fired from my previous position, only brought home to me the reality of my day to day situation. I was again being watched. The Securitate had caught up with me; someone had talked or spied upon me. I would never be free, really free. My every waking hour caused me to wonder when the next order would come. I could not allow them to arrest me again; for if I were, it would be the end. So I would revert to my old ways and avoid being friendly with anyone. My studies gave me an outlet and kept my mind occupied. The work at the University of Cluj for an Engineering Degree was very strenuous and involved a five year course when one could attend daily, which of course I couldn't do.

Unfortunately, and to make matters more difficult for me, there was a policy in Romania at that time which prohibited one from obtaining a degree in a second discipline.

To circumvent that 'minor inconvenience' I sought permission from Professor Ilie Murgulescu - the Minister of Education. He, fortunately, had forgotten about my previous request to attend the University of Bucharest and I didn't remind him. I would brave all to obtain my heart's desire. So, accordingly, in September '61, I sat for the entrance examinations. Having received notification of my acceptance, I joyfully started on the long and tedious road which was to last for the next nine years, for again, I had to do most of the work at home by myself. Only during the summer vacation was I able to attend the classes at the University of Cluj, a city in the far western section of the country.

Once more I was under considerable stress, for I never knew when the Authorities would discover my 'illegal activities' - I was, after all, breaking the law by trying to acquire another degree.

In the summer of '65 I took Florica to Granicesti to meet my parents. At once they liked her and within a few days were so pleased, that both my father and mother wanted to know why I was taking so long to get married. With their blessing, we decided, there and then, to tie the knot.

Florica was about thirty-one, full of life and happiness. She had short black hair and dark brown soft eyes, a straight shapely nose and full lips. She was slender, and about five feet seven inches in height. She had small hands and feet and a hearty laugh. We were very happy together and I knew then, I had made the right decision.

Michael, our first child, was born at the end of April 1966. Now, I knew God had answered my prayers made so many years before in the filthy dungeons of Jilava, Alba

Julia, and Aiud - my prayers to have two sons whom I would name Michael and Gabriel.

During the summer of '67 an incident took place in our plant which would have dire consequences. Four of our top management people were arrested and imprisoned - The Director, The Chief Engineer, Chief Mechanic and the local Coordinator for Industry. They had availed themselves of what they considered a 'good deal'. By buying some unfinished furniture from the plant and having some workers do the finishing at their homes they had saved themselves about six hundred lei. I had been offered the same deal but had refused because I already had good furniture at home; that was a lucky choice as it turned out. Without any warning, the Securitate were in the plant and the men in charge were marched off.

Taking their places were four rabid Communists; I realized I had to move and do so quickly. By this time, I had finished five years of study at the University of Cluj. I was very well qualified and had no difficulty finding a better job with professional colleagues at the Institute of Commercial Research. My position was that of Principal Scientific Researcher with a salary of 2,600 lei.

Still I was anxious and wary. As I went to and fro from home to work and from work to home, I was constantly looking over my shoulder. Was someone following me? Did anyone recognize me - someone who might be jealous of my accomplishments and wish to do me harm. He or she had only to mention my name to the Securitate. This was freedom! But there was nothing I could do but endure and hope for better days to come. Meantime, I tried to give my wife and small family, for by this time Gabriel had been born, a sense of security and a happy quiet life.

In June of '68 I was sent by the Institute to Constanta to look into the possibilities of setting up a supermarket there. It was a glorious opportunity to take my wife and older son for two days so they too could enjoy the sea and a change from the city of Bucharest. Paula, Florica's sister, took care of Gabriel while we were away.

One day while I was taking my lunch near the beach, I happened to see Michael playing in the sand. I excused myself from my companion and went to spend a short time with him and his mother. I didn't see any harm in my action for I did not neglect my work and any time I might have taken from the working day, I made up later in the evening. Besides, my job could not always be accomplished in eight-hour periods. Research and planning often took up most of my nights as well as my days.

However, my companion on this project, Dr. Gheorghe Alfiri, immediately phoned Bucharest and informed the Director of the Institute that I had spent sometime on the beach with my family. This man had been trained in Russia and therefore was a 'good' Communist.

When I returned to the city, the Director called me to his office. He was an understanding person but my relationship with my colleague was now ruined and I again felt that it would not take long for the Securitate to catch up with me.

I asked to be relieved of my duties and set about finding another position.

The following day I was accepted in the Romanian Academy in the Institute of Economic Research. Once more, I had found a better position with a salary of 2,800 lei. I was to stay in this very favorable situation for the next eleven years.

In the summer of '68 while I was sitting for one of my examinations in Cluj, I was called to the office of the Dean of the university. There I was confronted by two Securitate officers. They asked to speak to me in private. In an adjoining room, I was questioned by them.

"Who gave you permission to enter this university?" asked the senior officer.

"The Minister of Education, Professor Ilie Murgulescu," I answered, full of confidence.

They looked at each other, surprised and continued. "Why are you taking these courses?"

"I am preparing for a new profession in order to be more productive for our country."

To that they didn't answer and I was dismissed. But, I was badly shaken. Were they going to arrest me?

So this was freedom! The only thing free in Romania was the air and that was polluted. My heart was heavy. My God, I cried, give me the strength, the courage and the determination to forge ahead in spite of this diabolical system. I prayed for guidance. What should I do. I was trembling. I sat down to think.

After considerable thought and with great reluctance, I decided I should avoid the university for a while. I did not return for the examinations that Fall or Winter and therefore missed out on a whole year's work.

In August 1970, Florica and I took the children on a vacation. We went by train to Constanta to spend twenty-one days at the beach. We rented a little apartment and each morning departed by foot with all the paraphenalia necessary to shade us from the scorching sun - it was an unusually hot August. The children were delighted playing in the sand - making castles, digging forts, and looking for sea-shells. When they tired of those games, they enjoyed splashing in the water and running in and out while I watched. Florica was not a great swimmer, she much preferred to walk on the beach or lie on the sand in the shade.

Eleven days later, when we thought we were all getting acclimatized to the heat, Florica had a bad nose-bleed and didn't feel, at all, well. I went at once to the First Aid

Station and found a doctor. He examined her and concluded that she had pressure on her brain.

"Why did you come to the sea?" he asked.

"We came because a doctor in Bucharest recommended that the children get some sun." I answered.

The doctor then advised that Florica spend the rest of the vacation in the mountains.

I then bought tickets and we went to Putna in the north where my brother had a cabin. We stayed there for about a week enjoying ourselves, walking and visiting the local monastery. Florica seemed to be doing fine. Finally, we went to Granicesti to visit my parents for two or three days. The weather was beautiful; the countryside a garden of flowers. We spent one day making garlands and chains from the many beautiful flowers that were growing in the foothills of the Carpathians. We arrived home tired but very happy and we had necklaces of wild flowers for everyone.

It was the 20th of August. At about two o'clock in the morning, Florica came to me, as I was in a separate bed with Michael, and asked me to take her place beside Gabriel as he didn't allow her to sleep because of his kicking. She also complained of a little headache. She took a children's aspirin with a cup of water before she lay down beside Michael. She immediately went to sleep and so did I.

At five o'clock, she called me and complained of a severe headache saying: "I'm afraid something is happening to me. Probably the incident at the beach has something to do with it."

"OK," I said, "I'll go at once to call an ambulance."

When I arrived back at the house, Florica was crying. "Please take care of the children," she said and there was pleading in her eyes.

The ambulance arrived about an hour later and when the medics examined her they declared that she was probably suffering from an aneurism.

They put her into the ambulance and I went along with her to the hospital. All during the journey, I tried to talk to her but she could no longer speak to me. Only her eyes told me what she was thinking: "Take care of the children."

The Doctor was known to me and my family and Florica was given the best care. However, the hemorraghing continued despite all the efforts of the staff. She became paralyzed and within a short period was declared dead.

The next day an autopsy was performed on the body and the result was that Florica had a narrowing of a vital blood vessel in the brain which, subjected to unusual pressure, had ruptured.

The following day I had the body transported to my parent's home in a casket, but in order to transport the body to Bucharest, I had to have a second casket built.

Everyone was in shock. Such a young woman! She seemed so healthy. Then as their eyes shifted from the open coffin to the small children and my wan tear-stained face, there was intense emotion.

"Now it is your time of trouble and suffering," one man addressed me. "I know, the same thing happened to me," he confided.

August 23, was a national holiday celebrating the alliance of Romania with the Allied Forces. Bands, parades, and a festive mood swept the country. Flags, balloons and garlands of flowers were festooned on public buildings, private homes, and apartments as the truck, put at my disposal by Nicolae Chitan, bore the mortal remains of my beloved Florica from Granicesti to Bucharest. It gave me a strange eerie feeling; the incongruity of my surrounds - the gala atmosphere, the laughter, the carefree antics of young and old alike in the streets, on the road-sides, while within the truck my friend and I were silent, glum, preoccupied with our overwhelming sorrow.

We, eventually, arrived in Bucharest at about three o'clock in the morning and drove straight to the chapel Izvorul Nou. With much difficulty, I persuaded the keeper to allow us to carry the casket inside. There was limited space in the cemetery and unless one had already purchased a plot or knew someone who had one, it was impossible to be buried there. I remembered that my good friend, Dr. Ion Cardas, had just such an extra plot. I called him and explained my situation and immediately he offered to help me. Four days later, we buried Florica.

It was a beautiful day. They came in groups large and small - at least two hundred people, for she was greatly respected by her colleagues at work. Many of my friends from the Institute of Economic Research also came to pay their respects and I was deeply grateful for the outpouring of support and condolence. Yet, nothing and nobody could lift the heavy weight from my broken heart. We had loved each other so much. How short was our life together! She had been such a wonderful wife and mother and now I was alone with two small children. To whom could I turn for help? Who would care for them? My mind asked a thousand questions but gave no answers.

Florica, 1965   *Teodor and Florica, 1967*

Teodor and Florica, 1966

*Teodor, Florica, Michael
and Gabriel 1968*

*Good buddies, Michael and Gabriel,
1969 In Bucharest*

Christmas 1968 In Bucharest. Florica, Michael and Gabriel

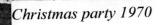

Christmas party 1970

Michael & Gabriel, 1969 before their mother died.

New family: Teodor, Iuliana, Michael and Gabriel, 1973

Chapter 11

A Tragic Time

And if the branches tap my pane
And the poplars whisper nightly,
It is to make me dream again
I hold you to me tightly.

And if the stars shine on the pond
And light its sombre shoal,
It is to quench my mind's despond
And flood with peace my soul.

And if the clouds their tresses part
And does the moon outblaze,
It is but to remind my heart
I long for you always.

Mihai Eminescu
- And if . . .

Florica's death was a blow from which I did not soon recover, but I had to continue with my work and the smooth running of my home for the sake of the children. I asked my youngest brother Ilie, then only a high-school student, to come to Bucharest. He could finish his schooling at night while during the day he would look after the children. This allowed me to work without worry. Paula, my wife's sister, came each day after work to prepare food for the family. She also helped with the cleaning.

After about three months, however, the task became too much for Paula and she was unable to continue. She introduced me to a woman whom she considered reliable. She also assured me that she would keep an eye on everything from time to time.

Three days later, before I went to work the hired woman, Elena, asked me what time I would be home as she wished to prepare hot food for me.

"Four-thirty," I answered.

"Fine, I'll have your dinner ready," she replied and went happily about her chores.

When I arrived home that afternoon I rang the bell but nobody answered. I pushed on the door and found it was open. When I entered the apartment, I soon realized that the servant was not there. The children, I discovered were playing alone in their room. I was very upset and went next door to ask if they knew anything about Elena.

"About half an hour ago, I saw her leave with two suitcases," answered my neighbor.

I returned to my home and found that most of Florica's clothes were missing. I called Paula and asked if she knew Elena's address. Her answer not only amazed me but made me angry. She had no idea where the woman came from. I then went to the police station and reported the incident.

There was little the police could do at that time. Several months later, while Ilie was on his way to school by bus, he happened to see Elena on the sidewalk. He immediately got off the bus and tracked her down. Taking her by the arm, he explained to the passersby that she had been in the employ of his brother and had stolen his possessions. He took her to the police station not too far off. What eventually happened to Elena I don't know for I was too preoccupied with the children to follow her story or worry about her activities.

I decided to call my parents and ask them to find a reliable woman from our village to act as a housekeeper for me. So it was that Tecla arrived in mid-November. She was to stay three years with us and faithfully discharged her duties during that time. To this day I owe this conscientious woman a deep debt of gratitude which I can never fully repay.

My first concern was always the children. I wished that they might attend school as soon as possible. There was a special Kindergarten set up for the personnel of the Academy which was within easy distance from my place of employment.

It accommodated children from ages three to five. At the time, Gabriel was only two and a half.

When I arrived at the school and showed the Director the children's birth certificates, she said she could only take one. For a moment, I was so deeply affected, I cried. Then, I said: "I can't separate these children. They have suffered enough having lost their mother only a few months ago."

Since there was nowhere else open to me, I begged the Director to make an exception. "I'll change his certificate," I said. "No one will be the wiser; he's a tall lad for his age."

I finally convinced the woman, having told my story and all that had happened since Florica's death, to allow the two children to be enrolled in the school.

So I was happy that I had succeeded in placing my sons in the best school available. It was close to Christmas - 'The Winter-tree festival'as it was then called in Romania, and Old Jack Frost would be coming to all good boys and girls - Communist style. I was appointed president of the parent group with the task of gathering toys and gifts for each child in the school to celebrate this special time of year.

I put my heart and soul into the job and the result was that the school never had such an abundance of gifts for all the children.

About six months later, an experienced teacher drew me aside one day.

"Mr. Gherasim, I observe that Gabriel is a little immature compared to the other children of his age."

In my mind, I realized that what she said was quite true; certainly Gabriel was less mature but he was several months younger than the rest. "Yes," I answered, "You are correct," but I did not enlighten her further.

She continued to elaborate. "From time to time we take each child in our arms. Gabriel will invariably ask each teacher in turn. 'Mama? Me 'mama?' At three and a half children do not have difficulty recognizing their mothers. And, again, his judgement is that of a younger child. He does not stop as the other children do before entering the ramp leading from one level to the next, instead he runs down the ramp at full speed and ends up falling at the bottom. Now we are obliged to take him by the hand to prevent him from hurting himself."

What could I say? I couldn't tell the truth. So I was forced to listen and concur.

The observant and concerned teacher gave me, yet, another example of Gabriel's slow development by stating that one day she saw him sharing his candy with all the other children around him.

Well, I thought, since when is sharing an immature act; I was about to question her judgement when she offered: "I said sharing, Mr. Gherasim, but from his own mouth!"

"I see," I said, "allow me to tell you something. Gabriel doesn't have a mother. He was only two when she died. I suspect he is feeling that loss very deeply. In time, he will catch up," I assured her.

About a year and a half after Florica's death, I was introduced to a young woman who was working in another department of the Research Academy; her name was Iuliana Ionescu. She had never been married and still lived with her parents and sister in another part of the city. Radu Demetrescu, the colleague of mine who introduced us was also known to Professor Goga Ionescu, Iuliana's father, and was determined not to listen to any excuses especially Iuliana's: "I don't know about him. He has already been married and what's more he has two small children. What will my father say?" These and many other comments were answered by Radu with very few words. "How long more are you going to wait, Iuliana? Surely, thirty-one is old enough to make up your own mind."

Not long after our first meeting, Radu arranged a get-together in Professor Ionescu's home. I was pleasantly surprised when I arrived at the villa, for not many people could afford or were allowed to have their own homes in those days when the Communists under the Secretary General, Nicolae Ceausescu, who was also President of the Romanian Republic, was in charge. But the Communists had already confiscated three other homes belonging to Iuliana's father which may have been a factor in allowing the family to keep one.

The exterior veranda and the large entrance hall greatly impressed me. Upon being shown into the livingroom, I realized that the massive ornate mahogany furniture was a throwback to better days.

The meal which followed was prepared beautifully and tastefully. It was accompanied by wine and followed by a light dessert.

Radu was the chief spokesman for the evening. He knew Iuliana's parents well and therefore took the lead in the conversation.

"It gives me great pleasure to introduce Teodor Gherasim," he began. "He is a colleague of mine; I have known him for the past ten years as a hardworking, honest man. He has two small children and anxious to build a new family having lost his wife two years ago."

Iuliana's father was surprised by this proposal. He looked at Iuliana and said, "You must realize that to bring up and educate two small children is a big responsibility. You believe you are capable of undertaking such a task?"

"Father, I'm not able to have children of my own. But I like children. I think I can manage."

For a moment Professor Ionescu was silent then he continued: "If you think you can take on this responsibility I don't have any objection!"

A glass of wine was poured to celebrate the moment and everyone relaxed. Both her mother and sister agreed that it would be a good match, and her father brought the evening to a close with the words: "Well, up to now this has been a house with three women and only one man, now I'm happy I'll no longer be outnumbered. There will be four men and three women henceforth. Quite an extraordinary turn of events."

Getting Iuliana's consent as well as her parents was the least of my troubles. The real difficulty lay in getting the children's approval. To accomplish this we went to great lengths. Iuliana planned what she though might be a good approach. It was close to the end of the school year. We decided to meet at a large Department Store, "Victoria's." She would appear to be a sales person when I arrived with the children to purchase new suits for them.

I checked several different outfits for both. She then came to help us decide saying: "I think this one suits Michael and that would be perfect for Gabriel."

The children were taken aback by this woman who seemed to be so interested in them.

When I prepared to pay for the suits, I found that I was short some money. Iuliana who had been playing with the children in the toy department, came to my rescue and paid the balance.

It was closing time and the customers were leaving. As we were about to exit into the street, Michael tugged on my arm and said, "Tata, I like this lady," meaning Iuliana, "and I want to invite her to our house to play with my toys."

I was surprised by this declaration especially coming from Michael. For I had not forgotten his rude forthright comment a few months before when I had occasion to introduce him to another woman. "You're ugly, I don't like you."

Since Iuliana had obviously won the hearts of my two small sons, we went home together. I invited her to stay to dinner and when it was time for her to leave, they still insisted that she stay. Having finally convinced them that she, too, had a home of her own with a mother and father, we decided to accompany her part way. We took the bus together and got out at the first stop. Then we three walked home happy.

Iuliana and I were married in August 1972, two years after Florica's death. As it turned out, she was an excellent mother and wife. She treated my small boys with care and affection, saw that they lacked for nothing, and brought order and discipline into their lives. For this I will always be grateful to her.

With the children settled in an excellent school and now having a mother to care for them, I turned my attention to obtaining my Doctorate in the University of Bucharest. First, I had to take an examination and having been admitted - because of my status in the Academy - I started on the three year special course. As well as the required studies, a candidate for the Doctorate program had to be a published writer. Undaunted, I set aside several hours each night to work on this specific part of the program. The result was that between 1971 and 1980, I published eleven books and a Thesis as well as presenting, at least, twenty-five papers and articles in different Research Institutions and in Reviews: 1. Energetics. 2. Metallurgy. 3. Modern Commerce. 4. Economic Review.

In 1968 I co-authored with Gheorghe Alfire a book entitled *The Supermarket in Modern Commerce*. It was the first time such a concept of self-service was introduced into the Romanian commercial system.

My books in order of publication:
1. Long Term Prognosis and Planning for Plant Directors;
2. Pricing Models and Examples to Predict Future Markets;
3. The Correlation between Marketing and Industrial Production (using W. Leontieff's method)
4. Method of Basic Pricing within Technical and Economic Parameters;
5. Technical Progress in Industrial Enterprises;
6. The Solution to Basic Pricing Problems in Our Country (Romania);
7. Pricing Models and Examples;
8. The Economic use of Metalic and Electrical Energy;
9. Economic Growth and Efficiency (Study: Library of Economics. Art. 29, Pg. 281);
10. The Theory of Pricing (Study: #14 I.C.E. 1970);
11. Prognosis for Future Development of the Steel Industry (Co-Authored. Paul Petrescu, Engineer. Pub. Bucharest Academy. Romania, 1980. under the title - World Economy -Horizon 2000, and others.

Finally, my Doctoral Dissertation entitled: *Technical Progress and Metalurgical Costs*. The coordinator for this project was Professor I. Rachmuth - member of the Romanian Academy.

Fourteen copies were distributed by me to the particular universities having both schools, Economics and Engineering, the purpose being to obtain the opinions and criticisms of the many professors regarding the merits of my work. Of all those who read my Dissertation, only one found fault and he, Gheorghe Cretoiu, had studied in Russia. He objected for the simple reason that I had not made any mention of the Marxist-Leninist theory in my work.

The date for my appearance before the board of examiners to defend my Dissertation was set. It would be January 9, 1984. When I and the designated professors arrived at the hall in which the examination was to take place, we found a note pinned to the door which stated: 'This Session is cancelled until further notice.'

I was very upset to learn of this decision and went to the office of the Directors; Ion Totu and Ctin Grigorescu.

"Why is the Defense of my Dissertation postponed?" I asked.

"Because you must leave on January 22, for Italy with your son, Gabriel, and it will be very simple to re-schedule when you return."

The two Communists I then faced, smiled. Once more they had managed to hinder my advancement. They knew I was not a Party member, therefore I had no business obtaining a Doctorate Degree. They had allowed me to work and publish, but they had no intention of granting me that final honor, the certificate stating that I had obtained my Doctorate.

Chapter 12

My Children

What is love? A lifetime spent
of days that pain does fill,
That thousand tears can't content,
but asks for tears still.

Mihai Eminescu
- What is love…

As the years passed and the children grew, I wanted them to have the best education possible. They received private music lessons and I employed a language professor to teach them English. Michael learned to play the violin and for two years we endured his practicing. He did, however, make it to the level of playing Vivaldi at a concert.

After he had performed he was so proud of himself that he asked: "Tata, I have talent?" "Of course," I answered. But in the end his teacher advised me against his continuing – "his talents," he suggested, "probably lay elsewhere." In fact, he was correct, for Michael very soon after showed a keen interest in mathematics. To foster this interest and obvious aptitude, I spent time with him on his homework and gave him extra problems to solve in a separate notebook to which he diligently applied himself.

With Gabriel the problem was different. Sometimes we found his bow outside in the bushes; he didn't like the violin. I bought him a piano, but after six months, that, too, was not his instrument. "Maybe," I discussed the matter with his mother, "he is still a little young," for he was only

171

five at the time. In talking about the problem with him, I said: "Gabriel you have tried the violin and now after all the trouble we have had to get a piano up to our apartment" - for we lived on the sixth floor and there were no elevators available to accommodate such a large instrument - "you now wish to discontinue your lessons. What do you really like?"

"Tata, I think I like to sing like Dan Spataru." Then Gabriel proceeded to sing: *Opriti timpul* (Stop the Time) to impress me with his vocal talents. After that he ordered me to buy all Spataru's records, so he could learn every one of the songs. Three months later, he had mastered the entire repertoire. Now, he decided, it was time to test his skill as a real artist. So when we travelled together by trolley car, he invariably entertained everyone, keeping up a continuous performance. As the passengers left each one thanked Gabriel for his lively contribution and advised me to send this obviously talented child to the Conservatory to study voice. But if Gabriel enjoyed himself on these occasions, his older brother was mortified. "How can he make a fool of himself in front of all these people, Tata?" Michael asked and there was pain in his eyes.

"Gabriel doesn't think like you, Michael," I answered. "And, besides, he's still a small boy and people find him cute." Michael wasn't convinced. "You must admit he has a nice voice and he's done a terrific job learning all those songs." I tried to assure Michael that Gabriel was not disgracing the family.

The next important event in the lives of the children as well as my own, occured in March '75 when I brought home our very first automobile; it was a white Skoda. Immediately, Michael named it, "The Swan". Both boys were so happy, they jumped for joy. Little did they know how long I had waited, and how dearly I had paid for such a luxury. It took three hard years of saving to be able to purchase it. In those days the full amount of money had to be lodged in a bank, which gave no interest, before one was allowed to buy a car. But I was a very proud man, indeed, when, finally, I was able to drive it home.

In June, I took Iuliana and the boys for our first vacation in many years to visit my parents' home in Granicesti. The weather was glorious, long sunny days, clear skies, and an abundance of wild flowers colored the fields and the ditches. We spent a week visiting the churches and monasteries for which Bucovina is renowned, then we left the high Carpathian mountains and descended to the Bicaz Valley where there was a hydroelectric dam and a huge lake which stretched into the valley for forty-three kilometers. We drove around the lake while I explained to the children the importance of this dam in the production of electricity. We passed the picturesque village of Bicaz Ardelean with its wooden church dating back to 1829. Not too far off the limestone cliffs rise straight up to a height of 200 - 300 meters above the river; at some points pressing so close especially at the 'neck of Hell', that the road is built directly into the face of the rock.

Leaving the Bicaz Gorge we went south-west to Lake Rosu. This lake was formed by glaciers and has a pink to reddish color. When one stands on the edge, the tips of a few pines still protrude from the water, remnants of the landslide which in 1838 formed this lake by damming the Bicaz River. I remember it was a good area for trout fishing.

Sovata was our next stop where we arrived just in time for lunch. This is a bathing resort set in the midst of beautiful forests and consisting of a series of lakes formed in old salt quarries. Fresh water on the surface of the lakes acts as insulation keeping the lower salt water at a constant temperature of between 30° - 40° c. all year round.

A most interesting experience on this trip, especially for the children, was our stop at Sapanta. Here in the 'Happy Cemetery', largely the work of Stan Ion Patras, we were amazed to see the beautiful colorfully-painted headboards. Some had portraits of the deceased, scenes from their lives or reminders of their professions; each plaque is accompanied by witty limericks - "who sought money to amass, could not escape Death, alas!" A mother's message to her son - "Griga, may you pardoned be, even though you did stab me."

We spent three days at the Felix Hot Springs enjoying the mineral waters and in general relaxing, taking walks in the nearby forest and visiting some old historical castles, and their museums.

Our next visit took us to the Ice Cave of Scarisoara. The cave is filled with 75,000 cubic meters of ice, 15 m thick, and it has preserved evidence of climatic changes over the past 4000 years. In several chambers there were fascinating and elaborate formations of stalagmites and stalactites. Towering pillars in the inner cavern gave it the special name of 'The Church'.

Alba Iulia was a city I did not want to bypass for three reasons: its historical import, its cathedral, and the fact that I had been imprisoned there for seven months.

The city is dominated by a huge citadel laid out in the shape of a star and the plateau on which it stands has been fortified ever since Roman times. Inside the citadel there is the Museum of Unification embodying the fact that Romania's history has been a long and bloody fight for national unity which, finally, was gained on December 1, 1918.

Other important buildings which we visited on that occasion were: The Orthodox Church built in 1921 where King Ferdinand and Queen Marie were crowned and the Catholic St. Michael's Cathedral built between 1247 and

1290. It is in the Romanesque style and it houses the tomb of Hunyadi, the greatest of Transylvania's warlords.

I wanted my sons to see the old fortress built during the Austro-Hungarian occupation, where I had spent my last dark days in a Communist-run prison.

While I stood outside the once drab, grey and crumbling walls, I thought of the thousands of brave men who had suffered and died within. I couldn't help making a comparison between then and now. A new coat of paint, renovations which converted the cold inhospitable cells into modern offices and businesses - what about the human tragedy that had occured in those very rooms? Again, I came face to face with the cruel, callous, and calculated indifference of the governing bodies of our country. How many innocent men, young and old alike, had been cruelly tortured and had died in that very building! Should it not have been preserved as a memorial to those countless heroes, as a shrine to the martyred, as a hallowed tomb, where generations, yet unborn, might contemplate and from that experience learn never to allow such atrocities again? For those who do not learn from the past are bound to repeat its follies.

To this moment, my flesh crawls, my mind rebels, my whole body shivers when my thoughts return to that 'Hell' of tortures, insanity, and death. My spirit alone rises up in defiance, and goaded now, as then, by some unseen force which I know as God, it will never be silenced or defeated.

It was in that city, Alba Iulia, in that fortress of evil that I endured the rigors of a hunger strike for six days. Among the injuries sustained there was the loss of several teeth, particularly my front ones, due to the method and persistance of the 'good' prison doctor, who, in his attempt to force-feed me, thrust a spoon between my teeth thus prying my mouth open. One was allowed to die of starvation, Communist fashion, but one dare not deviate from their particular form of starvation.

We stopped for a few hours in Ramnicu Valcea for lunch, after which, I took the opportunity to point out the school which, as a young boy, I attended. We spent some time near the lake in the Zavoiul Gardens and I told my children about my meeting there with my father and how we enjoyed listening to Maria Tanase's singing. Finally, we visited the cave which served as a bomb shelter during the American air-raids. Bucharest was our next stop and we were all glad to be home again. It was Sunday evening, my last few hours of vacation. The following morning, I returned to work.

At approximately nine o'clock on the evening of March 4, 1977, we had just finished celebrating Gabriel's ninth birthday and had retired for the night when the city of Bucharest was shaken by a violent earthquake - 7.4 on the Richter scale. I was sleeping at the time, as was the rest of the family. Juliana was the first to feel the effects; she looked out the window to see the waters in the lake rising and the earth in front of our apartment heave and roll. She called to me. Luckily, our building withstood the force. I woke the children, dressed them and prepared to leave the city. I realized that if we had one quake another would follow.

As fast as we could we drove through the crowded streets and headed for the Arnota Monastery high up in the Carpathean mountains.

On our way the scenes I witnessed remain vividly in my memory - buildings tumbled in a pile of rubble and dust, gas pipes exploded and burst into flames. The streets were jammed with traffic; back and forth, distraught people running, screaming, crying for help. In a matter of minutes complete chaos had engulfed the entire area.

In one place a block of buildings had collapsed. I heard the cries of those who had survived under the debris but when the rescue workers came on the scene they only made matters worse, instead of carefully removing some of the supporting beams, they cut them and as a result the inevitable happened, the rest of the building collapsed killing everyone. During this catastrophe, Mr. Ceausescu was away on a visit, so no one took any initiative. Eventually, when he did arrive home, a semblance of organization was evident. Such was Romania at the time, that only the Dictator could make decisions for the entire country.

Before we left the city behind us, we stopped by Iuliana's parents. By the grace of God, they were all in good health and the house had been spared any damage.

Arriving in the monastery, we were graciously received and given a room with three beds. Here, I felt that we would find peace and quiet and in our completely new surroundings, the children would soon forget the horrors of the night that had just passed.

The next morning, I was convinced that my decision had been the right one. We awoke with the chiming of the monastery bell; it was time for prayer. The birds were already giving praise to their maker and we gladly joined the nuns to express our gratitude to God for having spared all of us.

After prayers we were served coffee and bread. Then we went for a walk in the gardens, although the snow was still heavy and covered the ground, it was invigorating and a great distraction, especially for the boys.

After a week, we were refreshed and relaxed and ready to return to Bucharest. We were happy to find that our apartment and everything in it was intact. But all around in various parts of the city it was like a war zone. It would be a long time before things got back to normal — so many killed or wounded. No one ever found out for sure how many casualties.

In 1978, my father-in-law had an accident while crossing the street. He was hit by a car and broke his thigh. At that time, he was about eighty years old, so he had to spend many months in hospital. He realized the accident would shorten his life. For me and the children and especially Iuliana, it was a sad time. He had been a good educator all his life and my two boys had acquired much from his knowledge and expertise. He had attended the University of Leipzig - was a brilliant student speaking five languages, Greek, Latin, German, French and Romanian. His greatest contribution to Romania upon his return to his native land was to introduce the most advanced system of German agricultural technology. He founded the first high school for this type of education - operation and maintenance of agricultural machinery, the establishment of bakeries and the setting up of a system of land usage, surveying and conservation. This school which to this day bears his name - Goga Ionescu High School is located in the city of Titu near Bucharest, and has produced excellent results. It was a model which was quickly replicated in other parts of the country during and after World War II.

Two years later Professor Ionescu suffered from prostate problems. He was so sick that I had to call the emergency. When I spoke to the doctor in charge, he asked me how old the man was. I answered: "He's in his eighties."

"We don't have any place for him," he responded. "Anyway he has made enough pee-pee." And the phone was slammed down.

There was nothing I could do but go to the hospital myself making sure I had at least a thousand lei in my pocket. Having discussed the situation with the Director of the hospital and personally putting the money into his pocket, I was informed that there would be a place available immediately and that an ambulance would be sent posthaste to my address.

My father-in-law spent at least two weeks in the hospital, after which he was treated at home by Doctor Ion Cardas and lived for another two years.

During the 1970's the Romanian government started an intensive program to industrialize the country. Huge plants were built and the money was obtained from the International Monetary Fund. To support this large debt, the people of Romania had to pay dearly. Prices for food rose rapidly and large quantities of the best products were exported. For domestic consumption only the barest essentials were retained in the country. As a result there was never enough of anything - cheese, milk, butter, eggs, meat, although in theory these items were proportioned out to each customer, in reality the amounts were never adequate and often the supplies at the stores ran out long before everyone was served. The norm was long lines everywhere and as no one store supplied all the food items, consequently, one had to go from one long line to another to acquire a few groceries. I spent many hours after work queueing up for a few sausages, while my wife, Iuliana did the same at another store for a loaf of bread.

Of course all the people were not subjected to this treatment. Those of the "nomenclature" or the Party members, as well as the Securitate - Secret Police, had a special store where they could purchase anything they wanted. For these classes of people, Communism was an ideal system; they lived like kings.

Ceausescu, the Dictator, who ruled Romania at the time, tried to persuade the rest of the world and the West in particular that his was an independent and democratic state having nothing whatsoever to do with Moscow. This was merely a front to attract Western aid and investments as

179

was discovered in 1978 when General Pacepa defected. It was revealed that Ceausescu was, in fact, a double dealer - keeping Moscow happy while pretending to open the Romanian economy to the West.

Externally, Ceausescu was respected because he fulfilled his obligations - he repaid his debts on time, but within the country, he was a Dictator in the extreme, obliging his people to support the unsupportable and crushing all resistance without mercy.

Along with this "Open up to the West" attitude came one advantage - that of limited travel. Those in the Communist elite were allowed to journey to France, Greece, Germany, and Italy. But the rest of the population was restricted to the Eastern-Bloc countries.

I availed of this opportunity in 1978 and with my wife motored through Hungary, Czechoslovakia, Poland and East Germany.

We left Romania from the western city of Oradea and traversed Hungary towards the Czech border in the northwest. Most of this land is flat as far as the eye can see and consists of rich farms producing large quantities of grain and potatoes. Not until we arrived at the Tatras, the eight-thousand-foot peaks of the Carpathians which separate that area from Poland, did we see any high ground. This was a picturesque, romantic place which displayed the deep greens of conifers and other forest trees, reminding me of my beloved Bucovina. We travelled through valleys green with pastures and meadows, and perfumed with the heady smell of orchards. Fields and roads were bordered by rows of cherry trees. And along the river beds in the marshy lands barefoot children tended sheep and gaggling geese.

The population showed its mixed heritage - German, Polish, and Hungarian, for each race has retained its language and distinct ethnic racial diversity.

As we neared the city of Prague, we were hailed like conquering heroes by the passing motorists and pedestrians alike - with cheers, hand-waving and excited salutations. Our white Skoda was the attraction. Seeing our Romanian license plate, everyone immediately realized that their national product was appreciated in other countries besides their own.

The city of Prague is made up of two towns - the Old and the New. In the Old Town we discovered the quaint theater called Mozarteum where the great composer himself once conducted his works. There are two opera houses, one Czech, the other German which is not surprising in the land of Dvorak and Smetna. We enjoyed seeing the Castle, the Hradcauy which is today the seat of the government, and before we left we prayed in the beautiful Cathedral of St. Vitus with its Gothic spires where for centuries Bohemia's kings were crowned.

Poland is known as the land of the plains. Only in the southern portion lying near the Carpathians does the flat land give way to hills. It is a country of rich well-watered soil, raising thousands of acres of grains, potatoes and sugar beets.

Cracow was the first big city to greet us in this vast land. Situated on the Vistula it has for centuries been an important trade route to the East and was for three hundred years the capital of Poland. Its university, so old for it was founded in 1364, has become permanently black with the passage of time. We were surprised to hear the hejnal trumpeted from the tower of Our Lady's Church and were told it commemorated the saving of the city from the Tartar invaders.

My excitement was great when we entered Berlin - this the capital city of what I considered one of the greatest countries of the world. My mind went back to my years in prison and I remembered all I had learned from such

181

superior minds as Monsignor Ghica, Cisek Oscar Luca, and Alex Ionescu. It was almost as if I were entering a sacred sanctuary. This world of Goethe, Nieche, and Schopenhauer, of Beethoven, Brahms, Schumann, Mendelssohn and Wagner, of the writers: Schiller, Wieland, and Herder, of the world - renowned scientists and mathematicians, Einstein, Von Braun and Oppenheimer. I knew them all and felt I was about to greet old friends in their own homes and haunts. My wife was amazed when I told her so many details of their lives and loves as well as my familiarity with and understanding of the works of these brilliant men.

My first impression was a sorry one, however, and my heart bled when standing by the Brandenburg Gate, I beheld the Wall which divided the East from the West. Here we were prisoners, cut off from the rest of the world while a few feet away people went about their business in complete freedom - no wonder that Wall was known in Eastern Europe as 'The Wall of Disgrace'. We visited the university, the Reichstag, and many of the stores which, at the time, seemed so well stocked in comparison with those in Bucharest.

In Potsdam we had the pleasure of a guided and very informative tour of Frederick the Great's summer residence, Sanssouci. Set among the hills and meadows, lakes and woodlands, this magnificient palace is surrounded by a beautifully landscaped park. The palace was built in 1745 - 1747 according to Frederick's impeccable French-influenced taste. Every inch of the interior walls were adorned in extravagant rococo style.

At the end of a long avenue that runs through Sanssouci Park stood The New Palace (Neues Palais) which is much larger and grander than Sanssouci. Built after the Seven Years' War (1756 - 63) it has an indoor grotto hall, the walls and columns of which are set with shells, coral, and other aquatic decoration. In the upper gallery there are paintings of the 17th Century Italian Masters. A beautiful theater in which drama and opera are still performed is also a part of this floor.

The city of Potsdam is interesting for its stately domed church of St. Nikolai (1724) built in the Baroque style with classical columns. There is also an Egyptian obelisk erected by the architect of Sanssouci, Von Knobelsdorff.

The Schlossholel Cecilienhof, an English country-style mansion, is the place were Truman, Athlee and Stalin drew up the 1945 Potsdam Agreement. This was of particular interest to me since I and my beloved country had suffered so much from that Agreement which sold half of Europe to the tyrant Stalin.

We headed south from Potsdam and took in the cities of Dessau, Halle, and Eisenach on our way to Weimar. This latter city, the home of Goethe, I just had to see.

In Eisenach, we stayed only long enough for me to visit the site of eastern Germany's automobile industry. I was amazed to find out that they were using compressed cardboard to manufacture their automobiles. I hoped I wouldn't ever have occasion to buy one of them.

Erfurt, the city of flowers and towers was a delight. We learned that it was the center of eastern German horticultural trade and Europe's largest flower and vegetable-seed production.

The Cathedral with its glorious stained-glass windows and beautiful carvings holds the biggest free-swinging bell in the world - the Gloriosa. It was cast in 1497 and took three years to install. When I entered its hallowed walls, I knelt to thank God for his goodness to me, in allowing me to see such wonders.

On the Ilm River, Weimar seemed a small place to have acquired such a large name and reputation. But I knew that by the early 19th Century it had become one of Europe's most important cultural centers, as the poets Goethe and Schiller had both resided there. Johann Sebastian Bach had played the organ and Carl Maria von Weber had written some of his best music in that city. Liszt had been director of music there and presented the first performance of *Lohengrin* to its cultured citizens. It was here also that the first German democracy, Weimar Republic, received its constitution drawn up by the German National Assembly in 1919-20. Unfortunately it, too, saw the first congress of Hitler's New Nazi party after the collapse of the Weimar government.

To the widowed Countess Anna Amalia, Weimar owes much of its greatness. For in the late 18th century she went talent hunting, wishing to adorn her Saxon home with cultural figures. Goethe was her first find and he spent 57 years of his life in that city. Not far from Goethe's residence, is the Schillerhaus.

Entering into Goethe's home was, I must confess, the highlight of my travels. I had a vivid picture of where it was located and I knew each room and every bit of furniture as if it were my own home. The pictures of this beloved man had been etched so well in my brain by the equally beloved Cisek Oscar Luca, the Romanian Consul General to Geneva until 1953, while we were together in our prison cell in Jilava. I wept tears of joy on that occasion and was ecstatic to think that I had survived the horrors of Communism and was able to breath the air of superior minds - free minds, for a few short hours, at least, in the environment in which such greatness had flourished.

Again, my wife, was amazed at my knowledge of intimate details regarding Goethe's life and work. I informed her of the story of Goethe's first meeting with his future wife, Christine Vulpius, an uneducated woman. It was the talk of the cultured world of the period when he actually married her. The only attraction, it seemed, was his admiration for the glistening dew drops on her naked leg when he met her early one morning as he passed the public park on his way to the Foreign office where he was Minister of Foreign Affairs. Christine stopped Goethe's carriage and offered her brother's manuscript to him, letting him know that nobody wanted to publish it. He took the work and told her to come to his office in a few days; which she did. After that meeting, she was invited to his home and there she remained for the rest of his life.

Many have puzzled over the curious choice Goethe made - an ignorant, unsophisticated woman who eventually bore him two children, neither of whom amounted to anything. Some say the fact that the great man needed nothing from an intellectual counterpart made sense and if his wife looked after him and catered to his physical needs, his own superior intelligence supplied the rest.

Leipzig, the second-largest city in eastern Germany was always a major trading center. It was here that Johann Sebastian Bach (1685-1750) was organist and choir director in St. Thomas's Church. Richard Wagner was born in this city in 1813, and Goethe and Schiller both lived and worked there.

My chief interest was to visit the university; for it was at this university that my father-in-law, Professor Ionescu, received his advanced education.

Towering above the city is a 470-foot structure which designates the University of Leipzig. In the tower are housed office and lecture rooms, and a spacious campus is spread out below.

We also attended an opera in what is known as the first postwar theater to be built in Communist East Germany. Its solid unimaginative style is the subject of much controversy.

Dresden, the Florence of the North was the capital of Saxony dating back to the 15th century. It was considered one of the Western world's architectural and cultural treasures until the British bombers destroyed it overnight in February 1945, even though it was declared an "open city". If I had not decided to make a hasty exit, I think I would have cried tears of blood to have to witness the destruction, the utter barbaric and wanton devastation that the British air force wrought on that once glorious city. As it was, I saw enough; women piling debris, a few buildings under reconstruction, but the horror, I still can picture in my mind today, was the sight of twenty thousand wedding rings which had been collected from the charred hands after the bombing and which were preserved in a small museum near the Cathedral of Our Lady. Here also I learned that from the entire population of the city only 39, 773 were identified. Over half a million civilians and more than 55,000 fire fighters fell victim to this, Churchill's "fire storm strategy" - so called because the bombardment created a fire storm in the city center, a storm which was impossible to extinguish.

We journeyed through Czechoslovakia once more, this time traversing the western section. The city of Bratislava on the Danube was the largest town on our way and we were fortunate to witness a wedding party as we drove by one of its many churches. The bride did not wear white but was decked out in a multitude of bright colors; her headdress was made up of several layers of ribbons. It was a very quaint but attractive sight.

Our time in Hungary was considerably longer on this our return trip, than when we entered its eastern province on our way to Germany. I wished to see a friend of my father, Ianos Kovaks, in Dombovar, so while on route we stopped off to take in the sights of Lake Balaton, famous all over the country as a vacation resort. After leaving the lake, we travelled all night in order to arrive early in Pets where we remained for four days.

Ianos Kovaks, a Hungarian, had lived for many years in Tibeni a small village not far from Granicesti and our home. He had become good friends with my father during the war as they both served in the army in W.W. I together.

In 1940 when the Germans as allies entered Romania, the many ethnic groups were dispersed to their individual native lands following Hitler's orders. So it was that Ianos and his family departed and went to live in southern Hungary.

When I met him, he owned a small farm and seemed prosperous. We discussed the differences between our two countries. He pointed out that in Hungary things had changed a lot after the 1956 Revolution. There was freedom of religion and there were additional holidays in the calendar year. As a farmer he was allowed to have ten pigs, four cows, twenty sheep and two horses. This situation greatly reduced the possibility of hunger on the individual farms but, as in all Communist countries, the collective farms were also in operation, and every capable person was obliged to carry his own weight. In comparison with Romania, I concluded, this system seemed light years ahead. The farmer in my country could only have one pig, one cow, one horse, and five sheep. Most of his time was spent on the collective farm; consequently, he had little opportunity to produce anything from his own small holding - approximately 250 sq. meters around his house. Starvation and, as a result, sickness was more prevalent in Romania during those years.

One evening, I brought up the question of the border. How well was it patrolled? Had he heard of any escapes?

Ianos told me he had indeed heard of a few, but very few. It was well patrolled and dangerous to attempt a crossing.

Nevertheless, the thought of complete freedom never left my mind and I decided to check out the area for myself.

Iuliana did not favor the idea and was afraid. She also reminded me of the possibility of reprisal or revenge on our families.

I assured her that I did not intend to do anything foolish.

Having bade my friend farewell, we set out once more. Heading south for about thirty miles we arrived at a forested area. Proceeding further, we soon came upon a column of Russian tanks moving towards us. The commander ordered me to stop - "Pastoi! Where are you going?" he asked.

Iuliana froze.

"To Pets," I answered and tried to smile.

"Pets! It's not in this direction." He motioned with his arm for me to turn around. "Nazat."

So I was obliged to retrace my way to Pets and forget my fanciful idea of freedom and trying to escape the oppressive Communist system then.

We spent two days in Budapest and enjoyed every minute. A clean city with wide streets, fine churches and handsome bridges. We found there were also many good restaurants and its National Museum is prized as one of the finest in the world.

Reminders of the Revolution were still visible - bullet holes in many of the important buildings, and of course the inevitable burned-out houses, shops and offices that were either under reconstruction or left in their tumbled-down state.

I was stopped by a policeman as I crossed an intersection a second before the light actually turned green and for my indiscretion was fined 500 lei. But since I had only one hundred he relieved me of that amount instead. From that time on we were forced to sleep in the car and could not dine out, our food henceforth consisted of canned goods which we had brought with us from Romania.

Our next stop was Szolnok where we spent a few hours before making our way to Debrecen and thence to Oradea across the Romanian border.

I thanked God for my good friend, Kosa Ludovick who opened up his home and his heart to us. We spent one night with him and his family and then, refreshed, started out on the last leg of our long journey. Two days later we arrived home to Granicesti where the children were awaiting us.

We stayed in my parents' house for several days and it was during this time that the boys asked me to take them fishing. A small shallow pond not far away was our only hope that day. I thought to amuse the children by catching a few minnows, perhaps a frog or a couple of eels. Imagine my surprise when I caught several carp, and a bucketful of trout in a very short time. So many fish, in fact, that I was obliged to return home to get two more buckets. It reminded me of the miracle on the Lake of Galilee. When we retraced our steps that evening we had fish for the neighbors as well as ourselves. The children were delighted and considered themselves first-rate fishermen.

But all good things come to an end and our leisure time was drawing quickly to a close. We returned to Bucharest; the children were happy and content and ready for another year of work and school, Iuliana and I to a life of stress, hard work, and few rewards.

Chapter 13

Critical Changes

To exist! O, what nonsense, what foolish conceit;
Our eyes but deceive us, our ears but cheat,
What this age discovers, the next will deny,
Far better just nothing than naught but a lie.
Mihai Eminescu.
- Mortua Est!

Shortly after my vacation, our whole section at the
Institute, consisting of ten people called the Socialist
Economic Organization, was sent to the city of
Ploiesti to study the opportunities for increased economic
efficiency in the distribution of machinery, merchandise,
construction materials, and the management of the land in
that area.

This was an assignment that was well suited to my
expertise. After much work and research, I found a way to
save the State a considerable amount of money. My
proposal detailed the steps to be taken to eliminate the six
warehouses with their six directors and large staff and
replace them with one large warehouse. Considering the
fact that each warehouse had a general director, two
assistant directors and a staff of workers, and that each
establishment housed the same equipment for the various
departments of: Agriculture, Forestry, Energy, Metals,
Petroleum, and Machinery, I concluded that the most
efficient use of men and materials would be one general
director, two assistants, a manager and a staff of twelve
service people. This proposal, to which my colleagues

agreed, was submitted to the central government in Bucharest. Our group was happy. We had done a good job and come up with a sound solution to a glaring problem, so we returned home well pleased with ourselves.

Two months later, we received an acknowledgement of our work and the evaluation which considered it "good for nothing".

The Director of the Research Institute at the time was Ion Totu. When he spoke to us in those words, my answer was: "I thought our objective was to discover the weaknesses and deficiencies, not to make an inventory of what was correct and operational?"

"After I read and reread your report over a period of three days, I came to the conclusion that there is nothing good in our Socialist Economy," he answered. "And now, Mr. Gherasim, for your obviously prejudicial evaluation of our fine plants I terminate your employment in this Institute."

"Very well," I answered, "but I assure you that before long it will be too late to correct the situation." I sat down utterly disgusted with Mr. Totu in particular and the entire economic system in general.

After I spoke, Mr. Ihor Lemnij, a specialist in Technological Progress techniques, took the floor. "Director, if you have consulted with the six directors (for it was thus that Mr. Totu had made his final conclusion) it is only natural that they would challenge our report. They most certainly do not want to 'rock the boat', considering these men are nearing the end of their careers, for the most part, and looking forward to their pensions. The efficiency of production means new methods and new techniques. So I consider your decision based on the judgements and opinions of the six directors in Ploiesti to be incorrect."

Two more of my colleagues spoke but by this time the Director was very upset and there and then terminated the discussion. So much for constructive criticism under a Communist system!

Immediately, our group of ten experts was given notice. We had lost our positions at the Institute and were out on the street within the hour. Needless to say, I was not a very popular guy, since it was my idea, in the first place, which had led to this drastic consequence. That was August 6, 1978, and I was once again without a job.

Two days later, however, I was fortunate to secure another position, this time in a plant named Republica, which designed and manufactured piping and other conductive devices and which employed 8,000 men. My title on this occasion was chief engineer and my salary once more was increased from 3,640 to 4,020 lei. I could now laugh at the foolishness that had afforded me a better job.

I was to spend the next six years in that plant. During this period of my life, I was responsible for an invention which was to save not only energy but large quantities of steel. Working with the Director of the plant, Mr. Ion Moldovan, we compiled an extensive body of work entitled, *Modern Techniques for the Effective and Efficient Production of Pipes*. This book was published by the Metallurgical Department, Bucharest.

Within two years, I had another invention put together with the help of a team that I had organized. This was a flange which I devised using the steel remnants normally discarded. It would be used in a boiler plant in Ploiesti and was therefore a grave responsibility for the pressure exerted on this flange would be considerable and could cause extreme damage if it collapsed or the boiler exploded. Happily, for me, it proved successful and I was given a salary advancement from 4,020 to 4,450 lei in November 1980.

While I was working on that project in the Plant, I was also working at home compiling the dissertation for my doctorate. This occupied most of my free time and many sleepless nights over a period of three years.

At the end of 1982, a director from the Department of Metallurgy came to visit our plant. I was called by him for an interview in a private office.

"Mr. Gherasim, I have finally found you," was his opening statement.

I froze. Immediately I knew I was confronted by the Securitate.

"How many years has it taken, to find you!"

I answered: "Twenty-five. So what is wrong? I have always done my job to the best of my ability. I have been a good worker even though I was continually under extreme pressure and fear."

"You will be demoted from your present position as Chief Engineer," he said, a cynical leer on his puffy face, "to Project Engineer and your salary will be reduced to 4,020 lei."

This meant that I was demoted not one step but three. In his discussion with Mr. Moldovan, the Director from the Department of Metallurgy revealed that I had been in prison and had not stated that fact on my resumé; so it was his 'right' to punish me.

That evening I went home very dejected and frustrated. I had worked so hard, had made so many sacrifices to achieve my present position as chief engineer and now through the envy and vindictiveness of the Party, I was again unjustly punished. I could have cried but I knew it would only upset my family.

The next day I spoke to the Director, Mr. Moldovan telling him the truth about my imprisonment and the reason why. He advised me to 'lie low' for the moment. "Allow this wave to pass," he said, "and later we will find an opportunity to correct this situation." I knew that was the only solution.

It would take more than two years to rectify this injustice and then only by advancing my salary to half of what I had lost, 4,230 lei.

In 1981 Iuliana's father got very sick and had to be treated at home again by Dr. Ion Cardas. We had a hard winter that year and a great many difficulties driving the doctor to and fro from his home to ours.

In the spring of 1982 there was a symphony concert in the George Enescu Theater. I always bought season tickets and although the weather was particularly bad that evening, I didn't wish to miss the concert. Iuliana was unable to accompany me so I took Gabriel instead. We arrived a little late and could not take our usual places. Gabriel found a seat on the first floor, while I went upstairs. At that time Gabriel had just turned fourteen so it was a special treat for him.

It happened that during the concert Gabriel found he was seated beside an American who was having difficulty reading the program. Immediately, Gabriel came to his rescue and translated for him. During the intermission, he introduced his new friend, Mr. Jack Buzbee from Texas, to me. Then, after the concert, since it was still storming badly, I offered to drive Mr. Buzbee to his hotel even though I knew I was taking a risk because the Intercontinental Hotel, which was frequently occupied by foreign visitors, was off limits to us Romanians and was under constant and rigorous surveillance by the Securitate.

I immediately formulated my strategy were I to be stopped. I would tell the officer that as a Romanian I should be polite to foreigners and since the weather was so bad had merely offered to give the American a ride.

Mr. Buzbee got into the front seat while Gabriel sat behind. The storm continued and even gathered intensity. We arrived at the hotel and our guest alighted and graciously thanked us for our kindness. Gabriel then took his place in the front and we started off for home. Not long after, Gabriel discovered Mr. Buzbee's wallet on the floor of the car. Taking it up to examine it, he found a considerable amount of money, an I.D. card and his passport.

There was nothing to do except return immediately to the hotel. When we arrived a short time later at the parking area, we found Mr. Buzbee standing in the torrential rain, despair and anguish written on his face. Gabriel jumped out of the car with the wallet in his hand and ran towards him.

They both returned to the car and Mr. Buzbee once more thanked me personally. He then took Gabriel's hat placed it on his own head for a minute and handed it back with a twenty-five dollar bill folded up in the band. He told Gabriel he would be staying in the city for three days and if he, Gabriel, would be available as a guide to show him the sights, he would be very grateful. The following day, Gabriel went by the Metro and met Mr. Buzbee. He took him to many interesting places including the Royal Palace, the Museum of Romanian Villages, the University, and the Orthodox Cathedral.

Before he said good-bye to his new friend, Gabriel returned the money he had given him saying: "Mr. Buzbee this is not necessary. It was my pleasure to show you around and our duty to return your wallet. And besides, my father is an engineer and it would not be right for me to accept this money."

"But I must give you something in return for your kindness. Surely there is something you would like?"

Gabriel thought a moment and then answered. "Oh, yes, I'd like a Texan hat and a belt with two holsters."

Mr. Buzbee smiled and answered "Your wish is granted. As soon as I return to America you will have them."

A month later, I received a notice from the post office letting me know that there was a parcel from America awaiting me. I went to get it and after having opened it found it was indeed a Texan hat and two toy guns in leather holsters. I was told that the guns would have to be examined by the Director of the Post Office. Eventually, after being warned that those toys were in no way to be used to frighten little old ladies, they were released into my charge. So Gabriel got his gifts!

After that we hadn't a quiet moment in our house. All Gabriel's friends wanted to wear the hat and holsters especially when I took photographs. He became a famous personality in our area of Bucharest having had a special relationship with a 'Texan cowboy'. Iuliana sent some painted eggs and Romanian handwork to Mr. Buzbee in acknowledgement of his thoughtfulness while Gabriel continued to correspond with his new friend for the next two years.

* * * * *

One evening our door-bell rang and when I answered it an old friend of mine from my prison days was standing without. His name - Traian Turtureanu, he was accompanied by a young woman. He asked to be allowed to enter. Then he introduced me to his fiancee and, in brief, stated that he wished to get married and wanted me and Iuliana to be his witnesses. This request placed Iuliana and me in a dangerous situation for we were forbidden to ever associate with those who had been in prison once we were released. Traian had probably come to me in desperation.

We chatted for several minutes and finally decided to help them out. The wedding service was set for a few days later. Having obtained all the necessary information we made plans to meet at the Mayor's house and later to gather for the religious service. There was no celebration, no festivity, what a sad state of affairs! We were both too scared to even have a drink. We parted as I warned him not to visit us again for his safety as well as my own.

In the spring of 1980, Iuliana's father grew worse. We knew he could not resist much longer. The children had benefitted enormously from this talented and highly educated man. I had great respect for him and knew I would miss him for a very long time to come.

But he lingered and soon I became more worried about Gabriel's health.

Towards the end of spring 1981, Gabriel started to get sick. At first we noticed that he suffered repeatedly from tonsillitis. We took him to Doctor Georgescu in the Vitan Polyclinic. She perscribed penicillin and with this medicine Gabriel seemed to improve. But after one week, the malady re-occurred. I returned a second time to the clinic and the doctor repeated and increased the dosage but after two weeks, the same symptoms returned. No analysis of his urine was made and I believed at the time that it was necessary. Ten days later, I again went back to the Clinic with a sample of Gabriel's urine which was at that stage brown in color.

"This child is suffering from glomerulo- nephritis and must be hospitalized." the doctor said.

It was then I knew by the expression on her face that she realized she had made a mistake with her diagnosis.

When I arrived at the hospital, I was introduced to Dr. Alexandrescu, the physician in charge. He asked: "Why has Dr. Georgescu sent me this child at this late stage? He should have been here long before now."

I had no answer for his question. Then the Dr. responded. "His sickness is now chronic. Some organisms can respond quickly to a strict diet and medication, others don't. We will try to treat him as best we can. Please bring some honey, and tea. The rest we will provide."

I realized then that Gabriel was a very sick boy. Later I found out that had his tonsils been removed he might have been spared all the trouble and sufferings that followed.

Gabriel was forced to remain in the hospital for the next four months. His progress was very slow. As the school was within a short distance, the doctor allowed him to attend these classes.

The summer vacation seemed to give him back some of his former strength and exuberance. He was examined regularly by my good friend, Dr. Ion Cardas, who continued to visit us at home.

It was heart-breaking to me to see my once vivacious young son so lethargic and obviously deteriorating as the summer was drawing to a close. It caused a pall to descend on the whole family. I was at my wit's end to know what to do, when I heard of a saintly priest who resided at the Varatec Monastery.

Not long before Christmas, Gabriel had to return to hospital - this time to the Carol Davila where the best nephrologists worked. He was decidedly in a very weakened state.

When I heard the doctors' report, I was devastated. The medicine was not working and the specialists were unable to do any more for my son. I could no longer wait for human help so I set out that night for the Varatec Monastery in far off Moldavia.

When I entered the chapel where Father Vrajitoru held his prayer meetings and where he personally spoke with each one who came to seek his blessing or his prayers, I was surprised to see so many people waiting patiently in line to speak to the holy man.

Finally, my turn came and with tear-stained face and broken heart, I knelt before this saint whom I had travelled some 500 kilometers to meet. When I had told him my troubles, he gently took my hand and with deep penetrating brown eyes looked into the depths of my soul, saying: "You have two sick people in your house, an old man and a young child. Go home, the old one will go to his reward, the young boy will live."

With those words, my heart instantly felt lighter. I thanked the priest, received his blessing, and departed happy that evening.

Returning to Bucharest I went straight to the hospital where Gabriel nervous and anxious awaited my return. I gave him some holy water to drink and told him what Father Vrajitoru had said.

Immediately Gabriel responded. As if an electric shock had catapulted him back to life, he cried out, "I will be saved!"

Gabriel was to spend another year in that hospital. During that time one doctor, in particular, Dr. Penescu went out of his way to be nice to him, receiving him with open arms, and daily encouraging him with a smile. The regular routine of transfusions and injections, this extraordinary man made tolerable by transforming the horrible situation into a fantasy world. With his stories Gabriel had the power of Batman and could take the bitterest medicines bravely. To his credit also is the fact that although the medicine was very expensive and difficult to obtain, he, Dr. Penescu managed to find it on the Black Market.

Not only was this good doctor, supportive of Gabriel, but he also stretched out hand to encourage and support my wife and me.

In the early summer of 1983 Gabriel's kidney suddenly collapsed. It was now only a question of days before Gabriel would die.

Incredible though it may seem, a day or two later, Doctor Ursea, Director of the hospital who was a friend of

Mr. Ceausescu assembled all the doctors and told them to discontinue Gabriel's dialysis treatment. "We don't have machines to go around and besides his father is an enemy of the people."

For a moment, no one spoke. Then Dr. Penescu got to his feet and confronted the Director. "We have here a humanitarian case," he said. "We cannot neglect a child if we have the opportunity to save his life. If you won't allow this patient continuous use of the dialysis machine, I will resign immediately. And," he continued, "we must rise above politics and self-interests and act as conscientious human beings."

It was due to Dr. Penescu's stand that Gabriel was given a priviliged status and was treated the same as the Patriarch Iustin Moisescu and other persons related to the politicians who alone were considered for this treatment.

Shortly after this occurence, Gabriel's creatinine level rose to such high levels that it was impossible to sustain his life on a stable basis. The Director decided to give me a letter stating that in Romania there was no possibility to save Gabriel's life. All that remained was for us to emigrate to Italy or Austria to obtain a kidney transplant.

On the 12th day of February 1983 I remembered I had been in prison with Monsignor Agustine Francisc who was attached to the Catholic Cathedral of St. Joseph in Bucharest. I asked for an appointment to see this priest. With Iuliana I went to meet him the following day,

"I remember we ate bitter bread together in Jilava," were his words to me. Then when I told him my story, he went out of his way to help me. He immediately dictated a letter to Caritas in Vienna through the Bishop urging that a place be found as quickly as possible in order to save a young life.

My happiness knew no bounds when after twenty days I received an answer advising us to apply for a transplant in

Italy. With this assurance, I called Rome, Naples, Udine, and Milan. Eventually, the director of the Niguarda Central dialysis hospital in Milan, spoke to me and said, "I will keep a place for one month, no more."

With these assuring words, I made my way to the passport office, then I had to appear before five superior officers of the Securitate. The main reason for this meeting was to discuss who should leave the country with Gabriel, his mother or I.

At first, there was no question of my leaving, since I had been a political prisoner even though I had been designated as a donor. They then suggested that Iuliana accompany Gabriel not realizing that her kidney would not be compatible.

After three weeks of talking, while the Securitate waited for Gabriel's death, we awaited a decision. Gabriel however, had no intention of dying, so they again opened up the discussion of my going to Italy.

The Italian Red Cross, in the meantime, had contacted the Romanian Red Cross and alerted them to the fact that they were expecting a very sick child as quickly as possible. Through the insistance of Dr. Ligia Oradeanu director of the Romanian Red Cross, the Securitate ordered me to again appear before them.

Their objection at that time was that Romania could not afford to pay for a kidney transplant. Gabriel would be a liability the state was not in a position to support. "How, therefore, do you intend to pay for this treatment?"

I answered: "I'm an engineer and an economist. I will work, if necessary at two jobs in order to pay at least some of the money. And," I added, "I will sign a document to this effect that I will not seek any support from the Romanian State for this operation."

Secondly, the officers confronted me with the assurance, that were I to divulge anything regarding my treatment while in prison, or commit any indiscretion, I would feel the consequences.

Finally, they told me that I would be allowed to take no more than $100 from the bank out of the country. With this I was supposed to support the two of us until such time as I could get a job. Having worked for thirty years in the country, this was a shock from which I am still reeling today.

One of the officers seeing my dilemma, suggested that I collect some extra money through the Black Market. I looked at him and realized that he was setting a trap for me. I straightened myself, raised my head and replied. "I will go with God and a $100 and not another cent."

Chapter 14

Many Blessings

When death did not exist, nor yet eternity,
Before the seed of life had first set living free,
When yesterday was nothing, and time had not begun,
And one included all things, and all was less than one,
When sun and moon and sky, the stars, the spinning earth,
Were still part of the things that had not come to birth,
And You quite lonely stood... I ask myself with awe,
Who is this mighty God we bow ourselves before.

Mihai Eminescu
- A Dacian's Prayer

It was January 22, 1984. Gabriel had been allowed to come home from the hospital for his last night. All the family, my mother, brothers and sisters, had gathered for a final farewell dinner and as Gabriel put it later: "It was a sad yet happy time."

I looked out the window across the park towards the lake. All was quiet; a blanket of fresh snow covered the ground lending a pristine unemotional serenity to the scene. Turning away, I looked at my sick child. What was to become of him... of us? I asked myself. My heart was sick, heavy. But I had to be brave, steadfast, and strong for him.

The ambulance was at the door. I had no more time for daydreaming. A new life, in a new country was demanding my attention. I helped Gabriel down the stairs to the waiting car and the rest of the family followed accompanying us to the airport.

As we emerged into the cool morning air, Gabriel and I looked around the familiar surroundings for the last time as if trying to hold on to something that we both felt we were leaving forever. Gabriel bent and picked up a handful of dirty snow. Clinging to it, he held it tightly in his hand and would not be parted from it. Later, he told me he·kept it until it had dripped, drop by drop, from his warm fist; it was thus that the final tie with his beloved home-land was broken.

At the airport we said our good-byes and took our places on the plane. We were ready to take off when suddenly an angry voice over the intercom announced that there would be a delay. A moment later several Securitate officers boarded the plane and the one in charge shouted: "Gherasim! Where is Gherasim?"

I immediately answered: "I'm here."

"Come with me," he ordered. "And the boy, too."

"But he's a sick child. It's difficult for him to walk. He had to be brought here on a stretcher."

"Get a stretcher." The same guard ordered.

As we left the plane, the only words I heard were: "Must be a spy, a traitor"… and a woman mumbled: "We'll be late for our connections." "A disgrace," remarked an old man as I passed his seat.

In an underground room, we were both ordered to strip naked. At the same time two officers emptied out our few worldly possessions and ripped the suitcases apart, tearing the lining and zippers in their futile attempt to find the money they were sure I was carrying illegally from the country. How well I knew their cunning minds and cruel ways. I had been correct.

Were I to have one dollar more than the $100 they had so graciously permitted, our flight would have ended there. So the last humiliation, the final degradation had been done me and my child. There was nothing more they could do…

I was told to gather my belongings together and prepare to return to the plane. The suitcases were so badly damaged that they would not close so we were forced to use our pant belts to secure them.

Back on the plane again; an hour had been wasted and the passengers were furious.

"Where did you work?" a man asked.

"I'm an engineer and I worked in the Republica Plant."

"Ah! That's the reason then." he answered but wasn't mollified.

The plane, finally, took off rising higher and higher into the sky above Bucharest. Beautiful Bucharest lay beneath covered in snow and like the picture I still held in my heart of the serene park, lake, and surroundings near my apartment, this landscape, too, seemed remote and heartless. A tear fell from my broken heart that morning and I leaned over and whispered to Gabriel, "We will never return to this land."

After an hour's flight we landed at Leonardo da Vinci airport in Rome. There we were met by a friend who helped us to buy our tickets and get set-up for our flight to Milan which would leave within the hour. As the tickets cost $75, I was now left with $25 for food and shelter for myself. I could only think of the thirty years I had spent working hard and long for my country as well as my family and at that moment, it seemed it had all been for naught. Was there another country on the face of the earth that would treat its native sons with such contempt, with so little civility, nay, not even the basic humanitarian requirements were accorded us.

At the Milan airport the contrast between our departure that morning from our native land and the welcome given us by the smiling gracious Italians was extraordinary.

"Benvenuto in Italia. Siamo pronti di aiutare," were the first words to gladden our ears. They embraced us and took us immediately into their hearts, those three young doctors who had come in the ambulance that awaited us as we exited the plane. I noticed the soft white fresh snow which looked like down. It didn't seem cold and forbidding anymore - only soft and protecting.

Gabriel was taken at once by stretcher and I knew instinctively that he was in good hands and that everything possible would be done for him. God had already repaid my confidence in His goodness and power.

I was happy that I had not wasted my time in the dungeons of Romania. The Italian I had acquired there, now stood me in good stead and I was proud to be able to converse in that beautiful language. Gabriel used his knowledge of English to speak with the doctors. And I knew once again that God had been guiding me when I resisted the mandates of Communism and had paid for a special English teacher to tutor my young children.

When I realized that there was nothing more I could do for Gabriel, I relaxed and for the first time realized how really tired I was. A bed was furnished by the hospital so that I could remain close to Gabriel. I was fed and housed and shown such consideration and courtesy that I felt I could hardly bear so much warmth and kindness. I rejoiced that I had lived to experience human nature at its best. God bless Italy and its magnanimous people!

It took me several weeks to find a job. In the meantime, I stayed in the Catholic convent of the Suore del Cenacolo where I was to remain for approximately three weeks. After that an apartment was found and I was allowed to stay in it for over a year free of charge. When I eventually had enough money, I paid rent and utilities.

The first session in dialysis went well. However, on January 31 Gabriel had a very hard day. His blood coagulated and a vein was blocked so it was necessary for him to have an operation for a new fistula which was eventually carried out on February 3. After the two hour operation, Gabriel had to endure four hours of dialysis. I stayed with him the whole time until eight that night. We then had a break of two free days until he had to have dialysis again and once more I watched as my poor son had to endure bouts of vomiting and severe headaches while attached to the machines.

On February 9, a telephone to the Director of the hospital, Dr. Minetti, from the Bucharest Military Hospital stating that they now had everything necessary to save Gabriel's life and that they were willing to come to Milan with a military ambulance properly equipped to take him home.

I knew instinctively that this statement was a lie and became very angry. After all we had gone through, up to this point, at the hands of the Securitate, they were still trying to hinder, in every possible way they could, our successful solution to this life-threatening situation.

"Dr. Minetti, I wish to declare political asylum in Italy. Please find a lawyer and allow a representative from the hospital to accompany me to the police station so that I can accomplish this right away," was my answer when the doctor spoke to me.

Arriving at the police station, I filled out the necessary forms and without too much trouble received all the identification I needed to remain in Italy.

When the authorities from Bucharest again called the following day to confirm their suggestion, Dr. Minetti was prepared.

"If you have everything ready as you stated, why did you allow the Gherasims to leave the country in the first place? Now they have all their papers in order and have taken out Italian residency. Please don't disturb me again." He hung up.

After that, I had the distinct feeling that I was under surveillance by some of Bucharest's agents even here in civilized Italy. Often, I saw a car with a single person in it stationed not far from my apartment and on one occasion this man questioned the door porter. Were they going to kill me in cold blood? I asked myself.

Gabriel's health improved sufficiently in the weeks that followed to allow him to live outside the hospital. Unfortunately, that reprieve didn't last long. On February 27, during the night he developed a high fever, a cough, and was vomiting. I was convinced that he would surely die on that occasion. I summoned a taxi and took him as quickly as possible back to the hospital. He had, it was discovered, contracted pneumonia.

On the third of March, the eve of Gabriel's birthday, he had a visit from Dr. Joseph Lax.

"Good day, Gabriel," he said in Romanian. "I was born in Craiova and have worked in Milan for many years. I am now retired. I learned about you and know that you are here with your father. Will you allow me to help you?" he asked.

"Of course," answered Gabriel. At that point in time Gabriel's health was in a critical condition. He was unable to eat and was rejecting all the food that was provided by the hospital. I now entered the room and introduced myself.

Dr. Lax realizing the seriousness of the situation asked: "What is your favorite food, Gabriel?"

Gabriel's eyes lit up. "I love stuffed peppers with garlic and red cabbage salad." "Very well," the doctor answered. "Tomorrow you will have this treat."

True to his word, Dr. Lax found a Romanian woman who prepared this special dish and the following day he brought it to the hospital.

By the end of the month Gabriel's health had stabilized. He was once more allowed to leave the hospital. After that our new friend, Dr. Lax, came regularly each week-end to be with us. Gabriel and the doctor became really close friends and together we were eventually able to visit a few of Milan's important sites - The Cathedral of St. Ambrose and the Carnival.

Later I learned that Dr. Lax, who was Jewish, knew all about my time in prison and that I had risked my life for a fellow-prisoner who was dying of T.B. As it happened this prisoner had been a university professor in Bucharest and Tel Aviv and was also a Jew. I was impressed to discover how much our new friend really knew about me.

As soon as I could, I registered Gabriel in the local high school - Ungaretti. He went each morning to school and in the afternoon, three times a week to dialysis. One professor, Mr. Panzzini, came voluntarily each week to help him with his homework and to give any other information he needed.

Since I was working long hours, it was not possible for me to do the cooking as well, so we regularly frequented a small restaurant called the San Carlo. There we were served ample portions of soup and pasta - a more vegetarian diet suitable for Gabriel.

During these days of exile and great difficulty, I kept a journal from which I can now draw. On April 15, I telephoned home and invited my wife, Iuliana, to join me in Italy. I also sent money to the bank, enough to buy two tickets, but I later found out that Iuliana never received the money and consequently was unable to leave the country. Things were very bad in Romania then and in order to help my family there, I regularly sent coffee and cigarettes which could easily be sold for extra cash.

Soon after Dr. Lax became friends with Gabriel, he drew me aside one day and spoke to me about the negative side-effects of dialysis on the young body. The sooner Gabriel could get a transplant the better. He suggested that I allow him to talk with the director of the hospital, Dr.

Serchia. The result of this discussion was that Gabriel was put on the priority list for a transplant.

In preparation for the operation, the Reverend Don Bruno de Biasio from the Dergano church in Milan organized a prayer session in the Theological Seminary to encourage and support Gabriel. It was a very intimate and powerful experience for both of us and I will never forget how affected I was and how deeply I realized that without the help and support of Almighty God we poor human creatures can do nothing.

After receiving the blessing of the Reverend Doctor More, the Father Superior, and a special crucifix, Gabriel spoke.

"I am ready to undergo this operation with courage."

These words and the prayers of so many holy men gave me courage also and I relaxed and left everything in God's hands.

About this time, I had the good fortune to meet a Mr. Luigi Pagani from Bergamo. Our situation had been made known to the congregation in the Dergano church and I was deeply moved by the response. One evening, Mr. Pagani invited me to his home in Palazzolo. He had a car which he wanted to place at my disposal. It was a Fiat 500, light-blue in color. He told me he knew how difficult it must be for me to pay for an ambulance each time Gabriel had to go for dialysis, this car would, he hoped make things easier. I was overcome with gratitude and emotion and my esteem for the Italians grew by leaps and bounds.

Another unexpected surprise awaited me when a few days later, I opened my pay envelope from my second job at the Baroncelli Textile Co. Inside, I found 500,000 lire instead of my usual 250,000. I was sure there was some mistake, so I immediately went to talk to Mr. Baroncelli.

"There is something wrong here," I said. "I have received twice my correct wages."

"No mistake, nothing wrong," answered my employer. "I have done well this month and wish to give you a bonus."

I was so overjoyed that when I went home, I decided as long as Gabriel was feeling well, an outing to the theater would do us both good. So we took off to La Scala, bought tickets for the third balcony and took our places. That evening Gabriel saw *La Boheme* for the first time. It was a magnificient production which we both enjoyed and remembered for many days and weeks to come. When writing home, I tried to describe the opulence of the world's best known opera house - the plush red carpets, the velvet chairs, the magnificient murals and statuary, the beautifully dressed audience. I even sketched the interior so as to add to my verbal description.

I'm reminded of another incident which took place some time later but which was related to our being present at a performance of *Rigoletto*. While at the opera house, Gabriel became acquainted with a young man who had just arrived by bike in the city from Switzerland. Having nowhere to stay and nothing to eat, I invited him to spend the night in our apartment.

All went well until it was time to eat dinner. I had prepared our favorite Romanian chicken dish - chicken with garlic and other herbs cooked in cream. All I had to do when we arrived home was to reheat it. I served what I thought would be a real treat and in the words of Gabriel: "With a broad smile, I asked, 'And how do you like it?'"

The young man, I cannot even remember his name at this late date, didn't even lift his head but answered: "I'm eating it, am I not?"

Later when we asked him to stay the night, he excused himself saying he had forgotten something and when Gabriel accompanied him to the street to give him directions, he barely waited to say goodbye, but took off on his bike as if in dire need of a place to relieve himself. So were my culinary arts and our favorite Romanian food appreciated!

I learned that a very rich Romanian, Josef Constantin Dragan, who had a publishing house, lived in the city of Milan around the same time I was there. Here, I thought, was a good opportunity for me to make a little extra money. I would ask him to republish two of my text books: *Modern Methods for the Efficient Production of Pipes and The Elements of Mechanical Metallurgy.*

On ten different occasions I spent over an hour each time waiting in his secretary's office to get an interview with this man, only to be told that for some reason or another he was unable to see me. Finally, I asked the secretary: "Please tell me is there any chance that I can see Mr. Dragan? I want the truth; I don't have time to waste."

"I'm afraid not," was her reply. "He knows your case and is not willing to help you." Then she added lowering her tone: "He is, in fact, a close-fisted man."

Again I was disappointed in one of my fellow-countrymen and was all the more thankful for my Italian neighbors and friends.

Upon meeting again with Dr. Lax the following day, I soon discovered that, he too, had been disappointed with Mr. Dragan and his NAGARD publishing house. Two years prior to this time, he had submitted two manuscripts about Craiova, his birth place and the city of his childhood. Mr. Dragan had promised him that these works would be published but up to that time the only answer he had received was that they were being reviewed by the Party's Central Committee in Bucharest.

In our discussions together, I realized that the Central Committee had nothing to do with the publication of manuscripts and that his works would never be published.

It was a great blow to this old man for he never again saw his life's work as he had submitted his only copies.

On March 25, we were invited to spend the day with the Massola family. While in hospital, Gabriel got to know a Mr. Massola, who also had kidney problems and who died a short time later, leaving his large fortune to his grand-daughter Daniela. This young woman had met Gabriel during her visits to see her grandfather, and seemed interested in seeing more of him.

Both Daniela's parents were well-educated and successful people. Her mother was owner of a perfume company and her father a banker. Over a delicious lunch, we discussed many topics, including the eventual demise of Communist power, before we set out for a trip to Oltre il Colle near Bergamo where they had a holiday apartment. This beautiful area reminded me of the Carpathians - the lush green fields, the soaring mountains clad in pines and the fragrant warm air.

While we older folk went for a walk, Gabriel and Daniela remained in the apartment. It was obvious that Daniela really liked Gabriel. When I saw this situation developing, I was happy because I thought very highly of the young woman and hoped something might come of it.

For the next two years Daniela and Gabriel were good friends. She had her own car and often came to pick him up and take him for a drive in the country. At the time Gabriel was, however, too sick to consider any deep and lasting friendship.

May 12, 1984, we visited Bologna and Ferrara with Professor Manole Negoe from Bucharest who was a friend of our family. This gave us an occasion to see these cities and admire their monuments of antiquity. It also afforded me an opportunity to send a letter to Iuliana and Michael and to give all the details of our life in Italy.

Soon after the Professor returned to Romania, I heard from him and learned how Michael, although accepted in the Politechnic University was not allowed to attend the day classes, but could only take those offered at night. The reason given for this discrimination was that his father and brother were in Italy - a capitalist country. The same answer was given when he tried to follow a military career. Because of this arrangement, Michael's course of study took six years instead of five and like me, he was continually under stress and strain and aware of the all-seeing eye of the Authorities.

While awaiting the transplant, according to my journal, Gabriel continued the dialysis three times a week. However, during the month of July a young friend of his who lived in an apartment nearby and who had needed oxygen to sustain her life, had died. This was an awful shock to him and I realized, for the first time, that he had a great fear of dying. His reactions were quite alarming - he had leg spasms and cramps, his blood pressure rose, and severe headaches forced him to go to bed. Because of this, I had to take him to the hospital and I was obliged to lose three days of work. I was so upset, I believed I would lose him. I called his aunt Paula who lived in Udine to alert her. She came with her husband and stayed with us for a few days encouraging Gabriel and eventually through her patience and gentleness he gradually regained his equilibrium and his optimistic attitude. All would be well; he would get a kidney. The operation would be successful; he would have a future.

August 12, we went with Dr. Lax to visit Lake Maggiore in the north. This resort area set among the forested hills was a source of tremendous pleasure to Gabriel and he enjoyed swimming in the cool waters.

At the lakeside, we came upon a lovesick Romanian - Stelian Dragu. He had met and fallen in love with an

216

Italian, for whom he went to great lengths to show his sincerity. He parked a new Fiat near the lake with the words: *Valeria... ti amo ancora*, written all over it. He had hundreds of posters printed with the same declaration in one hundred and three languages, a picture of the car, and of himself holding a bouquet of red roses while standing beside it.

Yet with all this, I learned afterwards, he was unsuccessful in winning the hand of the beautiful Valeria because her father would not give his consent.

In the end of August, I found another job with the help of Mr. Sergio Randazzo and the brothers Giannattasio in a Computer Center: Airoinformatica. This was a good position; I was in charge as an engineer, and given double my previous salary. I was happy there and my employers were also pleased with my work. I would stay with this company for about two years and when I eventually had to move on, the company gave me an extra six months pay to carry me over until I got settled in my new home.

September came and went and in October one evening I experienced severe pain. During the night it became worse and I had the feeling that perhaps I was having an attack of appendicitis. At about nine o'clock when I could no longer support the pain, I called an ambulance. After consultation, the doctor's diagnosis was that I had a urinary disorder. He gave me some medicine and sent me home. But the pain didn't subside. Eventually, a neighbor, Pietro Mantovani, who had experienced similar discomfort in the past, offered to take me to the Niguarda hospital. Once there, the doctors recognized me.

"Now we have the two of you, first Gabriel, now papa," said Dr. Rovatti.

I was given an I.V. with medication to enable the breaking up of the crystals of uric-acid which had lodged in the urinary tract, as they suspected.

Because I still had pain after two days, they decided to take an X-ray. From this, they discovered that my appendix was greatly enlarged giving the appearance that I had three kidneys. After six days of rest and medication, the appendix returned to its normal size and I was released.

However, during the interum, Gabriel who remained at home alone, but was being cared for by Mr. Mantovani received a phone call from the hospital to say that they were ready for his transplant. Again our good friend, Mr. Mantovani drove him to the hospital. He came to see me there before going to the operating room. Having encouraged and assured him that I would be praying and that I was better and about to be released myself, he left in good spirits.

"I'll see you tomorrow," I said as he accompanied the doctors from my room.

Chapter 15

The Long Ordeal

Little heed the lofty ranging
That cold logic does display
To explain the endless changing
Of this pageantry of joy.
And which out of death is growing
But to last an hour or two;
For the mind profoundly knowing,
All is old and all is new.

Mihai Eminescu
- Gloss

The first human transplant was performed in 1967 by the eminent South African surgeon, Doctor Christiaan Neethling Barnard. The operation was successful but unfortunately the patient died after only eighteen days as a result of the destruction of his immune system by the drugs used to suppress rejection by his body of the donor heart.

Since that time, however, the organ transplant procedure has become a rather common occurrence and due to better drugs and continuous research those who undergo this type of operation are now living much longer and better lives.

A kidney transplant is a very serious procedure and even when the operation itself is successful there is always the risk that following transplantation, difficulties of rejection will set in. This may occur anywhere from a few weeks to a year or two after the operation has been performed.

Because everyone has antibodies whose duty it is to guard against invading foreign bodies, these react to protect the host when a transplant is made. Thus it is vital that various drugs be used to counteract this natural process.

I was released from the hospital the very day Gabriel was to have his operation. Eight hours after I had waved to him from my bed, I was standing beside his. As soon as he came to, I assured him that all had gone well and since there was nothing I could do I said: "I'll go get something to eat and then come back."

He nodded a drowsy reply and closed his eyes.

As I walked through the hallways of that large institution I thanked God we had come this far. But I knew we still had a very long way to go. How careful we would have to be. We had received this precious gift which gave Gabriel a new chance for a normal life.

The following morning I went back to see him and found him on dialysis. I was not too surprised for I knew it would take time for the new kidney to function on its own. So many parts, veins and tissues had to heal; time was needed.

After twenty-four hours everyone at the hospital was excited and happy. Gabriel's kidney had started to function! They concluced then that the operation had been a success. However, it was noticed that his liver had become enlarged and five days later the quantity of urine decreased. To counteract a negative effect - that of rejection, the amount of prednisone and cyclosporine were increased.

Gabriel's good friend Dr. Lax was present every day giving him encouragement and supervising his treatment. After a week, the kidney really kicked in and each day saw a gradual and positive improvement. A few days later, Gabriel was able to get around in a wheelchair and received a visit from his classmates from the Ungaretti High School. He was so happy to be able to converse and joke with them. They told him how they had been praying and brought a letter signed by all those who couldn't come.

Gabriel always had strange and, it seemed, whimsical tastes in food but after his operation they seemed to become bizarre. His first request was for peas. This desire was supplied by Madam Letitia Zaccherini. The next day he wanted pears and Madam Balasiu came to the rescue. These good people came from the Romanian community in Milan and were only too happy to help. The priest, Father Bruno, from Bergamo also came to see him. He blessed him and encouraged him to be courageous; everything would be fine, he said.

On November 8, Gabriel's name day - the feast of the Archangels, Michael and Gabriel, he was released from the hospital. That evening one of the professors from school with ten of his classmates arrived at our apartment to surprise him. They had collected some money and offered it as a gift. We spent a very nice time together and Gabriel was extremely happy. He was now in his seventeenth year and the transplant was working well.

On December 21, 1984, Dr. Lax who was visiting Gabriel opened the refrigerator door and saw that it was almost empty. "My goodness!" he declared, "your refrigerator is not ready for Christmas. Please come with me, both of you and we'll stop by the supermarket."

Once there, he ordered us to take a cart and fill it with whatever we needed. I placed several items in the cart watching carefully the price and the number, then I stopped.

"Why are you stopping?" the good Dr. asked.

"We have enough for two or three days," I answered.

"But it will be Christmas in two or three days," he said. "You don't want to make a Christmas like we had in Craiova, with sausage, and cosonac, nuts and candies, and a nice Christmas tree with all the decoration?" he asked surprised. At that moment, I realized, for the first time, that the old man was alone and wished to share Christmas with someone from his old country. So the three of us started choosing items until the cart was completely full. Then, not seeing a Christmas tree, he asked the manager where he might find one.

I never saw anyone so happy as Dr. Lax on that particular occasion. When we got to the check-out stand, he was proud to pay the bill of 720,000 lire and my thoughts turned to another, a very rich man, Mr. I.C. Dragan, who had not lifted a finger to help, who didn't even want to hear about Gabriel and his difficulties.

When Dr. Lax came to call on us on December 24, our tree was in place and we had decorated it to the best of our ability. He came carrying several tapes - Bach, Chopin, Verdi and Enescu as well as a recording of the Orthodox Church Choir from Bucharest singing traditional carols. He spent the whole day with us and we all thoroughly enjoyed ourselves. It was a day to remember.

"In the last twenty-five years, I have not had a more beautiful Christmas than this one with you and Gabriel," the old man said. "Now before I go, I would like to hear once more, the *Balada* of Ciprian Porumbescu."

As I was bidding him good-night, I looked into his tired eyes and saw a truly happy man and I was also overjoyed to have been able to afford him this small comfort and joy in exchange for all he had done for us. We had been able to speak and joke about our native land and the memories these stories and anecdotes brought to his mind were like a breath of fresh air invigorating every fibre of his being.

On Christmas Day we were invited to the Zaccherini family home near Bergamo. After church we travelled the fifty miles and arrived in the early afternoon. We were given a nice room with two beds and from the balcony we had a beautiful view of the Villong mountains.

Madam Zaccherini prepared a marvelous Christmas dinner, and being Romanian, herself, it was a feast with many different national dishes. I had met this good lady at church one Sunday morning some weeks before. At that time, she told me she would be visiting Bucharest and if I would like to send something home to my wife and son, Michael, she would be more than happy to oblige. Upon her return, she told me she had met Iuliana and had been informed by her that the Securitate had warned her several times not to communicate with anyone. Michael, at that period, was serving in the Army and was soon to be given a short vacation. Iuliana would say no more at that juncture, but she started to cry. It wasn't too difficult for me to understand what the Authorities in Romania were up to.

On December 27, we were asked to attend a reception at a restaurant in Bergamo. This was given by an Italian family whose name we were not permitted to know as they were the parents of the donor of Gabriel's kidney. The young man who had donated his organs was killed in a car crash, but although the parents were grief stricken, yet they were, in some small way, comforted to see Gabriel and to realize that his young life had been saved by this great gift from their own son.

Upon our arrival home later that evening, three 'bright sparks', regular customers of the San Carlos restaurant, were waiting at our door. The Three Wise Men, they called themselves, had come to visit us. One was eighty years old and was known by the name of Alfredo Pozzetti - the great eater. The second lively lad was Zanchi Giovani - the sweet-talker - he was only seventy-two, and finally, Fremagalli Dionsie - the pig, he too, was eighty and a bit.

I invited the venerable gentlemen into our apartment, offered them some wine and refreshments, while Gabriel put on our Christmas lights and played some Romanian music. They remained with us for several hours and when they took their leave, they declared they would never forget this 'una bella serrata.'

On the 31, December, Dr. Lax phoned asking us not to go anywhere. He wanted to spend the evening with us and to ring in the New Year Romanian style. He arrived sometime later with his arms full of packages - enough food and candy to make a special meal for this a very special night. Before he left early the next morning he wanted to hear the old Romanian verses the children repeated on this occasion:

Maine anul se inoieste,	*Tomorrow the year is renewed*
Plugusorul se porneste,	*The little plough tills the land.*
Plugusor cu partu boi,	*The little plough led by four oxen,*
Plugusor manat de noi,	*The little plough handled by us*
Hai, Hai!	*Hai, Hai!*

At the end of January, Gabriel returned to the hospital for a check-up. He was found to be doing so well that he was told he need not return for another three months. With this good news, he was able to return to school and I to work and our lives began to follow a more normal course.

Gabriel wrote to his friend Mr. Buzbee in America telling him of his transplant and that we had decided to seek passports for the U.S. In his reply Mr. Buzbee said he would be visiting Italy in June and that we would talk then.

As it turned out, Mr. Buzbee and a friend arrived in Milan around the same time as a very good friend and former colleague, Paul Petrescu. Paul's wife pitched in and made a wonderful Romanian dinner for everyone and afterwards we all sat around discussing what would be best for the future of Gabriel and myself. Mr. Buzbee suggested that he try to adopt Gabriel but for various reasons this turned out not to be feasible. He even solicited the aid of the well known Senator Phil Graham, who graciously sought to add weight to Gabriel's case at the immigration office, but to no avail. Gabriel was a liability and the U.S. was not willing to take on any more charity cases.

Our only hope of gaining entrance into America, was to seek political asylum. Were I to be allowed to enter the States, I would be able to support him since I was quite cabable and willing to work. So Gabriel called the American Embassy and asked for the necessary forms which were forthwith sent to us.

It was during this period that I had my first heart attack. The weather was oppressively hot. I was working two jobs to make ends meet and to pay my part of Gabriel's expenses. It was true that the Italian Red Cross and the Austrian Caritas had undertaken a large portion of the bill for the transplant but I had to make my contribution also. Unfortunately, a bill for four million lire was sent by the hospital to the Romanian Embassy around this time. It was a very upsetting state of affairs for me, because I had signed stating I would not cause the Romanian government any expense and if they were to pay, I figured they would probably extract the money someway or other from either Iuliana or Michael. Another factor which contributed to my attack was the stress of my primary job - I was working in a polluted environment of gas fumes, lacking sufficient fresh air. And to add to my difficulties, I had received bad news from home. Iuliana and Michael would not be given visas to travel to Italy; she had not received the money and parcels I had sent, and finally, Michael was not being cooperative at home. I was unable to rest or go to the hospital for proper care, so the doctors gave me medication and a letter to my boss at work.

My position was changed to a less exacting station and a cleaner environment, so I was able to go ahead despite the many difficulties that plagued me. Only God knows where I got the strength and energy to keep going, but, to this day, I thank God that I was able.

In January, 1985 T.V.R.I., the Italian T.V. station interviewed both of us, chiefly because Gabriel's case was unique. I took the opportunity to thank the Italian Red Cross, Caritas of Austria, and the Rhoda family for all the help they had given us. I also had an interview with Emiliano Ronzoni from the *Il Sabato* paper. The article ran in the April edition and was entitled "C'e un nuovo Ospedale che non ha muri" – "There exists a hospital without walls."

I expressed my gratitude to the Italians in general and the professionals of the Niguarda hospital in particular. Then I thanked the social worker, Marie Teresa Magni who went out of her way to find a room where I could stay while Gabriel was in the hospital.

I then recounted my difficulties in leaving my home, family, and country, and acknowledged the hospitality of Italy: "It is impossible to find such humanitarism in any part of the world."

For the bulletin from the Romanian Church in Milan, I also wrote an article. This was dated January, 1985 and had a photo of Gabriel.

A poster at the entrance of the hospital had caught my eye, at first I didn't quite understand but shortly afterwards I learned that it represented an organization dedicated to preserving life: "Auitami a vivere. Dai quello che poi." "Help me to live. Donate whatever is possible."

To this organization and to the excellent doctors, Gabriel and I owe a debt of gratitude that can never be repaid. I would like to mention the names of those dedicated men and women doctors: Drs. G. Serchia, L. Minetti, J. Lax, Iuliana Lefevre, A. Belli, Rovatti, Borghi, Civatti, Brando, and Busnach.

I concluded my short article by stating that Gabriel was improving each day and gaining weight. He was attending school and had many fine friends.

Some weeks later, I received a long letter from the Reverend Casian Bucescu who during the Communist regime despite much opposition, had the courage and fortitude to build a beautiful church in Granicesti. This man was arrested twice spending five years in prison. When he heard about Gabriel, he at once asked his community to pray as he prayed every day and recommended that each time anyone passed a hospital he or she should make three signs of the cross - one to thank God for all those who worked in that hospital; two, for all those awaiting operations or who were sick, and third for all those who passed by, that they never arrive there.

Ion Caraion was a well known writer and poet in Romania after World War II. He was condemned to death for high treason because of his connections with the French Embassy and anti-Communist activities. After almost twently years, he was released for lack of evidence.

I was honored to have met and befriended this man while in Jilava. I learned many of his poems and one in particular remains, to this day, in my mind.

THE SEASONS
Anotimpuri de malarii
Somn de ciur si maracine
Grota-s pune ochelarii
Ca sa vada cine vine.

The season of malaria
Sleep uneasy and tortuous
Blindfolded lest the eyes
Behold who is the next.

This internationally acclaimed poet had heard about Gabriel and me through the radio program - Free Europe, and the Monte Carlo T.V. He wrote to me immediately expressing his concern and wished us every success. It was close to Christmas and he, himself, was seriously ill; in fact he was dying of liver cancer as a result, he suspected, of his treatment in prison. He had been forced to work long hours in a lead mine deep underground - a man who had been a university professor, an editor, and the author of, at least, twenty-five books.

His last poem, *Ultimul Colind* he wrote and dedicated it to Gabriel.

Ultimul Colind

Saracute, straiele
De pe el...Si paiele
Nu prea tin de cald.
Gura de la gura,
Incropiti caldura.
Cresteti-l inalt.
Zvelt si nazdravan.
Cit altii-ntr-un an.
Mina de la mina
Plazmuiti-i lin
Camasuici de in,
Pieptaras de lina.
Nu-i de ajuns, plapindul,
Coperisul oii.
Mai dejuga boii
Si-adunati-i-cerc.
Mai suflati cu rindul
(Viata nu e joc)
Fiecare-n foc.
Uite, eu incerc.

Sa se-atite lemnele!
Proorocii, semnele
Si le-adeverira.
Va muri pe-o lira
In forma de cruce
Sfintul prunc din basmul
Celor mai uituce
Nazariri frumoase.
Si-o sa-i fie spasmul
Vesnica fintina.
Mina de la mina,

Tirnositi-i casa
Intr-acelasi loc
Unde-n staul acum pare,
Pare ca sa doarma.
Viata nu e joc.
Viata nu e floare.
Viata e o arma.

Cracium 1985
Ion Caraion

The Last Carol

In swaddling clothes poor
He was clad... And manger
cold, no warmth gave.
Breath of life
Exhaling heat
To nurture growth
Comely and sublime; -
As others attain in a year.
Each one in turn
Caress, mold him tenderly
Garment of cotton
Cloak of wool
Does not suffice, infancy,
The lamb's fleece
Yoke-free oxen
Surrounding.
Breathe warmth.
Life is no game.

Each at the fire
See how I do
Blow air on the embers.
Let the prophecies be
realized
He will die on the lyre
Shaped as a cross
Holy Babe of the Story
Of the long lost images
Let the Eternal flame
errupt.
United incense, the manger
Where now He sleeps.
Life is not a game
Life is not a flower
Life is a sword.

Christmas 1985
Ion Caraion

One of Ion Caraion's last letters was written to us in Milan. It was dated June 8, 1986. He died a few weeks later of cancer of the liver.

Lausanne, 8, VI, 1986

Dear Ones,
Who could have predicted that two years would pass without the opportunity of meeting and so little distance between us. But my severe sickness has hampered me and I fear will be the cause of my demise.

In a short time, I hope you will live in America. That would be a good decision. You will be successful hopefully with the support of someone and... you will reunite your family.

Poor Romanians! We have, over the centuries been trying forever to reunite our families. Forgive my writing, my hand shakes. It's difficult for me to squeeze a few words out. I answered Marin Mincu. You did a good thing when you gave him my address.

Send me, as soon as possible, the poem Anotimpuri and any others you remember, even fragments.

It would be wonderful if you could get permission to travel to the hills of Luzanne. For you and Gabriel to do what I was unable to do. In any case you must not try to return to the Inferno that is Romania.

From your photo, you look good and Gabriel exceptional. One day you four will be together, no doubt.

For my part and that of my family I wish you all satisfaction and friendship.

Ion Caraion.

Mr. Ion Caraion continued to work although in ill health while in exile. He published poems, articles, and books. One entitled *Comrade Hitler's Insects* he was gracious enough to send me as a gift.

During the period that Gabriel was recuperating from the transplant, we were introduced to the Manzzoni family. This name was well known in Italy as Mr. Alessandro Manzzoni's grandfather was a famous writer of classic literature. Young people today may still find his book - *The Betrothal*, an interesting read.

Filippo Manzzoni was an only child. He was about the same age as Gabriel and was, then, attending boarding school in Switzerland. During the vacations the two became good friends, often practicing speaking French together. Both refined, sensitive young men, they enjoyed playing the piano. Filippo was an avid stamp collector and Gabriel helped him augment his stock, since we were corresponding with several different countries in Europe and elsewhere.

Upon our first visit, Signor and Signora Manzzoni were curious to know why the Romanian people tolerated such a tyrant as the dictator, Ceausescu. They could not understand how such a rich agricultural land was unable to supply the demands of the population and why so many Romanians were fleeing to Italy in a time when the country was ruled by its own people.

I had many a long and lively discussion with these learned and intelligent Italians.

The Manzzoni home took up an entire block; it was a veritable palace and rose six or seven stories high. A large entrance hall built in the Roman style was supported by four huge columns. The floor was marble and as one looked ahead the magnificient broad marble stairs with branching arms led to the upper floors. Gold-framed oil paintings, mostly from the Renaissance period, decorated the walls. Signor Manzzoni explained that several of these paintings were handed down to him from his great-grandfather and were consequently quite valuable.

We were taken to a large elegantly furnished sitting room where we were served drinks from a revolving table. This beautiful room displayed taste and grandeur, yet we felt relaxed and at home and enjoyed the opulence and lifestyle of our gracious hosts as if it were second nature to us. I was among educated people who appreciated what I had to offer and with whom I felt completely at ease.

A sumptuous dinner followed and afterwards we spent the evening in lively and cordial discussion and inevitably the old questions returned: why so much hunger, scarcity etc. in Romania while the streets and markets of Italy were stockpiled with Romanian goods? "I was shocked when I arrived," I said, "to see so much merchandise from my country. I studied this situation while I was in Italy myself and being an engineer and economist, I discovered what was wrong," I continued. "After W.W. II, the Italian Communist Party had an exclusive monopoly to import meat from Romania. I also found out that this meat was imported at a very cheap rate and this allowed the Party to resell to the other European communities at market value." I explained, "This accounted for the long lines in the cities throughout Romania; people standing in the cold of winter or the heat of summer for hours on end to receive any bones or inferior parts of the meats when their turns came to be served, and added to that their portions were rationed. The final insult to our starving people was the disclosing of the fact that so many of these top Party officials held Swiss bank accounts. At this time, the Minister of Health, Doctor Ion Mincu, had the gall to propose that it would contribute to the health of the populace if there was less meat consumed substituting instead soy beans and salami made from soy with more vegetables.

"But it must be remembered," I continued, "that there were always special stores for those in 'high places' where everything imaginable was available at exorbitant prices."

"Is it true that each family in Romania is expected to produce at least five children?" asked my host.

"Yes," I answered, "whether or not they can support them is another situation."

Signora Manzzoni spoke: "How did you manage living as you did in the city of Bucharest, to feed your family of two sons, and a wife when food was so scarce?"

"I was lucky. My father was a good farmer and always supplied me with vegetables and meat when I visited my home during vacations."

So we spent many interesting and happy evenings with the Manzzoni family during the two years that we were fortunate to know them while in Italy. After we left we continued to correspond for over the next ten years and received from Signora Manzzoni the exceptional magazine *Bella Italia* as a reminder of our sojourn in Beautiful Italy.

We spent about two years in Milan. The climate in that part of Italy is mild; the rains come in spring and Fall, and summer is a time of azure-blue skies. Outside the city the countryside is a riot of color, the air is sweet and life is on the whole leisurely. Italians know how to live; they enjoy their foods, wines, and each other's company.

Easter 1985 we were invited by Giani and Liliana Grasso to spend the week-end in Carati Brianzza. Mario, their son was about Gabriel's age. Liliana was Romanian and often went to update her education at the University of Cluj, giving me an opportunity to send money and food home. On this occasion we enjoyed a traditional Romanian Easter celebration and partook of the usual foods including colored eggs.

We had the opportunity to listen to the Cluj Philharmonic Orchestra which was performing in a city nearby - Desio. The conductor was Emil Simon and the program included Enescu's Rapsodie No. 1, Strauss Waltzes, and Suppe's Overture. This concert was a huge success and we thoroughly enjoyed it.

A few days later, I phoned Bucharest trying to reach my wife. She was not home, so I called her sister Elena only to learn that Juliana was in the hospital. Elena would not tell me in which hospital, but she did say it was all on account of Michael's bad behavior. She began to abuse me over the phone blaming me for all their trouble. After listening to her for a few moments, as she berated me and called my son a violent person, I told her to cease this kind of talk for we were on an open line, which was monitored and her description of Michael could very well be taken literally. At that she hung up. I was forced to get information about my wife, Iuliana, through my good friend, Dr. Cardas. From him, I learned that things were not the same between us and

233

that she did not ever intend to follow me to Italy or anywhere else.

"How much, Lord, how much?" I cried from the depths of my soul. I felt like Job in the Bible - abandoned, deserted by all.

Gabriel had always been a kind, loving and outgoing child. He remained so as an adolescent and his nature was and is to this day prone to generosity and acts of kindness. An opportunity to show his concern and be of help came in the form of a little lost child. A little girl who was wandering about the street crying drew his attention. He immediately went to console her and taking her by the hand led her to a policeman. The distraught mother was eventually found and both happily united. I didn't know on that occasion who was more delighted Gabriel or the mother. I have never seen my son hurt a living thing and that includes flies. They're all God's creatures and need to be respected. I've seen him go out of his way to allow flies and other small bugs to escape when trapped in the house.

Shortly after Ion Carion's death, his wife, Valentina, and daughter, Marta in accordance with the poet's wishes, came to Milan especially to find out how we stood with regard to emigrating. They had made up their minds that if the American Authorities did not allow us to enter the U.S. they would do all in their power to facilitate our entry into Switzerland. Three days after they left we were informed our U.S. papers were under consideration. Now our minds concentrated on finding a sponsor.

A cousin of mine, Filon Morosan had left Romania some seven years before and was living with his wife and family of seven children in the Portland area. He had been allowed to leave for religious reasons. He became our initial sponsor but because Gabriel's problems were so serious it was necessary to have at least two persons responsible. So we had to look around for other possibilities. We got in touch with our friend Mr. Buzbee in Texas. Soon he had contacted his friends as to what could be done and eventually Senator Phil Graham was approached.

After much discussion and research, Mr. Graham came up with two ways to help Gabriel enter the U.S. The first solution suggested adoption, the second, entering the U.S. as a student. Unfortunately, neither option was possible. Gabriel's friend, Mr. Buzbee was not married so was ineligible for that responsibility and Gabriel, at the time, was a minor, under the age of eighteen and had no means of support. We were left with no alternative but to apply for political asylum.

Chapter 16

Beautiful Italy

"I swore that I would scatter them as wind upflings the foam,
And give my charger hay and oats in the Vatican at Rome...
Yet you before my legions imagine you can stand,
You ridiculous old dotard, with a bare staff in your hand?"
"To that old dotard, Emperor, aught one courtesy accord
For over all Wallachia 'tis he the chosen lord.
And wiser you would guard your words, nor yet too loudly
boast
Lest should the furious Danube flood engulf your fleeing
host."

Mihai Eminescu
- Satire III

I n June '86 we decided to move to Latina. Gabriel's
health had improved and since we were in the process
of seeking emigration to the United States and as the
Embassy had its headquarters in Rome, we thought it better
to be close by. Near Rome, to the south, and on the coast is
the city of Latina and in this city the Refugee Camp was
located. This was our destination.

But before leaving Milan, the city which had given
Gabriel a second chance at life, I want to express my love
and admiration for that glorious center of art and culture, by
highlighting some of my favorite and most frequented
haunts. The Cathedral has to be seen to be believed; one of
the wonders of the world with its white marble traceries,
pinnacles and flying buttresses, not to mention the 4,000

statues. Started in 1387, it was completed in 1815. It is also in this great city that one of the world's greatest paintings - *The Last Supper*, by Leonardo da Vinci is housed. And, since Italy gave us the opera, it seems fitting that one of the greatest geniuses of opera, Mozart, produced his first opera there when he was a boy of fourteen. I, as a poor refugee, enjoyed so many wonderful performances in the beautiful La Scala.

The journey from Milan to Rome, a distance of approximately 900 kilometers, took several days. It was the chance of a lifetime, a time to explore and get to know some of the glories that are Italy and have been for two thousand years.

The first day we drove through Cremona, the home of three generations of the Amati family and also of their pupil Antonio Stradivari, who about three hundred years ago made violins that have never been equaled. This town like other interesting cities of the Lombardy Plain was founded by the Romans in the early 220's B.C. Modena, where Italy's beloved Luciano Pavarotti has a home, is an area of lush green pastures, orchards and vineyards. Bologna, our next stop, is the major passage of the Apennines from the plain to the peninsula. This town, the seat of an ancient university, has two leaning towers dating back to the thirteenth century.

"La Serenissima" is the term that has been applied to Venice. "The most serene" perhaps can be best attributed to the beauty of this city for its past was anything but serene. This, one of the strongest bulwarks of Christendom against the expanding attacks of the Turks, was also for centuries the unrivaled mistress of trade between Europe and the Orient. A city built on water, it was created over a thousand years ago on mud banks and swamps and today is still considered one of the most beautiful cities in the world.

St. Mark's Basilica and the Dukel Palace are exotic mixtures of Byzantine, Gothic, and Renaissance styles. In Venice one has to walk everywhere and where you cannot walk you go by water in a gondola or by Vaporetti - water buses.

St. Mark's Church is, without question, the heart of the city and one of Europe's most beautiful churches. It is built in the form of a Greek cross and topped by five massive domes. It did not become a cathedral until 1807, although it was begun in 1063 and erected to house the remains of St. Mark, which were taken from Alexandria two centuries before by agents in the employ of the doge.

Down the ages, the church has stood as a symbol of Venetian wealth and power and has been called Chiesa D'Oro - Golden Church. The four bronze horses over the central doorway are copies of the originals which are on view in the Museo de San Marco and which were taken from Constantinople in 1204 along with a lot of other loot. Just inside the door, in the porch, there is a medallion of red porphyry set in the floor marking the spot where Barbarossa, the Holy Roman Emperor, and Pope Alexander III were reconciled through the efforts of Doge Sebastiano Ziani in 1177.

One of the unique features of this church is its roof of brick vaulting, rather than wood, enabling the ceiling to be decorated with mosaics. The interior is dark. There is a massive iconostasis and Byzantine chandelier. These features, as well as the Greek cross floor plan give San Marco an exotic aspect - Oriental magnificence blended with Christian belief give an awesome impression.

We spent a whole day in and around this beautiful church - in the famous piazza and the Museo Correr. The next day Gabriel and I visited the Accademia Gallery; the Venetian paintings there were simply fantastic.

In the Museo Correr there is a vast collection by the old masters, once the property of the aristocrat Teodoro Correr - hence the name. He donated them in 1830 to the city.

The Accademia Gallery houses perhaps the most extraordinary collection of Venetian art in the whole world. Notable among the works are: Bellini's altar piece from the Church of San Giobbe, his *Madonna with St. Catherine and the Magdalen*. There is also the huge canvas - *Feast in the House of Levi*. Titian's *Presentation of the Virgin* and *The Tempest* by Giorgione (1477-1510).

My heart and soul were fed by these masterpieces for days to come and I look back reverently upon that blessed opportunity which was granted to us to become immersed in the glories and riches of the human mind. This surely was education in its highest and most enlightened form and I was grateful that Gabriel, for all his sufferings, was able to be exposed to such magnificence.

We could have spent a month in Venice and not seen all that it had to offer. But, we could not leave without seeing the great Gothic-Renaissance structure of pink and white marble called The Palazzo Ducale. It was more than a palace combining a sort of White House, Senate, prison and torture chamber all rolled into one. The Venetian government set up in the 7th century as a participatory democracy, provided for an elected ruler - the doge, who served for life. He was in practice just a figurehead. Power rested in the General Council. Laws were passed by the Senate - a group of 200 elected from The General Council - which could have as many as 1,700 members.

The entrance to the palace is an ornate Gothic Porta della Carta which opens onto a huge courtyard. Ahead lies the Scala dei Giganti - Stairway of the Giants, which is guarded by towering statues of Mars and Neptune.

Inside, the walls and ceilings are magnificently decorated by Venice's greatest artists. Those best known are the paintings of Tintoretto - *Bacchus and Ariadne crowned by Venus* and Veronese's *Rape of Europa*. The world's largest oil painting - *Paradise* by Tintoretto (1518-94) can also be seen in this building in the Great Council Hall. It measures 75 by 23 feet and takes up the end wall of this great hall.

Rimini on the Adriatic was our next stopover. We had a twofold reason for making this city a focal point. We had heard that each July an art exhibition was held there, to which some of the greatest artists of Europe were invited. Among those thus honored was a Romanian, Camilian Demetrescu, some of whose work had already been commissioned by the Vatican. I was looking forward to meeting this great man.

When we arrived at the designated area, the first object to attract our attention was a colossal wooden sculpture - *Cristos Pantocrator*, which looked down on us with hands extended as if to embrace the whole world.

Upon reaching the pavillion assigned to Demetrescu's work, I was overawed. *The Dragon and Utopia* was the theme of his display. Inside, there were seventy-two pictures and four large tapestries; the symbolism of these was explained by a series of four dialogues. The first was based on Plato's idea of Utopia; then came the Liberal notion of Utopia; thirdly the Totalitarian form was explained and, finally, Anti-Utopia as represented by Christ's philosophy.

Summarizing his concepts, Demetrescu argued: "Our age is a product of what is an 'ideal' society. Starting with Plato and continuing until to-day's Marx, all have a common theme - Utopia... Utopia, where it is believed possible to eliminate 'evil' and substitute 'good' by a decree of the State." Demetrescu goes on to explain that the kernel of all modern Utopias is to be found in Plato's Republic: property in common, material things, though good - even objects of affection, e.g. wife and family, religion, - must be relinquished, sacrificed. The State alone dictated the scope and content of education, closely censoring poetry, philosophy, history, and politics. Supression of subjective ideas and sentiments were in order. State liars and informers must be honored. Those who lived in rural areas were despised and disparaged while those who adhered to hedonism and obligatory 'happiness' were encouraged. Uniformity and conformity to set rules and patterns must be strictly enforced.

He concluded by asking the question – "what does the future hold?" Then answered by declaring that in today's world of materialism where the objects for consumption are promoted by inferior art symbols, thus spreading materialism more easily worldwide, we are living in a jungle. "Debased life-styles corrode the human spirit because man is being manipulated by artificial, utilitarian, unnatural interests, needs, and necessities which have surpassed any limit or measure. How else can the commercials of today be interpreted when they are geared towards industrial, political, pornographic or pseudo cultural interests that are symbols of a decadent "art"! In fact they are twice decadent - first by content and secondly by misrepresenting or incorrectly classifying the symbolism. In other words there is no food for the soul and no symbolism other than signs of degradation - of political, economic, and social power, the ruin of civilization and the destruction of humanity."

In speaking about this same theme, Pope John Paul II in his encyclical 'Solicidudo rei socialis' refers to the decadent art forms of the two worlds, East and West, as repositories of sinfulness. And Pope Leo XIII in the 1891 encyclical 'Rerum Novarum' predicted over a hundred years ago the collapse of Socialism from two causes: The destruction of private property and unequal distribution of wealth with no respect for human rights.

The artistic and cultural values of the Camilian Demetrescu exhibit – *The Dragon* and *Utopia* have, according to the critics in the mass-media in Europe and Italy, itself, been highly acclaimed. "In the exhibit," mentioned above which was so successful, "the artist brought to light the conflict between diverse life-styles within society and the denial of human liberty... (Utopia) This chimera completely dominates the masses like an arrogant and all-powerful Sphinx with a thousand different faces - the brutality of power-based weapons and also the insidious slavery of Communist society with its new mechanical idols, its 'necessary' objects invented or imagined... These forces are seeking to reduce man to an unthinking being without individuality and without transcendental horizons, and to degrade man to just a statistic in the greater mechanism of collective life... When talking about Utopia, it is found to be a 'nasty' common dominator of destinies in our century. While Demetrescu realized that the transcendental destiny of man has been suffocated and stifled by the ideologies of 'Real Socialism' (Communism). The Absolutism - Judaic - Christian Values, may be the only means viable to reestablish communion between spirit and intellect."[18]

The weather was good as we arrived in Florence. The city was making heroic strides to reclaim and repair all that the Arno River had destroyed the previous year. The streets were still full of mud; many priceless works of art had been damaged or destroyed, but the artists were at work, hundreds of them.

The Palazzo Vecchio with its Slender Tower begun in 1298, and the arcaded buildings housing famous picture galleries, a library, and the Archives of Tuscany were all being repaired. Florence - the city of flowers - is the intellectual and artistic center of Italy. The Cathedral, a stately marble structure, we were privileged to visit. Nearby, what is probably the most beautiful campanile in Italy, rises as a spectacle of delicate tracery - The Shepherd's Tower designed by the great Giotto. Of course we stopped to visit the baptistery with its bronze doors by Lorenzo Ghiberti which Michelangelo said were "fit for the gates of Paradise."

Leaving Florence, I headed northwest as I wanted to see the famous marble quarries of Carrara. Then, we decided to go to the city of Pisa; we could not leave this part of the country without seeing first-hand its world famous Leaning Tower.

On our way south to Rome, we came to the city of Gallese Scalo where the artist, Camilian Demetrescu, had his home and to which we were invited for a few days to visit with him and his family. This, we considered a great honor and to this day cherish the memory of the pleasant time we spent there.

His house, which has two floors and which also serves as his studio, is an art gallery in itself. The walls are covered with tapestries of wool, cotton and silk, and all are woven together with silver and gold threads using variations of the arazzi technique. The works displayed thus of special interest to me were: *The Berlin Wall* 1987, *The Triumphant Lamb*, *The Centaur*, *Freedom*, and *Utopia*, *The Custodian of Demogogy*. These works, in my estimation, demonstrated the prophetic talent of this artist. I had time to study these and other works as I read the many and various commentaries and critiques in the different art reviews, editorials, and other presentations. All concluded that this gifted Romanian artist's work was the ultimate representation of truth in the artistic movement of the latter part of the 20th Century and the beginning of the 21st.

One of his proud moments was when he showed me his contribution to the town of Gallese. In 1977, Demetrescu and his family with their own hands restored the 10th Century Romanesque church which had fallen into ruins. They made every effort to retain the unique style, sculpture and symbolism peculiar to that period. Today, the church is a place of interest historically, artistically, and structurally because it is a rare example of the Romanesque architecture which existed in Italy in A.D. 1,000, and also in many other parts of Europe.

It was with much emotion and great reluctance that we left this place of inspiration. The companionship and enthusiasm of this extraordinary man and his family had renewed my enthusiasm for life and given me confidence in the future. We have corresponded for many years on a regular basis. And I take great pleasure in writing about my friend for newspapers and magazines making the work of this Romanian artist known here in America.

* * * * *

Rome, The Eternal City

Rome, The Eternal City, the capital of Italy, is perhaps at first more interesting as the former center of the Roman Empire and the seat of the Christian Church. It is a place of ancient palaces, forums, temples, and circuses, of arenas, aqueducts, baths, triumphal arches, and paved streets. Marble colannades and architectural marvels reminiscent of Etruscan, Greek and Roman days. It was the greatest empire of antiquity. Today one stands in awe at the majestic Cathedral of St. Peter's and marvels at Via Nazionale or enjoys the Piazza Venezia.

In Rome it is usual to leave the city in the summer. Anyone who is anyone and even those who don't consider themselves in that category schedule their vacations so as to be out of the city and either in the mountains or at the beach during the months of July and August. But Gabriel and I chose this particular period to enter that most beautiful metropolis - July 17, to be exact.

We intended to spend several days exploring as much as we could before setting up house in Latina. First, being Romanian, we had to visit Triain's Column which depicts the historical events during the occupation of Dacia Felix - Romania today - by the Roman legions. I was exceedingly pleased to see this monument erected, in ages past, to the existence of the Romanian people. Not too far away was the place where St. Peter and later St. Paul were imprisoned. At the time we were there, the location was being renovated and we were not able to enter the exact chamber but we could view it very well from outside.

Next we went to visit the enormous monument of King Victor Emmanuel II, and from the terrace could see all across Rome to the domes of St. Peter's and St. Andrea della Valla. The Colosseum and later The Temple of Saturn, which is now reduced to eight pillars, were also on our list.

The magnificent gardens of the Palazzo Colonna brought me back time and again. I learned that the Palazzo was begun in the 15th century by Pope Martin V, who was himself of the Colonna family.

No visitor to Rome of course can leave that city on the Tiber without seeing the city within the city - The Vatican. St. Peter's with its colonnaded piazza, its fountains, its yellowish-white stone glistening in the bright sunshine, is undoubtedly the most magnificent church in the whole world. It took 120 years to build under the supervision of some of Italy's greatest artists: Bramante, Raphael and

Michelangelo. I give thanks to God everytime I think of my stay in Rome. The beauty, the treasures of hundreds of years of civilization - to have had the privilege of viewing all these firsthand is something that I will cherish till my dying day. Beside the Basilica of St. Peter, the palace of the Popes, built at the same time as the great church, has eleven hundred rooms - Raphael's frescoes adorn many of them. The rooms are open to the public. I spent hours enjoying and studying these wonders of art and beauty - the Sistine Chapel with the paintings of Michelangelo, the libraries, and museums. Then the gardens laid out in the Italian style, the statuary, the walks and groves, everything so arranged as to produce stately harmony.

The city of Tivoli situated about thirty miles east of Rome, dates back to the Paleolithic period as affirmed by fragments discovered in 1953 and now on display at the Pagorini Ethnological Museum in Rome. However, we did not go particularly to view the city but the world famous gardens. It took us a whole weekend to see them properly.

Begun in the time of Hadrian, the Emperor (A.D. 118-130) the Villa named for him was built in stages. Fascinated by the achievements of the Hellenistic World, Hadrian decided to recreate these marvels of the classical period for his own pleasure. After his death, the Villa was sacked by the barbarians as well as the Romans, themselves. Still the Villa and gardens are a pleasure to see; oleanders, pines, and cypress have sprung up among the ruins adding to the majesty of the surroundings.

Villa d'Este is the main attraction in the town of Tivoli. Ippolito d' Este was active in political affairs in the 16th century. He was a cardinal because of his grandfather, Alexander VI, an infamous Borgia pope. Ippolito had part of a Franciscan monastery torn down and the river Aniene diverted to build his villa and gardens. Extraordinary feats of engineering and beauty, the numerous fountains and waterfalls cannot be imagined, one has to experience the wonder of it all to appreciate these marvels.

At this time, we couldn't delay longer in the Eternal City as I was obligated to present our Romanian passports at the Refugee Camp in Latina, where, eventually, we received all our Italian identification papers and turned in our Romanian passports.

From the end of July to the end of October we remained in the Refugee Camp in Latina. The conditions were not good there, mostly because it was overcrowded and there were too many small children in confined quarters. Refugees from all over Eastern Europe, particularly Poles and Romanians jostled one another for space. The Poles, differing from the Romanians came with their entire families, their cars, trailers, etc. Whereas, the Romanians were lucky to escape with nothing and usually alone. Because of the overcrowding in Latina, it was not conducive to healthy living, particularly for Gabriel whose immune system was not in peak condition. The food was inadequate and not well prepared, so Gabriel suffered as a consequence and was often sick. I was forced to buy special foods for him but I was lucky because I had received six months severance pay from my former job at Airoinformatica in Milan.

While staying in the Camp, we were invited by the Suciu family to visit their home in the city. This family was related to Bishop Ion Suciu from the Greek Catholic Church in Blaj.

This brilliant young man with six other bishops was imprisoned by the Communists in 1948. After that, the churches were destroyed or confiscated as well as all other properties belonging to the Catholic Church: schools, homes, and charitable establishments.

In this way the Communists hoped to rid themselves of all those capable and educated people who might influence the youth and elevate the aspirations of the people at large.

Bishop Ion Suciu received his initial education in his native city of Blaj. Upon finishing his studies there, he went to Rome where he received his doctorate in Theology. In 1931 he returned to Romania to teach at the University of Blaj where he became an outstanding orator and teacher with a special interest in and leaning towards the youth who in turn were drawn to his charasmatic personality. Because of his activities and work he also attracted the attention of the Communist authorities.

With such outstanding qualities, gifts, and talents, he very quickly won recognition from his superiors in the Church and was consecrated Bishop at the age of thirty-one, making him the youngest Catholic Bishop in the entire world.

After the Communists came to power all those who were affiliated with the church were initially denied any salary while teaching in the schools and universities and then they were finally arrested.

Thus at the age of thirty-nine, this brilliant, promising young bishop was thrown into prison where he was tortured and died in 1953.

It was therefore a great honor to be invited to spend time with this family and to learn more about their martyred relative.

While I was at dinner, I was introduced to another Romanian, a lady doctor, Balenty by name, who ran her own hospital in Germany. After dinner, since I had had a heart attack in '85, she offered to check me over. From her, I learned ten valuable rules to protect my health which I should like to pass on to posterity in this chapter of my book.

1. Watch weight;

2. Diet - plenty of fruit and vegetables;
3. Always leave the table able to eat more;
4. Bathe in moderate water (not too hot not too cold);
5. No alcohol;
6. No hot or cold drinks;
7. No strenuous efforts;
8. Proper rest;
9. No heavy lifting;
10. No fast pace running or long distances.

All during our stay in Latina the weather was beautiful. Long sunny days and balmy nights with clear skies from which a myriad of twinkling stars could be seen.

One evening while I was helping Gabriel with his math problems - he always had problems with math, I heard a knock on the door. Upon opening it, I was surprised to see a fine looking gentleman who immediately introduced himself as Dr. Emilian Dobrea.

"I arrived last night in Latina."

I asked him to come in. When he was seated, I offered him a glass of juice; he didn't drink alcohol or wine.

"How did you escape?" was my first question.

"A friend of mine, Stefan Voin, and I swam across the Danube during the night. We blackened our bodies with shoe-polish, then we tied one wrist to each other - if one of us got in trouble we had decided the other would be there to help. We had practiced for two years for this venture and finally pulled it off twelve days ago." He was jubliant as he told his story.

"Doctor," I answered, "you took an enormous risk. Tito is two-faced. How many refugees have been returned to Romania in exchange for salt or iron products!"

"I know this well," he replied. "We slept in corn fields and in hay lofts and anywhere we could hide during the day and did most of our travelling by night until we reached the Italian border near Trieste."

Because the conditions in the Camp were less than ideal, we decided that he would remain with us. He was content to have a place on a mattress on the floor and I was happy to have a qualified doctor for Gabriel.

Dr. Dobrea spent at least a month with us until he found more suitable lodgings.

One day soon after meeting with Dr. Dobrea, I had to go to Rome to get some special medicine for Gabriel. It was about 10:00 a.m. when I arrived at the train station. While I was awaiting my train I stood, like so many others on the platform, watching the other trains coming and going. As I glanced at the passengers alighting from the train which had just pulled in, I noticed a very pregnant woman. With difficulty she reached the platform and then started to push a perambulator in front of her all the while huffing and puffing as she waddled along.

When she drew close, I realized she needed help. I didn't have too much time, but I couldn't abandon a human being in need.

"Madame, parlez-vous francais?"

She answered, "Je ne parle pas francais."

I then spoke to her in German, Italian, even Russian, but I got the same response. In desperation, I then blurted out in Romanian, "what is your native language?"

"Romanian!"

We both began to laugh and I said: "Then for God's sake speak it." And I realized that another refugee from Romania had somehow managed to escape all alone and in dire need. I decided she had to go to the Camp at Latina. She had no where else to go anyway. I took the pram from her and told her to follow me. I hailed a taxi and paid for her to be taken to the Camp.

Just before the cab took off she stuck her head out the window and asked my name.

"Teodor," I answered. Then the taxi sped away.

251

When I returned from Rome, she was already in the hospital and had delivered a baby boy.

Some two weeks later, the woman began to make enquiries about me. She asked around for a man named Teodor. Eventually, she was told that a Teodor Gherasim was staying in the Hotel Fogliano. She came to visit bringing her new-born baby and told me that she would like me to be the child's god-father at his upcoming baptism, and that she wished to call him Teodor. To which I gladly agreed. She thanked me profusely.

During the discussion which followed, I discovered that she not only lived about two blocks from my apartment in Bucharest, but that she had a husband and two daughters still in that city. Since life was so difficult for all of them, she decided she was going to try to escape. She had a sister living in Italy and on the pretext of visiting her, she obtained a visa for two weeks. Knowing that her child was due about that time, she set out with the intention of giving birth in Italy, thereby assuring that her child would be an Italian citizen. Having fulfilled her desire, she now applied to emigrate to Canada. Her next step would be to file for reunification of the family. This could take up to three years and in the meantime this valiant woman was prepared to do all she could to keep herself and her baby alive while awaiting her husband and other children.

Finally, she did emigrate to Canada and was, after several years, reunited with her loved ones.

During our stay in the Hotel Fogliano, which was situated near the beach on the Tyrehenian Sea, we took advantage of both the warm waters and the sunshine, spending longer periods each day in the open air. It was on one such occasion that I met Mr. D'Attilia, a member of the United Nations. He was interested to know how the youth of Romania perceived Communist ideology as opposed to Western Democracy. To this end he asked my permission to speak with Gabriel. For several days they spoke at length. And when, finally, Mr. D'Attilia had to leave, he came to congratulate me and tell me how proud I should be of my son. He only wished the young people of the West had such a thoroughly deep and realistic appreciation of what Western education and freedom really meant, and he concluded that Communism had, indeed, not achieved its goals as far as the youth of Eastern Europe was concerned.

On another occasion, an official from the mayor's office in the city of Latina fell into conversation with me. He was interested primarily in three topics: The role of the Pope in the Anti-Communist Movement; Why the standard of living was so low in Romania and other Communist countries; What does Communism really mean.

In my answers to the above questions, I explained that the Pope was enemy number one of the Communists. This particular Pope, John Paul II, from his youth in Poland had had a long fight, although non violent, with the Nazi occupants and then the Communist forces. He, unlike many, did not leave his country but remained as a leader, in both a civil and religious capacity. Then, when elected Pope in 1978, he was a strong supporter of the Solidarity Movement and Lech Walesa.

Lech, the organizer of Solidarity, was a worker in the shipyards of Gdansk. He had the courage to declare a general strike. Poland had had enough of Communist tactics. For the first time the workers in a worker state revolted. The result was that the Poles acquired their freedoms - of religion, of movement and, eventually, their salaries were increased.

But it had been a hard fight. In speaking to the first national congress at which 892 Solidarity delegates representing 9,457,584 members were present, Walesa said: "Each of us individually does not count much. Together we are the strength of millions who constitute Solidarity." He added: "We shall open a vista for a better Poland only if we act in solidarity. The struggle is going to be long and hard but we shall win and we shall make Poland a country of our dreams."

In tackling the second question, I had no difficulty and could have spoken for hours on the topic. Having lived through the years of Russian take-over and domination, and eventually survived the dictatorship of our own puppets of Communism, I was perfectly familiar with the state of affairs in Romania and the results of the long years of such abusive power.

"Romania and the other countries occupied by Russian forces paid dearly during and after W.W. II. All natural resources were confiscated; taxes, too high for most, were levied to pay for wartime expenses. This made it impossible for people to save or better themselves. Added to these trials, Romania lost at least half a million men to the Eastern Front and another half million were slain fighting with the Axis powers. After the Communist take-over, 300,000 men and women died in prison of starvation under the rule of Dej and Ceausescu." Finally, I tried to open the eyes of my Italian Communist listener by telling him that for simply expressing an opinion, over one million men, women, and children were deported to the Danube Delta, Baragan, and the Prut Valley to survive as best they could.

To his last question, I answered: "The Communist ideology supports the notion that all things are common to all men, therefore all must work for the common good. I then asked the man, "Have you a car?" He answered immediately in the affirmative. Then I responded, "You are not a Communist." "Why?" he asked. "Fine, give me your car, because I wish to go to Palermo. This is what Communism means. What is yours is mine also!"

He asked no more and like the rich man in the Bible went away sad.

As the summer was drawing to a close and it would soon be time to register Gabriel for school, we decided to make the most of the time left to see more of what Italy had to offer. Pompeii, Naples, and Salerno were the highlights of our next trips.

Pompeii, the city buried by the devasting eruption of Vesuvius in 59 and 62 B.C. was of great interest. We spent several days in this ancient pleasure resort of the Romans. From the recent excavations we learned that the city was beautifully laid out, its streets in parallel lines much like a modern city today but, unlike our modern buildings, the homes and public structures were made of stone and intended to last. The life of the city was in many ways superior to that which we consider so modern and advanced in our times. In the city center, the government buildings housing the ruling bodies where facing a long impressive plaza which was flanked on both sides by magnificient temples - to Appolo, Jupiter, etc. The art, architecture, mosaic work and murals, in the homes and public places were of such beauty and grace that to see anything similar today one would have to visit art galleries or museums.

Naples, the city on the bay with its blue, pink, or violet stucco houses climbing the hills, is an overcrowded and noisy place. Yet, it possesses numerous artistic treasures. In the Community Museum the statues of Triain or Trajan and Decebal - King of Dacia in the time of the Emperor Trajan, 106 A.D. were placed in the entrance hall making one feel proud to see one of Romania's ancient monarchs displayed and remembered side by side with a great Roman Emperor.

Although many parts of the city are unattractive and dirty, one is amazed to suddenly come upon a gem of rare beauty and splendor such as the Church of San Domenico Maggiore 'a jewel of Gothic architecture'. This church was

255

built in the 14th century and remodeled in the 19th; the distinct baroque influence is obvious in the interior. Unfortunately, many of the works of art were destroyed during World War II, but, miraculously, the belfry was saved.

Not far away is the Cappella Sansevero. The church was built by Giovan Francesco di Sangro, Duke of Torremaggiore. Suffering from a life-threatening illness, he vowed to show his gratitude if he recovered by building a chapel for the Madonna della Pieta, which he did in 1590. In the 18th century, important works of art - sculptures and frescoes - were added. Today it is a curious combination of the sacred and profane. One of the most important works associated with the chapel, however, is Giuseppe Sanmartino's statue *Cristo Velato* - the veiled Christ - sculpted in 1753. This remarkable work portrays the thinly veiled body of Christ.

The different architectural and artistic styles incorporated into San Lorenzo Maggiore give a detailed account of the development of art history in Naples. Commissioned by Charles I of Anjou the work was begun in 1270 and completed in 1275 on the site of an early 6th century church. Nine chapels extend from the apse including the magnificient Cappellone di San Antonio. Also, the 15th century panel of St. Anthony surrounded by angels is noteworthy.

We could not leave Naples without taking a boat ride to the famous Isle of Capri near the southern extremity of the Bay. The island is known as *un pezzo di cielo caduta in terra* (a piece of paradise fallen from the skies). Living up to this reputation, it has long been romanticised. John Dryden, sailing around it in 1700 coined the term to describe its wild beauty: romantique. It has been the playground of many of the worlds most celebrated writers, playwrights and poets from Turgenev and Dumas to Joseph

Conrad, George Bernard Shaw, D.H. Lawrence, Hans Christian Anderson and today's Graham Greene.

The Caprese like to think that the island's name comes from capra (goat) a nickname given to Emperor Tiberius for his hairiness and sexual appetite.

Capri is an island of kaleidoscopic caves often named after their colors - green, blue, white, or red. The world famous Grotta Azzura was not the only one that we visited but we were fortunate to see Grotta Verde and Meravigliosa as well.

At the end of October we moved to Rome so that Gabriel could attend the Avogadro School of Science and Mathematics. He was to remain there for the school year following the courses offered.

While Gabriel was attending class, I spent some of my time in the library. My objective was to study the geography of the United States in depth so as to come up with a good decision regarding our future place of residence there. My final selections included the States of Oregon, Connecticut and Georgia. I chose these states because, in my opinion they offered: the most equitable climates; opportunities for employment; local resources and conditions favorable for future development. Of these three states, Oregon was the one I liked best.

But, while living in the city which boasts more masterpieces per square foot than any other in the world, I could not allow any opportunity to slip by. I must see all!

What had I not seen? I asked myself. Ancient Rome came to mind – the ruins of the Roman Forum, the Capitoline Hill, and the Colosseum. Then, having visited these revered monuments, one gets a feel for the epicenter of the ancient world and an appreciation for what Michelangelo did to transform the Capitoline Hill - the seat of ancient Rome's government - into a Renaissance showcase. The Colosseum, perhaps Rome's most famous monument was begun in A.D. 42 and opened a few years later with a program of games and shows lasting a 100 days. More than 50,000 people could be seated in this arena, faced with marble and decorated with hundreds of statues. It had a velarium - an extraordinary system of sail-like awnings rigged on ropes and manned by sailors - to protect the audience from the sun and rain.

On the weekends Gabriel would accompany me; he was just as interested as I in the wonders that surrounded us on all sides. He was a good student of history and everything he saw only broadened his knowledge and gave color to the facts he already knew.

The Pantheon, one of Rome's most perfect and best preserved ancient monuments, was built on the site of an earlier pantheon in 27 B.C. by Augustus's General Agreppa. Hadrian had it rebuilt in A.D. 120. The hole in the ceiling, I learned, was intentional. The oculus at the apex of the dome signifing the 'all-seeing eye of heaven.' I also learned that the proportions of the central frame are condidered the most perfect in the world. The original bronze doors date back more than 1,800 years.

We spent most of one Sunday traversing "The Queen of Roads", the Via Appia Antica which was completed in 312 B.C. by Appius Claudius, who also built Rome's first aqueduct. But while we walked this ancient highway, we took time to visit two of the most important catacombs - San Callisto and San Sebastiano. The former is perhaps the best preserved underground cemetery. A friar escorted us acting as a guide and pointed out the markings and drawings of the early Christian worshipers. We also saw the excavated area in the wall where Mass was said in times of persecution.

The 4th century catacomb of San Sebastiano got its name because the saint was buried there. It is four levels deep and it is from this particular one that the word "catacomb" originates, for it was in an area where the road dips into a hollow - catacumbas as the Romans called it. As time passed the Christian cemetery which had existed there since the 2nd century came to be known by the same name.

In March '87 we had an interview with the American Consul General, Ms. Lynn C. Nelson-Parieta. We spent two hours discussing the pros and cons of our situation. At first it didn't appear that we stood a chance of getting into the United States, Gabriel was too much of a liability. I could see that Ms. Nelson-Parieta was not at all happy with our case. In the end, she proposed that I should get one sponsor for myself and two for Gabriel. I left very despondent and discouraged and wondered if I would ever hear from her again.

But God has a way of doing things of which we poor mortals never dream. While on a trip back to Milan for Gabriel's check-up, we took a sleeping compartment which we shared with a professor, Thomas Donaldson, from Loyola University in Chicago. He was travelling with his wife and child en route to the University of Milan.

We naturally got into conversation with each other and discussed many topics from the Russian crisis to the intolerable conditions of the Eastern European countries under Communism. Finally, we talked about my own situation and the perilous condition of Gabriel's health - our future expectations and our difficulty in finding sponsors to afford our entry into the U.S.

This man was extremely interested in our plight and by the time we reached Milan had promised to see what he, himself, could do to help us.

Two weeks later, when he returned to Rome, he called me and set up a time for us to get together. During our meeting, he drew up a petition of great length and outlined many reasons why we should be allowed to go to America. This petition was sent to Ms. Nelson-Parieta.

During this time, the administrators of the Latina Refugee Camp, were also aware of the difficulties I was encountering and knew that a Ms. Margaret Montgomery working with the Presbyterian Church World Service was looking into the status of refugees in Europe. They drew her attention to our plight. As a result, our case and several others, was written up in the review *Exodus* published by the Presbyterian Church (U.S.A.) Vol. V. No. 4. 1987. This review was sent to the White House and the American Embassy in Washington. D.C.

On June 17th '87, I had another interview, the result of which was that the U.S. approved our visas. At this time, Ms. Nelson-Parieta apologized for the long delay explaining that our initial sponsor - The Romanian Church and Filon Morosan had withdrawn their support. She was forced, she said, to look for a new sponsor and through the help of the World Episcopal Church found one. "As a result you will have to spend another month in Italy until all your documents are in order."

But I didn't mind another month. I was so happy to get this wonderful news.

In the meantime, a good friend of mine, Mr. Paul Constantinescu, living in Chicago wrote to the Consul in Rome offering to sponsor us also. By now I had four sponsors. Ten days later, I received the visas and tickets for our departure to Oregon which I had indicated earlier was the state in which I preferred to live.

When I had left Romania some three years before, I was allowed to take only $100.00 and two suitcases with a few articles of clothing. Upon leaving Italy I considered myself a rich man. I had accumulated six large boxes of books which I sent on by boat to my friend Richard, whom I knew would take good care of them until I had a permanent address. Thus the forces that sought to destroy me had, in fact, only given me a greater incentive to do even better than I had done before. I had lost my extensive library, acquired over thirty years in my homeland, but I would begin anew. One day, I believed, I would have all these treasures of inestimable worth in my possession again.

Before leaving Italy for good, I had one final job to do. I decided to donate my Fiat 500 to Mr. Nicolae Bujin as a gift to the Romanian community in Rome, to be used in transporting penniless emigrating individuals and families.

Gabriel after kidney transplant, Milan - 1985

Gabriel and Teodor; Easter, Brianzza - 1985

Gabriel In Anzio Beach - 1987

Gabriel in Portland,
Oregon - 1989

Teodor in Neptuno -
1987

Part IV

America!

Chapter 17

A Dream Come True

One wish alone have I!
In some calm land
Beside the sea to die;
Upon its strand
That I forever sleep,
The forest near,
A heaven near,
Stretched o'er the peaceful deep.

Mihai Eminescu
- One Wish Alone Have I.

The sun was setting in a golden glow in the western sky and the lights like a myriad glittering gems appeared below us as our plane dropped from the fleecy clouds over the city of New York. What a sight! What a glorious wonderful sight! I think only an immigrant can truly appreciate the first glimpse of the Statue of Liberty. Majestic, strong, guarding the entrance to the 'Promised Land,' the land of the Free. This awe-inspiring lady brought tears to my eyes and a rush of deep emotion to my heart when I beheld her that evening bathed in the dying light.

We had indeed arrived. I was not dreaming. In a few moments we would put foot on the blessed soil that was to be our future homeland. The great plane dropped her wheels and the captain turned on the fasten-seat-belt sign.

The usual orders were given as the mighty engines slowed significantly upon reaching the runway.

We were an hour late. That meant that many of us who had to travel further had missed our connecting flights. We were told to stand by and await other arrangements.

The efficiency, the stark almost antiseptic cleanliness of Kennedy International Airport was my first impression when we deplaned. There was, however, no friendly stranger to offer assistance. No casual hello or welcome to New York from a passer-by. So completely different from our landing in Italy where people are either shouting, laughing uproariously, or in one form or other displaying emotion. Here in the hubbub of this immense airport there was little display of human feelings. People awaiting friends or loved ones very politely shook hands, some actually embraced, a few quiet words were exchanged and they were on their way without a second glance at anyone other than their own personal acquaintances. It seemed, it never entered anyone's head to salute a stranger, and to talk to one, I gathered, was taboo.

But I had no more time or opportunity to observe the inhabitants of this new planet for I heard our names called and we were told that a bus awaited to take us to a hotel for the night.

By the time we reached the hotel we were ready for bed but sleep kept her distance for a long time. Finally, she played a tug-of-war with my tired body and mind. "You can't sleep now, it's not time to sleep. It's time to get up," she argued. "But I have to get up to take a plane in the morning," I shouted back. "I must sleep now." I must have won the fight for I don't remember anything after that until I was awakened by a phone call and told I had one hour to eat and get ready to be transported to the terminal. I had another day's journey in front of me.

The flight across the continent was memorable. The weather was good, the skies clear and we had a marvelous view of the great expansive landscape as we travelled from east to west. What a rich and beautiful country, I thought. With God's help we'll do well here and when the family is reunited we will be happy again.

We arrived in Portland in the late afternoon. It had been a glorious summer day that 29th July 1987. At the airport, my cousin, Filon Moroson, and his wife Anca as well as the Viorel Nutu family with their pastor, the Reverend Kovach, were waiting to welcome us. It was a wonderful feeling to be met by some familiar faces and to hear one's own language in a strange new land.

We were taken to a buffet dinner, the first of its kind that we had experienced. I could hardly believe the number of different dishes and when I was told that I could serve myself as often as I liked, I was both skeptical and amazed. My friends were amused at my hesitation and then laughed as I sparingly helped myself a second time cautiously glancing over my shoulder to see that nobody was watching me.

After we had eaten well, we were taken to a little apartment on Glisan St. This Filon had set up for us and we were deeply grateful to have our own place at last. I still had a little money left so I paid my cousin his out-of-pocket expenses.

The next day we went grocery shopping in the nearby Fred Meyer store and I set about the business of cooking. My primary task during the following weeks was to take care of the many forms and requirements of the State Department and The United States Government. Since I was not fluent in English this was quite a challenge.

Getting from one place to another in the city was another difficulty I had to overcome. Initially, I purchased a bus ticket and had to depend on that service to transport us to and from downtown to the many offices where we were required to file unending papers and forms. We were also obliged to attend English classes at Mount Hood College and initiation courses explaining the American lifestyle and other facets of everyday living in the United States.

On Sunday we were invited by Filon to attend services in his church but since we were practicing Orthodox Christians affiliated to the Romanian Orthodox Church, we were not ready to relinquish the old religion. I made up my mind there and then to try to establish a church for the Orthodox community living in Portland. A short time later I was to find out that a Mr. Alex Filipoi had already tried to organize the community to this end so I was happy to join him in formulating plans for a church and obtaining a priest, but as in all undertakings of some magnitude, time was essential.

My chief concern at the time however, was obtaining a job. This I was fortunate to get through the intercession of a member of a certain Christian church. I was so happy and with enthusiasm went by bus to Vancouver to start my first day's work. It was a construction job and although I had never done such work, I was elated to have a chance to be financially independent. I was received with warmth and consideration that first day and as a consequence I worked hard and did my best to satisfy all the demands of my boss. Imagine my disappointment when after three days I was told not to return, the reason given for this termination was that I was not affiliated with that religion.

What was I to think - here in America it was no better than in a Communist country. One had to belong to one "Party" or another before one was eligible for a job. But all wasn't bleak at this time. I soon learned that there was an Orthodox Church not far away - Greek Orthodox - A beautiful church, well established and easily accessible to us.

We attended the Sunday service and became acquainted with the priests. Through an interpreter, I told him of my difficulty in obtaining work. That was my lucky day. I was soon put in touch with a Mr. Boros who as it turned out was looking for workers. He had acquired an old apartment building and, lucky for me, he needed help in renovating it. Also, Mr. Boros was Romanian, so we had no difficulty in communicating. I was overjoyed. I had found permanent employment. Over the next few months Mr. Boros and I became good friends. He was honest, hardworking, and generous

Because I had to work ten hours a day, six days a week, I was no longer able to attend the English classes. But I was making a good living and soon was able to save. In two years I had acquired a savings of $10,000. Now I could move to a bigger and better apartment and start to prepare the necessary papers for the reunification of the family.

As the summer holidays were coming to a close for Gabriel, I had to decide where he would attend school in the Fall. The Central Catholic High School was not far from our apartment, so I considered that would be the best choice. But of course that was a private school demanding high tuition fees. There was no way I could afford these fees, yet I would not be discouraged. I went to the highest authority - the Bishop. In talking with this gracious man - this I was able to do in Italian - I explained our situation. I told him how we had been helped by the Catholic Church in Italy, by Caritas and other like organizations. When my interview was over, I was assured of a place for Gabriel for the upcoming school year.

My heart was overflowing with gratitude to Almighty God. Life was looking good. I would make it in this strange but wonderful land.

One day I left by foot, as usual, to mail a letter. As I was standing on the corner of the street waiting to cross, a gentleman in a car pulled up beside me.

"Where are you going? Can I offer you a ride?" he asked.

I told him I needed to get to the post office. Although my English was still poor, we managed to understand each other. He asked me where I came from and eventually, I was able to tell him a little of my background. I invited him to our apartment and there he was able to speak freely with Gabriel who filled in all the gaps.

This good man, Mr. Richard Larson was so moved that he at once offered to take me to his home and when I got there he said:

"I want to sell you this car. You need a car."

"I'm sorry. I can't buy it. I have no money," I answered.

"Do you have a dollar?" he asked.

"Sure," I said.

"Then it's yours," came the reply.

I couldn't believe it. I was now the proud owner of a Datsun 375 - a bright yellow Datsun, I might add. This was a real Godsend. And to add to our pleasure Mr. Larson presented Gabriel with a bicycle. He was now independent and could get to school much quicker.

I felt so proud and happy the following Sunday when I arrived at the Greek Church in my new acquisition and when I told my friends that I had bought the car for a mere dollar, they were dumbfounded. They laughed and joked and remarked that for a guy who didn't know English, I was sure making my way around.

My first encounter with the police came about because of my yellow Datsun. I was chugging along at about forty miles an hour on the freeway one day when I was hauled over by the awful flashing lights and shrill siren.

"You're going too slow," the officer said after he looked at my license and asked me to step out of the car.

I told him the car wouldn't go any faster. "If I tried to go faster" - here I demonstrated by coughing - "the car makes same noises."

The officer smiled, scratched his head and told me to get moving. I was glad to get away, for by that time I was perspiring profusely and was getting very nervous. My previous encounters with the police in Romania had left their mark. I had no desire to have any further encounters with the law in this country.

On another occasion, I ran out of gas on Barbur Blvd. I had to get out of the car, leave it by the side of the road and walk to the nearest gas station. There I was fortunate to find two young men who were sympathetic. I told them I had no money, no gas, and no way of getting home. They gave me a few dollars worth of gasoline in a can and wished me well.

"I'll be back at the end of the week to pay you," I said as I left.

They smiled but I could see by their expressions that they didn't believe a word I said.

When the following weekend came and I got paid, I returned to repay their money and kindness; they were so surprised, they greeted me with the words: "You're the only honest man we've ever met." We parted good friends and they were left with the impression that all Romanians were to be trusted.

After about eight months, my working hours with Mr. Boros were reduced to a five-day, forty-hour week. I found extra work erecting booths at the Saturday Market. This job demanded that I get up at four o'clock in the morning because all had to be ready for the opening at 10:00 a.m. For this work, I got $20 for each booth. This increased my weekly income by at least $200, all of which I gave to

Gabriel to purchase organic produce because he was so allergic to the toxins in the regular food.

Gabriel became interested in promoting the Romanian culture in the city of Portland. To this end, he sponsored and ran with the collaboration of Carmen Costan and Ion Pirva a weekly radio program. Included in this broadcast - *Vocea Mioritei* - were Romanian folktales, history, music and items of local interest to the Romanian community. He was very successful and remained on the air for about three and a half years.

After high school, Gabriel decided he would like to be a doctor. He started to attend classes at Mount Hood Community College. He was showing signs of being a gifted writer and contributed articles on a regular basis to several Romanian papers.

On the 9th of February 1988, my wife, Iuliana, filed for and was granted a divorce. She had stated that I had left - deserted without telling her where I was going or contacting her.

I had written to the White House asking the President, Mr. Reagan to intervene on my behalf in regard to unifying my family. Hence my complete astonishment and shock when I received an answer from the White House telling me that my wife had no intention of following me to America. To add to this tragic news was the fact that this decision would also affect Michael, my son. I was devastated. But I would not give up hope and on July 7, I called Bucharest to wish Iuliana a happy birthday. I had set up our new apartment and was really looking forward to having the family together again.

After I offered her my good wishes, she answered by telling me not to call her anymore. When I asked why, her response was: "I'm not your wife now." I continued to press her for reasons but she would give me none. So what I had heard a few months before had a basis.

I immediately called my son, Michael, in Bucharest. He had left home, was now working by day and attending school at night. For some reason, he had had a falling out with his mother. I asked him if he knew about the divorce. But he, too, was in the dark. He had heard nothing and had no communication with his mother.

Distraught, it was extremely difficult for me to accept the news. My background, all that I had been taught, my religious beliefs, had instilled the sacredness of the marriage bond. It was a contract, binding till death parted us. How could such a thing happen to me. In my whole life I had never known any member of any relative to have experienced such a serious break-up of the family.

Soon after, I received the divorce papers and learned that Iuliana had applied for divorce early in the year without communicating the slightest word or giving me any warning. She had hired a lawyer to present her case before the civil court in Bucharest. Her motives, I do not know, even at this time, but she cited her reason as being - Desertion. I had left the country as of December 31, 1986 and that she had never again heard from me. I was, according to her, completely to blame for this situation.

This was such a blatant lie and had struck such a cruel blow that I feared I would never again be able to trust anyone - my wife of 18 years to treat me so, was beyond comprehension. The woman in whom I had such confidence, to whom I had confided all, even my most secret hopes and aspirations . . . Had she, too, betrayed me to the enemy? If she were able to divorce me so easily, perhaps she, was indeed, just a 'plant' in my house, someone the Securitate had made use of to keep an eye on me over the years. So many troubling thoughts, so many bitter feelings; I was beside myself with grief and unhappiness. Over the past few years while I was engaged in fighting for the life of my child, while I worked two jobs in order to pay my share of the expenses and while, at the same time, I had sent money and food home to Romania, my wife, had, it seemed, had no intention of joining me and merely profitted from my generosity and sacrifices without giving me the slightest indication of her real feelings and resolve.

Life had surely laughed in my face. Would I never know real security, real peace, true, sincere love and companionship? These questions I asked myself as the worm of despair and utter dejection knawed at the inner recesses of my heart and soul.

The next few days were a confused and distracted time for me. I thought, at one period, that I was losing my mind. I had to do something to distract myself.

A friend of mine, Stefan Voin, whom I sponsored when he wished to come to Portland, had recently bought a new car. He wanted to take a trip down the west coast to Los Angeles and then east to Las Vegas, the Grand Canyon and take in all the sights in between. He asked me to come along with him. Gabriel urged me to go since it was summer vacation and he could get along very well without me.

I bought a tent since we had decided to spend as little as possible on this trip. We took the coast route Hwy. 101 and stopped off that first day at the Redwood forests. Magnificient! Fantastic! I hardly had enough superlatives to describe those majestic giants that reached up, it seemed, to touch the sky and were so large in diameter that an automobile could easily drive through at the base of the trunk. The experience was like that of entering a colossal cathedral. One stood in awe and wanted to pray. Here surely, I said to myself, is what the mighty hand of God hath wrought.

The whole trip down the Oregon coast with the attractive fishing towns and the view of the vast expanse of the Pacific until we entered California was a totally new experience and gave me back the strength and clear headedness I needed to face the drastic change in my life.

After San Francisco, that beautiful city on the Bay, we continued south. Sometimes we would stop off at a motel for the night to get a good shower and a more pleasant night's sleep but we found the campsites quite safe and the accommodations adequate most of the time.

Nature and the complete change had a beneficial effect. My heart, little by little expanded, opened up to the beauties that God was casting before me as each new day dawned. I began to take interest in the world around me and allowed my mind and heart to be comforted and refreshed by all I saw and heard. The world was full of pain and injustice - Christ, Himself, had been betrayed by those whom He loved most. Could I ask for more?

When we arrived in Los Angeles, our greatest desire was to visit Disneyland. We had, like so many others, suffered from the illusion that this place was merely a fairytale haunt for children, but were soon amazed to see that it was really a marvel of modern technology designed to fascinate and instruct young and old alike.

We spent one whole glorious day in Disneyland and came away with a new and hightened appreciation for America's ingenuity and creativity.

Our trip to Las Vegas was... well 'out of this world' as they say in America. I had saved $50 to play the slot machines. At first I won and was feeling quite complacent, even proud of myself. Perhaps I might still be a rich man! But all too soon I was brought back to reality. Not only did I lose my $50 but all I had won besides.

The night life in Las Vegas with all its exotic entertainment far outstripped our meager budgets so we decided to leave it all to the 'rich and famous'.

We headed northwest to Death Valley and for the first time in my life experienced the meaning of a real desert. As far as the eye could see arid, treeless land - only sage and low-lying cactus plants. I marvelled that these could survive the heat and lack of water. It was hot!

Our next stopover was Yosemite National Park. We spent two days exploring and enjoying the beauty and freshness of this famous place. It was a treat after the heat and dryness of the previous days.

The Capital city of California, Sacramento seemed less impressive than I expected. Of course I was looking at it with a sense of the dramatic - I had, one must remember, come with a background of some of the worlds finest capitals vividly in my mind – from the majesty of Rome to the glories in architecture as exhibited in Berlin or Budapest. The modern, unimaginative buildings of this sprawling city in the desert is, to say the least, a lamentable disaster. We did visit the Military Academy there and I was interested in their program and courses of study. But, perhaps, what struck me most was the informality and friendly atmosphere of this establishment, and I couldn't help contrasting it with our military schools back in Romania, where the buildings were formidable, stark and forbidding and one was never allowed, as a casual visitor, to enter those 'hallowed' halls.

We took I-5 Highway north after that, arriving in the late afternoon at the mountainous pass which, at the foot of glorious Mount Shasta, led to the Oregon State line. We were told that we should rent chains to negotiate the summit but as we were experienced drivers, who had been used to ice and snow for six months in our native land and having the added luxury of good tires, the officer allowed us to proceed. As it turned out the ice and snow at the top gave us no trouble.

We spent a few hours at The Wild Life Safari in southern Oregon before wending our way toward Eugene, Salem, and finally, home to Portland.

Chapter 18

Getting to know America

How many a star burns in the firmament,
How many a wave the sea before her throws,
Gleaming and sparkling fair, yet no man knows
What may their meaning be, or their intent.
Mihai Eminescu
- How Many a Star Burns . . .

I arrived home to find Gabriel had managed fine without me. It was true our apartment hadn't faired so well but I was happy to know that he was now mature - a man, in fact, and could run his own life and fend for himself.

For the next three weeks, besides working on remodeling an old house, I also tried to get our own apartment back in shape. About this time, Gabriel presented me with a Greyhound Bus ticket which would take me anywhere I liked in the U.S. This would give me the opportunity to visit the eastern part of the country and spend some time with my old school and prison friends.

On the 15th of August, I boarded the bus in downtown Portland and took off for my cross-country trip. In general, we took route 84 and enjoyed the beautiful scenery that highway has to offer - passing along the Columbia mile after mile until we eventually left the Gorge and the river behind. Near Hermiston we climbed into the higher plateau of grain fields on our way to Pendleton - famous for its woolen mills. After that the highway turned south-east towards LaGrande, Baker, and Ontario.

Along the route, the bus stopped at certain restaurants to allow the passengers to clean-up and eat. Those who wished to remain or who had come to their destinations had their baggage removed while the rest had twenty minutes to be on board again. We travelled day and night with a change of driver every six hours. The bus was air-conditioned and had an emergency toilet - all in all, a fascinating way to see the country.

Beside me was a young man who had come from California and who was to accompany me for several days as he was on his way to see his parents in New Jersey.

In front of me sat a young couple so quaintly dressed that I enquired where they were from. I was curious when I saw they wore sandals which resembled the Romanian 'opinci' and both had long homespun overcoats. In the conversation that ensued, I found out they had come from Canada and that their parents were Scots.

Behind me sat an Indian couple - He was the chief of the Sioux Indians and impressed me with his candor and warmth. He invited me to visit his home but, unfortunately, I didn't have time.

By noon the next day, we arrived in Boise, Idaho, where we stopped and ate a hearty lunch. I decided to see a little of this the capital city, so I retrieved my bag, found a motel and went off by foot. Happily, the main attractions were centered in the Julia Davis Park. Here a State Historical Museum preserves the pioneer features of the past. There is also a pioneer village and a zoo and a 1890's style Boise Tour Train took me on a tour of the city. I saw the old historic district and the Capitol as well.

The following morning, I resumed my journey having been refreshed by a good night's sleep and a glorious hot bath. I enjoyed the changing scenery as we travelled from west to east. The luxurious greens of western Idaho gave way to vast tracts of arid lands and I soon realized that we were travelling southeast towards the great State of Utah and the famous Salt Lake City. At Ogden we somehow lost Highway 84 and, before I knew it, we were following 80, which had started in San Francisco, ran all the way to Chicago, and from there, as I found out later, it didn't stop until it entered New York on the east coast.

I decided I wasn't going to miss seeing Salt Lake City so I was obliged to change busses again. Taking Interstate 15, I travelled due south and before I knew it I had arrived. Again, suitcase in hand, I found a motel and having freshened up went to see what I could see. Nor was I disappointed. Founded by Brigham Young in 1847, Salt Lake City's Mormon heritage is evident everywhere. From the heart of the city, Temple Square is dominated by the monumental Temple and its six Gothic spires. The spacious and luxurious Beehive House was the official home of Brigham Young and one of his 27 wives; while others lived next door in Lion House. The Pioneer Memorial Museum houses a fairly large art collection. I was interested to see the dinosaur exhibit at the university as well as the simulated mine with its 6,000 mineral and gem samples. The Fine Arts Museum, I was surprised to learn, housed ancient Egyptian, Italian Renaissance, and Asian art. My final stop that day was in the State Arboretum where I saw the world's largest Russian olive tree and in the Red Butte Gardens, exquisite orchids and tropical plants which I had never before seen.

I found out that I could take the bus coming from San Francisco on Hwy 80 and continue my journey as if I had never interrupted it, because at a little spot called Echo, I had lost Hwy 84 anyway.

Majestic, strong, bold, the mighty Rockies towered all around. I had grown up in the foothills of the great Carpathian Mountains of Eastern Europe and had travelled over them many times during my life in Romania but compared with the Rockies they were gentle, lady-like creatures decked in stately greens from crown to toe. The Rockies, too, could boast such radiant hues but only so far, then they lay naked, rugged and wild, striking fear and awe as they rose to meet the azure above. I marvelled at these masterpieces of nature and raised my heart and soul in thanksgiving to their Maker that I should see this day and had been given the opportunity to behold such wondrous beauty.

When we neared Laramie, my mind was quickly transported to the many cowboy movies I had seen on T.V. back home. I was able to picture the Old West, the wooden sidewalks and gaudy taverns, but when we came to the city limits my dreams and memories were suddenly dashed. Gone were the rugged boardwalks and the rowdy beer halls and instead a sedate city of modern stores, streets and houses had taken their places.

I'm glad nature didn't completely forget Nebraska. She gave it the Platte River. And the U.S. Government made a wise choice when it built Hwy 80 almost parallel to it for several hundred miles. I was sorry to leave it behind as it turned northeast not far from a tiny place called Doniphan for after that Nebraska had nothing to offer, as far as I was concerned.

On the outskirts of Omaha, Hwy 80 again turned northeast and then cut straight across the flat plains of Iowa in the direction of Des Moines. By the time we had reached that city, I was anxious to get to my friend's home in Chicago and looking at the map decided I hadn't too far more to go so I stayed put and did not give in to the temptation of exploring the State Capitol.

As we sped along the well-paved highway and across the vast plains stretching out to the horizon on all sides, I marvelled at the expanse and the obvious richness of this great land. And then I thought this plain, this seemingly unending prairie stretched from the southern states all the way to northern Canada. It was too vast to comprehend.

I called my friend, Paul Constantenescu, to confirm my arrival time. I was excited to see him and his family again after so many long years, approximately ten. He had spent two years in prison with me in Jilava. We would have a lot to talk about. What comparisons we would make between the old world and the new. How many aeons lay betwixt the two.

He was waiting for me when the bus arrived and we both embraced amid tears of happiness. He was exceedingly proud and excited to take me to his home to show me what he had accomplished in ten years. For my part, I was not only surprised but overjoyed to see his beautiful house - a modern spacious two story building with all the conveniences that were available at the time. Added to this achievement was the fact that his son, Doru, was attending the university and majoring in business administration. My friend, Paul, had certainly been a busy man but also a happy and contented one.

The first day with Paul and his family was spent catching up on the intervening years. They were very sad and disappointed to hear of my divorce and encouraged me to forge ahead. That night I slept well. I was very tired but well-pleased to have come that far.

The next day, Paul and his wife Nuti, who had taken several days off work so that we might be together, suggested we go to see the sights in and around Chicago. We took a route which led north along the lake for many miles. I was amazed at the mighty industrial complexes that occupied so much of the waterfront.

On our return trip, we stopped off to see the great column designed by the Romanian sculptor, Brancusi.

The world-famous artist had visited Chicago in 1939 to address an assembly of artists and curators. In an interview with the Chicago News, he spoke of his wish to build an 'Endless Column' similar to that at Targu-Jui in Romania, but having an interior with space for an elevator so that visitors could see the city from the top.

After W.W. II the column was built to the north of the city not far from Lake Michigan. When it was finished, it was 95 stories high and furnished with a bar on the highest level and beneath that, a restaurant.

It was Brancusi's wish that succeeding generations be inspired by his work: "Each generation should have its own version of an Endless Column so that it might be reminded that humanity's goal is to rise to perfection."

Of the artist's 600 works, 300 have found a home in America. Brancusi, himself stated: "Without America I would not exist." It is true that America was the first country to recognize the genius of Brancusi who received his inspiration from ancient Romanian art. His best known works are: *The Prayer*, *The Kiss*, *Wisdom of the Earth*, *Sleep*, *Maiastra*, *Mademoiselle Pogany*, and the *Endless Column*.

Knowing my penchant for art and all that is beautiful, Paul took pains to show me the best Chicago had to offer. The Magnificent Mile — the expansive Michigan Avenue with its wide selection of elegant shops. Water Tower Place, a mall with atrium named for the fortresslike tower that survived the Great Fire of 1871. Here also is the John Hancock Center, an office structure which offers a most impressive view of the city.

River North, once an area of warehouses and commercial buildings, now supports an artist's colony similar to New York's Soho district. I was told that there are more than 80 art galleries located in this section. The Terra Museum of American Art on North Michigan Ave. was very interesting and informative with its displays of 18th, 19th, and 20th century paintings by American artists.

Before I bade my dear friends goodbye, Paul arranged for my last evening to be something really special, something I would, in fact, never forget. We would spend the evening in the company of another Romanian friend whom I hadn't seen in many years. This was a big surprise for I did not expect to ever see Virgil Ivanescu again.

We all gathered in a fancy Romanian restaurant in downtown Chicago. The cuisine was excellent and my appetite good and I enjoyed the familiar tastes of my native land. We were entertained with a musical program featuring a singer and a dancer from Romania who were wearing national costumes. I felt very good; in my mind I was home again in beautiful Bucovina. The fine food, the wine and the music brought back fond memories and enkindled anew the old flame of patriotism. I was alive again. I was optimistic. Life would be good and I would not only survive this harrowing blow, this unexpected, cruel blow to my family and myself, but, I felt at that moment that I was still capable of achieving great things.

So, we three long-time friends parted once more. We, who were all born in the same year, although in different parts of the country, and who were destined to suffer like injustices and hardships in our native land before being reunited in America. However, before we shook hands that night on the almost deserted street in that great American city, we promised each other never to lose touch. To this day we speak regularly by phone and follow with interest the events and happenings in each others lives.

I continued my journey east on Interstate 80 the next morning. My destination was Hartford, but I would stop off one night in Cleveland and hopefully spend a few days in New York before meeting another good friend in Hartford.

As I did not know anyone in Cleveland, I spent the first evening there resting. I had suffered from a severe toothache while visiting Paul in Chicago. In fact it was so bad and I was in such pain that I had to consult a dentist but since I could not delay long enough to get the needed care, he gave me some pills and antibiotics to enable me to continue my journey. In addition, Paul armed me with a small bottle of 'tuica' - a Romanian alcoholic drink made from prunes. This I intended to swish around my mouth if the pain became too bad.

I was told that I could see several museums and the Garden Center in close proximity to one another. In the Temple Museum of Religious Art, I was impressed with the collection of Judaic art which included ancient Torah hangings from the 17th century, ceremonial artifacts and antique pottery from the Holy Land.

The Rockerfeller Park Greenhouse featured a water garden, tropical plants as well as other flowers then in season. A Japanese garden and a Peace garden were also interesting.

Not too far distant, I was happy to visit the Cleveland Museum of Art. It is considered to be one of the finest in the United States. Its collection includes outstanding works representing every culture and historical period. I found the Asian and European displays to be particularly outstanding.

After a good meal and an early to bed evening, I was ready to launch forth for the 'Big Apple'. The journey took longer than I expected; so when I arrived in that blustery, frantic city, I was rather tired. As that was the end of the line and the end of Hwy 80 also, I was obliged to find somewhere to stay. I had intended spending a few days in the great metropolis. But, after fighting my way up 44th street, down 45th and then be jostled by the crowds for several blocks on 46th and having failed desperately in my attempt to engage even one New Yorker in conversation, finally, I was so frustrated, tired, and afraid I'd get hopelessly lost, I figured the best thing for me to do was get out of the city as quickly as possible.

Before the day was spent, I had boarded a bus for Hartford, but not without losing my 'tuica'. As I was about to step aboard, the driver spotted my little bottle.

"What's this?" he asked.

"Oh, that's my medicine," I answered very innocently.

"Yah. Looks like liquor to me."

"Certainly, it's alcohol," I said.

"You can't have that," he snapped and put out his hand to take it. As there were several passengers waiting behind me, I offered it to him and said, "OK, you take it. It's very good."

He merely took my precious potion and flung it in a bin without comment. Heavens! I thought, New Yorkers don't even have a sense of humor.

Richard, another buddy from way back in my school days, was waiting with his wife, Nina, at the bus station when I arrived in Hartford. He, like my friend, Paul, was proud of his accomplishments in America. He had a lovely home, his sons were doing well - one had graduated from the university and was married. The other was also a graduate and was involved in research at the university.

We spent the first evening together talking and catching up on all that had happened in our separate lives over the years. Richard's old mother was living with them and I was glad to meet her again. She also had her tales of hardship and sorrow to tell. She and her husband had been well-off in Romania before the Communists took over. They owned a Textile Plant and she had been a teacher. Apart from the pain of finding out that her son would not be allowed to graduate from the university because he was the son of an exploiter of the people, she also suffered the loss of their business, and eventually, her husband's death in Austria, before they had time to really enjoy a quiet and peaceful life in America.

We spent the next two days sightseeing. The Hartford Insurance Company was a most palatial building and boasted that it sold life insurance to the first President of the United States, George Washington, himself. We visited the Botanic Gardens which had specimens from all over the world and we stopped off at the Wadsworth Atheneum, America's oldest continuously operated art museum. In the city center in Civic Center Plaza the Nook Farm with the homes once occupied by Mark Twain and Harriet Beecher Stowe were interesting and unique for me.

I noticed that the architectural style of most of the buildings resembled those in a European city and were so completely different from what I had experienced in Oregon and out west.

Before I left on my homeward journey, I made sure to send some of my books, which Richard had kept for me during the past several months, by mail, while the others, my pride and joy - 50 Elite books entitled the *Story of Universal Art*, I parceled up to take with me on the bus.

It was a beautiful summer morning when I bade my dear friends, Richard and Nina, farewell. The sun was just above the horizon casting a rosy light on the already bustling city. As we headed south on Hwy 84 and then southwest on 81, for I wished to return home by another route, I was aware of the picturesque countryside. Surely this was a great and magnificent country - so rich, so abundant and I was reminded of the words:

"America, America God shed his grace on thee,

And crowned thy good with brotherhood

From sea to shining sea."

I felt fortunate indeed, to have been able to see so much of this great land, to have experienced, first hand, its glory; its beauty, its vastness, and above all its abundance. Surely, this was the 'Promised Land' this was the 'Land flowing with milk and honey'. And I thanked God over and over again for the many blessings he had given me in enabling me to come to such a place to spend the latter days of my life.

At Harrisburg, I changed busses and took route 70 for Columbus, Indianapolis and eventually Kansas City. Land unending - great stretches of prairie, rich, fruitful beyond imagination. I could never have conceived of so much richness, and such abundance had I not seen it with my own eyes. And again my heart cried out and the tears wet my cheeks as I realized God had not turned His face from me but instead had opened His arms wide and 'shown me all the beauty of the earth and the fulness thereof.'

I needed a break when I finally got to Omaha, but not in the way it turned out to be. When I left the bus supposedly for a light lunch, I misjudged the time and was late returning. The bus had left without me and worst of all had my baggage and precious books. What on earth could I do? I was very upset. Then I went to the bus office and explained my dilemma.

"Not to worry," said the clerk.

Within minutes he was in touch with the driver of my bus and when he told him what had happened to me and that my books and luggage were still with him, he said he'd take care of everything.

I might have known - I was in America! All was in order, and awaiting me when I arrived at the next stop some hours later.

From Omaha I changed my route and took Hwy 29 towards Sioux City. Then, at Sioux Falls, I again changed the bus and followed Hwy 90 throught South Dakota into the northeast corner of Wyoming and on to Montana.

By this time, I was tired of the seemingly endless prairies, flat land stretching out on all sides. I, who had been born at the foot of the verdant Carpathians, longed to see a hill, a mound, a rise in the surface of the earth. As we neared Rapid City the famous Black Hills afforded me that wish and I felt safe again and comforted, for now, all I wanted was to get home. I had enough travelling to last me a very long time.

Close to Butte we crossed the Continental Divide and I really felt I was in familiar territory. How many thousand miles I had traveled, I hadn't yet calculated. It was baffling, incredible. I would have so much to tell Gabriel and perhaps, in time, my grandchildren. I felt like a pioneer, like a great conquering hero.

Only one regret entered my mind about this time, I had not been able to see the Grand Tetons. Perhaps I would get the opportunity another time.

From Spokane, it was only a day's journey. I would be in Portland by nightfall. I felt like an old horse, as it nears home, my mind and body gathering strength and momentum. I counted off the miles and soon the beautiful Columbia gave me the feeling of... ah, at last!

I took two days to rest after my Continental trip; then I returned to work remodeling and reconstructing houses and apartments. Saturday and Sunday mornings I spent several hours erecting booths for the Saturday Market in downtown Portland.

My mind was more at ease. I was now resigned to the divorce and decided I had to get on with my life. In time, God would provide. I would put my trust in him and prayed.

Gabriel started to make a name for himself as a writer, contributing to the school's newspaper. Several of his articles featured studies of the ancient churches in Romania and were written with flair and enthusiasm. He made me a very proud parent, although sometime later, I became very confused when he came up with the bright idea that it was all because of him that I was a parent. "You see, Papa," he said, "if I weren't your son you wouldn't be a father. A parent cannot be a parent without a child, therefore the child is the parent of the parent." Very profound words! I thought.

Chapter 19

Michael

Men merely live by stars of luck
And star-crossed fatefulness,
We have no death to prove our pluck
Nor place or time possess.

Mihai Eminescu
- The legend of the Evening Star

It was December 17, 1989. The news of the massacre at Timsoara made the headlines of all the world's newspapers. I became alarmed. I knew the Romanian people had reached saturation point. The country must revolt.

For twenty-four years, the dictator Nicolae Ceausescu held sway over the daily lives of the people of Romania. In fact, according to Doina Cornea, an outspoken dissident, Romania in the 1980's was a 'Huge Prison'. In writing to President Ceausescu she said: "We are, in fact, occupied by an invisible army of Securitate men under your direct leadership. They have infiltrated everywhere, even into the privacy of our homes. You have crushed people's innermost being, humiliating their aspirations and their legitimate claims, humiliating their conscience, and compelling them, under pressure and terror, to accept the lie as truth and the truth as a lie." Again she writes: "Institutions hardly function anymore. They have been abolished and merely figure as names: justice, army, party, education, etc."

Although her letter was blunt and to the point, Doina justified it by saying that, "the urgency of the conditions" in which the population was living and the regime's repressive policy, "even more devastating than the economic disaster" was caused by Ceausescu.

In her letter Doina Cornea also asked the President to stop persecuting journalists and printers, "whose only fault lies in no longer being able to live a lie." Three journalists were arrested: Petre Mihai Bacanu, Anton Uncu, and Mihai Creanga for printing leaflets criticizing Ceausescu's politics.

In a second letter Ms. Cornea describes her own ordeal as a result of the regime's reaction to her protests. She said, she lived in almost total isolation and suffered many forms of harrassment including beatings at the Securitate offices.

She reminded Ceausescu that, "history does not forgive" and certainly would not forget that he had, "started pulling down the country's centuries-old villages, destroying their natural order," that he had also demolished, "The oldest and the dearest" churches and leveled the medieval rulers' tombs. She concluded by warning the tyrant that he would, in the end, be judged by his "moral actions" and not, "the gigantic, useless, and hideous concrete construction" with which he was trying to replace spiritual needs.

Ceausescu paid no attention to Cornea's letters, nor indeed to similar protests by the poets Ana Blandiana and Mircea Dinescu. Instead, in February 1972 he, personally, took over the management of the DIE, the Romanian equivalent of the CIA or KGB. His intention was to take advantage of the eagerness with which the West embraced those who showed even the slightest sign of independence within the Soviet bloc. "We must make cleverness our national trait... Stop showing a sullen, frowning face and clenched fists to the West. Start making it feel compassion for us, and you'll see how fast Western boycotts change into magnanimity. Let's present Romania as a Latin island in the Slavic sea... Our millenia-old traditions of independence are now up against Moscow's political centrism... A pawn between two super powers..."

These bold philosophical statements were immediately followed-up by practical application. The DIE started planting hints of independence in the West in order to gain political and economic advantages. To bolster the DIE in the new venture, Ceausescu increased its ranks from 700 to 2,800 and upped its budget eightfold. This new operation was given the code name "Horizon". His objective was to give the West the illusion that his Romania sustained a different kind of Communism - free of Russian influence, deserving Western support.

This operation covered all bases: overt and covert propaganda in the West; hints and suggestions found in concealed microphones found in the Romanian embassies all over the West which were set in place to send misleading messages; there were documents "signed" by heads of foreign governments supposedly lost in luxury hotels or leaked to the West in various ways; intelligence officers posed as ambassadors or clerics; Swiss bank accounts for corrupt, high-ranking Westerners who agreed to present Romania as a "maverick"; and of course the age-old trick was played using intelligence officers as lovers to recruit Western agents of influence.

Charles Powers writing in *The Oregonian* March 22, 1988 entitles his article on Romania: "Nation and People pay the Price as Egoist feeds Appetite for Glorification." He succinctly evaluates the plight of that country at the time and quotes Saul Bellow's description of Bucharest's streets as an "exercise in a prison yard. The people line up on pavements sticky with the mud from the president's massive demolition and construction projects, to buy plastic bags of chicken parts - the feet and wings. No one seems to know what happened to the rest of the birds.

"That's on a good day. Many butcher shops, in fact, have simply closed. Those remaining sell slabs of pork fat and a kind of gray sausage. No one has seen a potato in the markets for months. There are carrots, beets, onions and small spotted apples. For the seventh straight winter, meat, butter, sugar, and cooking oil are rationed.

"Also heat and electricity. For the month of January, a family of four was allotted 35 kilowatt hours of electricity, resulting in rooms dim with 40-watt bulbs, and those who violated the restrictions were faced with electric bills equal to a month's salary."

Mr. Powers continues his account: "Romania's blessing this year has been a mild winter, but guests at the opera still wear their coats throughout the performance and hundreds of thousands of residents in the apartment blocks ringing the old city begin cooking their pork fat and carrot stew at 10:00 p.m. when the gas comes on.

"The city sinks at night into a gloom that seems unreal for the capital of two million people. Store windows are unlit, the few restaurants close by 8 or 9:00 p.m. Half the street lamps are turned off. The winter mists rise out of the damp streets, casting halos around what pale light there is, amplifying the rasp of footsteps in the dark.

"Late at night, the policemen - the ones in uniform and in teams of three - stop the few citizens who dare to be out at so provocative an hour, check their papers, ask where they've been and where they're going. It is like a place at war."

Despite all these signs of a collapsed economy, the occasional visitor from the West is assured that "there are no shortages of anything in Romania. Sometimes, however, there is a problem with supply" - from a hotel guide in Bucharest.

On December 20, 1989, Nicolae Ceausescu returned home from Iran to convoke an assembly of the citizens of Bucharest in the Central Plaza. All were required to attend this meeting on the morning of December 21. This was to be the biggest mistake of Ceausescu's entire life. As the uneducated dictator, who could not even speak his native language correctly, addressed the throngs gathered before the Central Committee Buildings, he tried to explain that the situation in Timsoara had been the work of fascists, anarchists, unruly mobs and common criminals. The people, as a whole, who had never, in fifty years, voiced aloud their true feelings were surprised when from among their numbers small groups of 'dissidents' spoke up contradicting the President. The sound of shooting was heard in the distance; whether real or taped no one was quite sure, but it was, certainly, a rouse predetermined by the Securitate (Secret Police) to intimidate the citizens of the capital.

The President left the podium and the crowds dispersed but not all went to their homes or work. Groups gathered in different areas around the city. There was a feeling of tension; soon the police clashed with the agitators and injuries occurred. When the leather batons did not quell the crowds which had quickly joined those who were fighting, guns, and tanks were mobilized and all-out battles were fought in the streets of Bucharest that night. However, by morning's light the streets were empty and exceptionally clean. There wasn't a spot of blood to be found, even though hundreds had been killed or injured. Later, it was learned that the injured had been carted off to hospitals where they were killed lest there be any witnesses to the slaughter of the previous night.

The following morning, in Michael's words - for I received a letter from my son describing his experience during the Revolution, - "I went to work. I was in charge of coordinating the work of several sections of the plant. I had no time to talk to anyone, but soon I found myself without workers. It was then that I learned that one man had already been fired because he lit a candle and placed it in a conspicuous place in honor of those who had fallen the night before. After that, about 80% of the workers walked off the job, I included. We reached the streets only to be joined by others. We noticed, as we passed, that one plant had its gates welded together, thus making sure none of its employees were able to leave the facilities.

"When we reached the Central Plaza in front of the government buildings we were told that Mr. Ceausescu would again address the crowds.

"This time, as the President began to speak, the crowd responded with loud booing and shouting 'Timsoara, Timsoara, we don't forget the dead. Down with Communism, Down with Ceausescu.'

"The dictator was visibly shaken. Once again shooting was heard but instead of frightening, and contrary to all expectations, the people remained firm. At once they took banners and communist slogans which they were carrying and set fire to them. They cut the hammer and sickle from the Romanian flag and held it aloft. Ceausescu was advised to leave, making his way with his wife to the roof-top of the government buildings where his helicopter awaited him.

"Meantime, the Securitate who were in strategic positions in the buildings surrounding the Plaza, opened fire on the crowds below. Again the population as a whole rallied and did not move, but in a show of defiance, when their fellow-workers fell, went to their aid. But, eventually, seeing the futility of trying to resist the power of bullets and armed tanks, the workers of Bucharest dispersed.

"I took shelter in a children's theater with some other co-workers until the police had left the area; then we went out to join others in disrupting traffic and other vital operations."

Thus began the downfall of Communism in Romania, or so we Romanians in exile hoped and prayed.

Michael is my older son; he was a student in the University of Bucharest. I suspected the students would be deeply involved in any anti-communist movement. I became alarmed. I knew the heart of this young man and was well aware of what his response to the current situation would be.

Upon my departure from Romania in 1984, I had no alternative but to leave Michael behind. After Iuliana refused to come to America, Michael left home and was forced to fend for himself - working by day and going to school at night. He had been denied admittance to the day classes in the university because he was the son of "a dissident, an enemy of the people."

I couldn't do what I so ardently desired; I could only pray and await the day when I would, eventually, be able to bring him to America where I hoped he would be appreciated not only for his fine upright character, hard work, and responsibility, but for his drive and ambitions as well. I had told him before I left Romania, while he was still in high school, to work hard and, since he was an excellent student in math, to study to become an engineer. This profession was held in high esteem and challenged the brightest students. I was, indeed, a proud and happy man when, Michael in 1989 despite many hardships - received his degree in engineering.

Soon word reached the West that the students of Bucharest had taken to the streets and where fighting using whatever methods or means possible. They scattered nails, and broken glass in all the main arteries of the city. They used stones and bricks, stripped the iron railing from store windows and front gardens to attack the Securitate and their followers. Eventually, members of the army joined in the battle on the side of the students and with them a supply of the much needed guns and ammunition.

A curfew was declared in the city and throughout the country the following day. Yet the students persisted; twelve hundred were killed during those first days of fighting.

I called Iuliana trying to get news of the extent of Michael's involvement in the revolt. She answered in code: "For the last three days he has been in the University Square where he signed the roll declaring his presence." I understood from this message that he was participating in all the student activities relating to the uprising. I was both proud and yet fearful.

In March of '90, Michael wrote for my birthday; it was only then that I really found out how completely involved he had been in the Revolution. His words brought tears to my eyes when he described the fervor and animation of the young people of the city in their efforts to bring freedom and democracy to their beloved Romania. He spoke of the young women who enthusiastically used their precious lipsticks to write on walls and windows "Down with Communism; Down with Ceausescu; Up with the Revolution; Up with Democracy; Freedom for Romania." He told of the food-store personnel who handed out supplies free of charge - when those who had not eaten all day asked to buy food. Eventually, on Christmas eve Mr. Ceausescu and his wife, Elena were put on trial and shot. People danced in the streets. New elections were promised. Romania would, at last, join the rest of Western Europe and be a free soverign nation again.

Food supplies, clothes and blankets poured in from America and other countries, he said. The currency was re-evaluated. There was an air of expectancy. People spoke freely. On Christmas day they went to church openly. The spirit of the old Romania was alive and strong. This state of affairs, the euphoria, lasted for about a week. People returned to work in the new year - the elections slated for March would bring great changes.

Michael went back to work with everyone else. He described the scene which followed his being accosted that morning by The Party Secretary - each plant had a member of the Party as an overseer. This man had not taken part in the fighting or in anyway supported the Revolution.

"You were among those who rose up against the State and our Socialist Republic, you son of a bitch."

"Yes," answered Michael and in his rage because of the disparaging and foul language directed at his dead mother, whom he idolized, Michael rushed at the man, delivering a resounding blow; then he walked out of the plant.

A few weeks later, word reached the West that a coup had been instigated in Romania. It was no accident of circumstances that propelled Mr. Ceausescu and his wife Elena to their deaths, but rather a well-timed plot to oust the dictator, who had already fallen from favor in Moscow, and replace him with the neo-communist Iliescu and his followers. Once again, the Romanian people had been deceived. The Democracy for which the youth of the country had given their lives was a dream which to this day has not been fully realized, "Neither the post-Ceausescu government of reformed communists nor the current five-party coalition has lived up to the expectations that soared so high when tyranny collapsed..." the words of Mr. Steven Erlanger of the New York Times, as quoted by the Oregonian, November 10, 1999.

Months passed. It then became clear to the people of Romania that the new government was merely a change of faces; the old ways and the old policies remained the same - long lines continued to be the norm outside the stores supplying food, and those who thought that free-market

301

economy would be a fact of life were quickly disillusioned. Many exiled Romanians, including myself - who should have known better - rushed to the aid of the land of their births only to find that any business venture or private enterprise was doomed to fail. The government regulations, the bureaucratic hurdles, the exorbitant taxes levied on the struggling entrepeneurs were such that it was impossible for anyone to succeed.

Crime and dishonesty seemed to be the vices which quickly flourished in the new Romanian Republic. The black market became a way of life, bribes and nepotism commonplace. Inflation soared, the lei was devalued, bringing it in line with Western currency, which meant it was worth only a third of its former value to the Romanian people. Salaries did not keep pace with the new prices of goods, thus contributing to the failure of many banks and businesses.

Chapter 20

Never too late for Love

O remain, dear one, I love you,
Stay with me in my fair land,
For your dreamings and your longings.
Only I can understand.
Mihai Eminescu
- O Remain, Dear One...

It was a mild dry evening, unusual for mid-December 1990 in Portland. I had heard that there would be a Christmas concert at the Greek Orthodox Church and that a Romanian conductor was to present the program. I looked forward to having a pleasant evening and possibly hearing some Romanian music. My friend, Dr. Dobrea, whom I had met in the Latina Refugee Camp in Italy was visiting the United States and came to spend some time with us. I invited him to accompany me to the concert.

The musical program for the evening was well chosen, however, I was disappointed to discover that there was nothing remotely Romanian included.

The orchestra began to tune-up and the noisy audience quieted. I looked at the program again and started to read the notes about the guest artists who would perform with the orchestra. One of the soloists was a soprano - Louise Warnock, a native of Ireland, who had been educated in Europe, obtaining A.T.C.L. and L.T.C.L. from Trinity College, London. She had also studied in France and had later received B.Mus. and an M.A. degree in the States. I was impressed and looked forward to hearing this particular singer.

The usual Christmas music, Ave Maria, and Oh, Holy Night were eventually sung by this soprano and I was delighted by the sweet sympathetic voice that rose above the orchestra.

"The voice of an angel," was a comment from a woman behind me, and I concurred mentally.

After the performance, Dr. Dobrea and I went to congratulate Louise. She was gracious and spoke to us for a few moments. Unfortunately, my English was not too good, so I could not converse at any length, but as is usual in such instances there were others in line waiting to talk to her so we moved on.

Several months later, at the end of June, 1990, I was invited to a celebration in a friend's house - The Filipois. As it turned out, Louise was also known to this Romanian family whose three daughters were all musical. Emilia, the oldest, had just graduated from high school so her parents had planned a big party to which they invited me as well as Louise.

I had to work late that particular day, so consequently, I arrived late, and many of the guests were leaving, among them Louise. As she was saying goodbye to the Filipoi family, I recognized her and went forward to greet her.

"I remember you," were my first words. She was taken aback and obviously didn't know who I was.

"Well, I'm sorry but... " she tried to recollect.

"At the concert, the Christmas concert last year," I interrupted. "I and Dr. Dobrea came to congratulate you after the performance."

"I'm sorry," she responded. "But I don't remember. You must forgive me, however, for there were many people there."

Ignoring the answer, I looked about. "Where... where, your husband?" I stammered.

"My husband! I don't have one; he died five years ago," she answered.

My heart missed a beat. I had to act fast. She was about to get into her car. "Oh," I said, " then may I... I have your number, I... I...." No more words came. But I had my notebook ready.

"My number!" Louise exclaimed. "My goodness, I'm sorry but I don't give my number to strange men, or those I don't know," and she opened the door of her car.

"Wait, wait," I said and without delaying for a reply, ran back into the house and grabbed a napkin from the table. As I approached her car once again, I said, "I'll give you mine," and I proceeded to scribble down my telephone number. I gave the napkin to her across the roof of the car as I did not wish to delay her longer. "You... call," I pleaded.

She laughed. "Maybe". She got into her car and drove off.

I returned to the party and asked Rodica and Alex what they knew about Louise. They said they knew her for quite some time and thought a lot of her but they did not give me much information or encourage me to pursue what was obviously my intent.

I waited a week - a very long week for a phone call but none came. I realized that I had to tackle this problem another way. Somehow I'd have to get her phone number. Surely, Rodica had it. So I called her but she told me she had promised Louise not to give the number to anyone. What was I to do!

The lady had, it seemed, all the qualities I liked in a woman - a slim shapely body, intelligent, she seemed to have a good sense of humor, was well educated as well as having a beautiful voice. I told Gabriel of my dilemma. He was encouraging at the time saying "Try Papa, try," but I later found out that he doubted very much whether or not I would succeed in winning the hand of my 'fair lady'. My English was so poor - how could I even communicate with her. Still, I would not give up. There was something about the woman which drew me to her. I was determined to get in touch with her.

For the next four months I bombarded Rodica with telephone calls; she just had to give me Louise's number. Finally, I prevailed and towards the end of October, I was in possession of the number I desired most in all the world.

The first night I called, she was surprised but not upset and realized I had badgered Rodica until she could take no more!

"I like hear expensive voice." were the words I struggled to articulate over the phone. After that I was wordless.

Louise understood my difficulty and spoke slowly; she also, I found out had studied several languages, French, Latin and some Italian so when I was forced to substitute words from these languages she understood what I was trying to say.

Our first date took place on November 8, 1991. It was Gabriel's name day - the Feast of the Archangels Michael and Gabriel. I invited Louise to join us at an Italian restaurant in downtown Portland.

On that occasion she made some excuse or other about how difficult it would be for us to find her house. So it was decided that we meet at a local shopping center. At seven-thirty sharp, Gabriel and I were at the designated area. Shortly after Louise came and parked nearby. Gabriel had warned me to keep quiet - not that I could do much more - he would do the talking. So, I dutifully sat in the back seat while my son drove and entertained Louise. By this time

Gabriel's English was excellent; he had no trouble holding forth for the next few hours.

The first opportunity for me to say a word came in the restaurant when having ordered dinner, I also asked for wine to be served.

When the wine was poured I raised my glass and looking at Louise, said, "To us!"

She was surprised and answered, "My! you sure work fast."

I knew she was not offended and I was extremely happy, enjoying every moment of our time together.

When eventually, we drove her to her car, I again sat behind allowing Gabriel to act as host and when we reached our destination, I alighted, kissed her hand and asked, 'Did I do a wrong?"

"Certainly not," she replied immediately. "In fact I had a most enjoyable evening, thank you both very much."

She seemed pleased and I went home a happy man that evening. But if I wanted to get to know her better I would have to learn more English. I decided to read everything I could since it was impossible to attend English classes. I read aloud to myself and when Gabriel was present, he would correct my pronunciation and translate the words I didn't understand. At other times, the Romanian-English dictionary was my constant companion.

I continued to call Louise each evening after I came home from work. For the next month until Thanksgiving, our conversations over the phone did not amount to much. Then one evening, I was surprised by a call from Louise inviting me and Gabriel to join the Filipoi family at her home for dinner. On that occasion, the Filipois whom we met at a pre-arranged stop were our guides to her home.

We had a lovely evening. I presented her with a large bouquet of flowers and was impressed by the beauty of her home and garden. My heart sank, however, when I discovered that I was not the only male guest. I was introduced to a doctor who later was seated at the head of the table. What chance had I. Still, as I sat beside Louise at dinner, I felt all was not lost. She was attentive to me and wished to know more about me. I was encouraged and decided I would send her my resumé. She seemed to be interested in my background and education. And I told myself, I too, am a doctor and probably have much more education than the fellow at the other end of that table.

We had an enjoyable evening together and when it was time to leave I accosted the doctor in the hallway.

"When you were born?" I asked in my imperfect English.

For a moment, he was taken aback, then by way of a joke, he said: "I am older than you, if that's what you mean. I'm sixty-seven," he said.

That answer made me feel happy, because I was sixty one at the time. Surely, Louise would choose a younger man!

Several weeks later, I again asked her to join me at a restaurant. Of course I wished to pick her up and drive myself. I called seeking directions to her house.

It had turned out to be a very bad evening. The wind was howling, the rain pouring, as only it can in Portland, and it was dark - very dark. I arrived safely in the area and followed all the directions given, but could not find the house. In despair, I decided to turn around and head for home. This woman is playing me for a fool, I thought, she must have given me wrong directions.

Then, on an impulse, I stopped the car and told myself that if the next person to drive by didn't know the address, I would be on my way and forget Louise altogether.

A pick-up was heading towards me. I got out and waved it down. There were two men inside. I showed them the address and asked if they could help.

"Is the lady's name Louise?" one of them asked.

Surprised that these men knew her by her first name, I answered, "yes."

"Then follow me," the older man said.

I got into my car, turned it around and followed the men down the hill and into a cul-de-sac. The men parked in what was their driveway and smiling at me pointed to the house next door. "That's where Louise lives."

I was dumbfounded. Was this fate? Surely this was Destiny, herself, speaking! Of all the people in the world to meet on a stormy winter's night but Louise's next door neighbors. I was overjoyed. I brushed the rain from my clothes, grabbed my bouquet and presented myself at her front door.

That was one of the most memorable evenings of my life, because instead of going out to dinner, Louise had prepared a sumptuous meal which we enjoyed together in the warmth and comfort of her home.

We did not meet over Christmas but I sent her a card which was ordered especially for her - a musical card with the Christmas song, *Rudolf the Red Nose Reindeer*. I heard afterwards that she laughed when she got it but didn't particularly care for it. That was too bad because I paid a whole $8.00 for it when I was making only $6 an hour. My intentions were good, anyway.

New Year's Eve was fast approaching. I wanted more than anything else to celebrate it with Louise. The Romanian Community always celebrates with a bang! A delicious dinner, wines, assorted drinks and dancing at a prearranged location is the norm. This event is usually well attended. To accompany me for the 1990-91 New Year celebration, I had my heart set on Louise. I sent her an invitation and asked to pick her up. But she thought better to go with the Filipois and meet me at the hall.

I bought a new jacket, my shoes were sparkling and I also had a new tie. I thought I was quite the guy. My flurry and excitement were such that I even forgot to take the tags off my new jacket, consequently they were fluttering from my sleeve all night.

My happiness was reaching explosive proportions when at the stroke of midnight, I offered a toast to Louise while on the dance floor and asked her to marry me.

She opened her eyes wide, hesitated a moment, looked straight into my eyes and then said, "Yes".

I could hardly contain myself, what a beginning to 1991! The following day, we were both invited to dinner at the Filipois. It was on that occasion that I announced to all present our intention of getting married.

May 17th was cloudy but dry, however, rain was predicted for the afternoon. I was as excited as a young lad going on his first date. Louise's family had been gathering from the four winds the day before - from Canada, California and even Ireland.

We had ceremonies in both churches beginning at 2:00 p.m. Since I was Orthodox and Louise was Catholic, we thought this would be a nice idea. Little Rodica Filipoi, who is an accomplished violinist played Porumbescu's *Balada* and Louise herself sang Gounod's *Ave Maria*, and the *Our Father* during the Catholic service. At the Orthodox service, the choir from the church responded to the priest's intonements.

Our rings were two plain gold bands on which we had inscribed the following words: "My Queen" on hers and "Te iubesc"–I love you– on mine.

Afterwards we went to St. Anthony's hall for the reception. We had hired a band and asked them to play the old-time favorites: waltzes, fox-tarts and polkas. All went well and we arrived home, finally, to the opening of many gifts and the warm and enthusiastic greetings of Louise's brothers and sisters who had preceded us to the house.

Thus began our married life together and the happiest time of my life to that point. In the years that have intervened, I can only say that I grow to love Louise more and she says she never regrets for a moment the decision she made to marry me.

Chapter 21

A Visit to my Homeland

Now though e'en I roamed that country
How could I its charm recall...
Where has boyhood gone, I wonder,
With its pool and woods and all?

Mihai Eminescu
- O Remain, Dear One...

Michael arrived in America in February 1992 on a visitor's visa. Our joy and anticipation was overflowing. I had left when he was a boy, now I was about to meet him as a man.

Amid tears and unspeakable emotion I embraced my beloved son. At last! I could look at him face to face. I could hold him to my heart as I used to do when he was a small lad. 'My cup was full to overflowing'; I had my two wonderful sons safe and in America. We were once again a family.

The next few days passed in catching up on the happenings and events of the many lost years of separation. Soon, however, Michael wanted to support himself so he looked for a job. At the time none was forthcoming in his field as an engineer. He, therefore, went to work at whatever was available - Shari Restaurant, gas stations, etc. Eventually, he broke the news - he was in love. His girl-friend, Carmen, was waiting for him in Bucharest. He couldn't stay in America without her. I felt an ache in my heart. After all this time, the efforts expended to facilitate his arrival in America, the hopes for a bright and successful future for him in this country, Michael had decided he would return to Romania within the next six months. He would have to get a job here that would pay him a decent wage and, when he had what he considered enough money, he would return to marry Carmen.

It was a time of deep sorrow. Why couldn't he wait, get himself settled, apply for permanent residency and have Carmen join him in this country? These and other questions which seemed logical and sensible to me, didn't occur to him. In the end, I was angry. "It's your life," I said. "Do with it as you please."

Later, in the spring when Michael had found work and Gabriel was at school, Louise and I visited Romania. I, to return home to see my mother whom I had not seen since I left for Italy with Gabriel eight years before, and Louise, to see my beloved country for the first time.

We intended to make this trip one of the highlights of our lives. Landing in Frankfurt, Germany, we were met by a very good friend of mine, 'Hitler' Seher, who drove us to his home in Stuttgart where his wife, Virginica, a doctor, met us with open arms. We spent several days there resting but also visiting the city of Stuttgart with all its beautiful sights. Virginica and 'Hitler' were lavish in their hospitality, not only wining and dining us but, when we were ready to leave, they offered us a car to allow us to travel more freely and at our own pace.

I must explain why I called my friend, Vasile, - Hitler. When he arrived in Germany - for he and his wife were originally from Romania and I had met him, initially, in prison - his name was considered a tongue-twister for the Germans. At the immigration office, the authorities proposed that he change his name to one that would be more easily pronounced. Vasile immediately came up with the name Adolf. A cheer arose from those around as they welcomed a new Adoft to Germany. When I heard of this, I thought the whole affair a big joke and thereafter called him 'Hitler'.

We left Stuttgart early in the morning as we planned to reach the Hungarian-Romanian border by nightfall. We had decided to spend the night in a zimmer on the Hungarian side and cross into Romania early the following morning. On this particular journey, we did not intend to do much sightseeing, I being anxious to get home as quickly as possible. The sightseeing could wait until our return trip.

Arriving at the border crossing near Oradea we encountered the first inconvenience of Communist bureaucracy and inefficiency. We had no trouble whatsoever crossing the borders from Germany to Austria and then into Hungary. All was done quickly, quietly and graciously. But upon entering Romania, the scene was one of long lines of cars, disgruntled travellers, confusion, disorder and for my wife, who had never before experienced such chaos, it meant several long hours in the hot sun even though we were considered the privileged ones. As we had a Germany license, we were ushered into a separate line and given priority status. Some Romanian travellers, we heard, had been stranded with their entire families for three days or more. That meant living in their cars for all that time.

"It's ridiculous, absolutely ridiculous!" Louise exclaimed.

"Not so loud," I said as I eyed the guard strutting up and down nearby. "Give them an opportunity and they'll really cause a problem." Besides, I had been a political prisoner, a man with a record and they had only to phone Bucharest to find out all they wanted about me. I wished therefore to get across with as little problem as possible. As always, I knew what to do in such cases. I had armed myself with some fine German whiskey and quietly withdrew it from the trunk as the custom's officer came by. Under the pretext of

315

opening up our baggage, I pushed the bottle into his hand. He pretended to rummage about for a few moments, then left ordering me to remain with my baggage open while he took our passports, supposedly to be checked at the office some distance away. About twenty minutes later - one wonders what they do in the intervening time - the officer came back to our car, looked in the luggage again, fussed about and then said we could proceed.

"Where are our passports?" my wife asked.

I repeated her question in Romanian to the officer and was told that we would receive them when we actually got to the barricade leading directly on to Romanian soil. After that ordeal, a further surprise awaited Louise. Having lived for over forty-five years in Romania, nothing was too far-fetched for me.

When we, finally, got free of all the nonsense at the border, we were confronted by filth and chaos of another kind - the gypsy population of the country, it seemed had come to greet us. They had their goods and chattles strewn pell-mell across the road, and in all directions for several miles.

"My God!" don't tell me this is Romania," said Louise and I didn't need to be told further what her first impression of the country was.

I tried to tell her to wait a while until we left this particular area. Knowing the gypsy people as I did, I had no illusions as to why they congregated so close to the border. Why they were allowed to do so creating such a poor image of the country to foreigners and visitors, I did not understand. But on further consideration, realized that the whole country suffered from apathy and lack of self esteem. Why should anyone care? Mr. Iliescu was in charge and he gave the orders, just like Mr. Ceausescu before him, and nobody else gave a damn. If Mr. Iliescu didn't care, why should anyone else?

We soon reached the city of Oradea but did not delay. I wanted to get as far away as possible from big cities and police officers and Securitate. Out in the open countryside, my heart felt less constricted and my mind relaxed. The knowledge that I was only a few hours from home, that I would soon see my dear mother and the family buoyed me up. I could drive all day and all night. However, I knew that would be too much for Louise, who by now, I was happy to perceive was also enjoying the beautiful countryside.

Towards evening we arrived in Vatra Dornei. We thought about staying the night and went to check the local hotel. I needed gas, but there was no gas station open - so much for accommodating tourists. But one never says 'No', or gives up too easily in Romania, otherwise the country would surely fall apart. I spoke to the hotel proprietor, who without hesitation siphoned off a half a tank of gasoline from his own car into mine. Having seen the beds and the accommodation which Vatra Dornei had to offer, Louise and I decided it was better to continue our journey over the Carpathians to Campulung to where my sister lived.

I was glad I had traversed those mountains and that particular road many times in my youth. The road built by the Roman soldiers in the first century A.D. is still intact today. Although it is narrow compared with today's motorways, it is sturdy and has less potholes being formed from stone. I was happy Louise didn't see the precipice which lay on the right side as we were climbing into the heights, but I was also sad because the views of the valleys below could be spectacular. I made up my mind to traverse this way again in the daylight; Louise just had to see the pristine beauty of the majestic Carpathians.

We arrived in Campulung at approximately 2:00 a.m. having travelled about two hundred and seventy miles. I soon found my sister's house and received a real Romanian welcome. Louise was happy; we had a nice clean bed and although we were too excited to sleep, at least we were able to rest and enjoy Veronica's fresh bread with a hot cup of tea.

Knowing that we would see Veronica and her husband again - certainly there would be a family reunion, we left early next morning on the last leg of our journey, bound for the small village of Granicesti, on the eastern side of the Carpathians, not far from the Russian border.

It was a beautiful day. The second week of May, 1992. Flowers in profusion everywhere, green fields and only the lowing of cattle or the easy clip clop of a horse-drawn dray disturbed the still, wet, perfumed, warm air.

As we drew close to the village, peasants working in the fields stopped to wave to us. Ours was the only car on the road.

'What backbreaking work!' Louise exclaimed. She realized that those tilling the land were doing so by hand with a hoe. "My God! don't they have any tractors, ploughs, etc?" she asked. "How in the name of all that's good and holy can they hope to ever get such a large area ready for sowing using such crude methods?" she continued.

"They do," I answered. And remembered how my poor mother and sister, Zanica, were forced to work on the collective farm doing this same kind of back-breaking work. But then it was for the 'common good' - I might add, of the elite Party members only.

When I opened the gate to the courtyard in front of my home, my mother was already standing outside the door. With arms opened wide, as I had remembered so vividly from childhood, she embraced me while the tears ran down her cheeks. At once, she also gathered Louise into her arms and from that moment they both fell in love with each other. They were and are to this day kindred spirits; there is a great bond of understanding between them even though my mother didn't comprehend a word Louise tried to say.

The days that followed were fantastic. We met several of my friends and many relations. We were wined and dined everywhere. People could not do enough to show their appreciation for the fact that we took time to visit and converse. One old man came running after us as we walked down the road for an evening stroll. He wanted to give Louise a gift. The only thing in his home that he had of real value to him was his pillow. This he took from his bed and offered it to my wife. Realizing his intent, she graciously told him it would not be possible to take such a large gift on the plane to America. But, she said, she was very appreciative of his gesture and thanked him profusely. One could not leave any house without partaking of food, beverage or at least some gift as a keepsake. Although poor in material things as compared to American standards, yet they were ready to give the little they had when a stranger honored them by stopping by.

Louise was deeply touched and at times overcome by such genuine, generous outpourings of friendship and love. "These people are so warm, so giving," she said more than once, "they remind me of the real Irish - those from the west of Ireland."

We took time to visit the churches of Bucovina - the many built by our great king Stefan. On several of these occasions, Mother accompanied us and while she prayed, we went to see the glorious paintings that adorn the walls within and without these churches.

The cities nearby Granicesti - Suceava, Radauti, and of course Putna were also part of our sightseeing tour and because we had such a good car everything was made that much easier.

Although Putna is not a big city as such, it is, in fact, a very old and thriving community built around its famous monastery. Begun in 1466 upon the initiative of Prince Stephan, later known as the Great (1457 - 1504) the church was the first building to be erected and in due time other buildings were added including a princely residence with defense towers.

The monastery soon became an outstanding seat of Romanian mediaeval culture. A famous school where grammar, rhetoric and logic were taught was also set up in the late 15th century and was functioning all throughout the 16th century. One of its most famous teachers was Eustatie, a Romanian who composed music for several of the psalms.

This monastery with its important contributions - cultural and artistic, is a symbol of a period of remarkable economic, social and political progress and a extraordinary assertion of the aspirations and struggles of the Romanian people for liberty, independence and national unity.

We went to the Orthodox service in the local church, that first Sunday in Granicesti. A beautiful church which I helped build, during and despite the Communist regime. There was a large gathering of people most of whom were either known to me or my family. I was very proud when Louise sang the Our Father in the Romanian language at the service. Afterward, we were invited to the priest's home for dinner. This was a very fine gesture and gave me a feeling of really being welcomed to my village. Such an honor is not given to all nor given lightly. The Reverend Constantin Hrehor, who is the pastor of St. Michael's Orthodox Church in Granicesti, is a highly intelligent and well-educated man - a poet, an artist, and an avid reader, he has published several books and articles over the years. He is also an outstanding Christian, devoted to his family, church, and country. In the short time that we were acquainted with him, I could see that Louise thought much of the man and his family.

I took time to check out my old favorite haunts - the lake where I had caught so many fine fish, the old school where I received my elementary education. The desks I used are still there; the very same - no new paint, that would spoil the look! The graveyard, where my father and grandparents and many generations are buried. I went into the fields, the orchards, and the forest nearby. Nothing had changed. It was as I had left it forty odd years before. And I realized how really small and insignificient we are, how quickly life, our lives pass away, but the great Carpathians, the forests, the land, the dark rich earth of Romania would remain for eons to come, for generations who will, like myself, love, cherish, and work for and in the soil that gave them birth.

Our visit to Bucharest was to be an emotional and, at times, devastating event for me, the city where I had lived, worked, and suffered for over 36 years.

Where was my beautiful city, the city I knew? Gone were twenty-four churches and monasteries where I often went secretly to pray - the nicest of which was St. Vinere, so popular that most of the city's population possessed, at least, a fragment of its brick facade. The Art Institute, the Operetta Theater and all the schools in the southeast sector of the city had been torn down in order that Ceausescu might build his gigantic palace - perhaps the biggest in the world-capable of housing 300,000 people, greater by far than the palace of Versailles outside Paris.

The old fear returned when I set foot in familiar surroundings - Blv. Repuglicii and Mihai Bravu street, that fear which had been my constant companion for thirty-five years. I was transported in a mesmeric state to those far off days; my stomach contracted as my pores oozed perspiration. Louise noticed the change in me and asked if I felt all right.

"This is a city of fear." And in the old way, I glanced about me and with the efficiency of long years of practice, processed the possibilities of there being Securitate or other

Agents in the immediate vicinity. "I'm OK, but I still feel I must be careful."

"Then, let's get out of here," answered Louise.

"But there are places you should see," I replied and some beautiful buildings left to admire. This was once known as the 'Paris of the Balkans' remember."

We visited the Natural History Museum and saw the plaster cast of Trajan's Column depicting the conquest of Dacia by Rome as well as the collection of golden jewelry and artifacts in the cellar. A most impressive display was the 6,000 year-old Dacian figure with the head of an animal, the body of a fish, and the tail of a bird as well as the fifth-century Hen with the Golden Chickens, a twelve-piece treasure fashioned by the Goths.

We spent a pleasant afternoon in the Cismigiu Garden amid flowering shrubs and beautiful trees and walked near the lake to watch the row-boats, while in the distance an amateur band sent discordant sounds in our direction.

We had lunch at the Manuc Inn. This garden restaurant was originally built in the nineteenth century by an Armenian merchant, Manuc-bey, as a caravansary for other visiting merchants. It is a two-tiered structure with wooden porches carved by craftsmen from Maramures. A legend is told about the founder who when he visited Paris, stopped to consult a fortune-teller. She predicted the day of his death, but Manuc-bey only laughed at her. However, the fortune-teller made sure her prediction did not fail. When she learned that he intended to make a trip to Russia for the period during which she had predicted his death, she arranged to have him poisoned on his journey.

Louise was delighted with the rich decorations, the twisted pillars and arches which form the exterior of the University of Bucharest. They represent the Brancoveanu style popular in the seventeenth century, to which were added Oriental and Venetian flourishes to the Dacian, Roman, and Byzantine elements that had existed before.

The Patriarchal Cathedral located on the highest point in Bucharest - the hill of Unification 1859 - drew us in to attend a service because of the extraordinary beauty of its choir.

It was time to return north and spend a few more days at home with my mom before once more leaving my beloved country.

Before leaving the city, however, I made a point to talk seriously to Carmen. I tried to tell her what I thought was best for both of them - that she should follow Michael to America. But like all young people who are in love, she too, did not understand my point of view.

On our journey north away from Bucharest, I was appalled and saddened to see what had happened to so many old villages along the route. Similar to what had taken place in the capital, the 'great dictator' had planned and carried out the demolition of numerous villages and communities which had existed for hundreds of years. His intention being to create a huge agricultural area where the "happy" peasants would work together all day long and, return to their new barrack-like housing, erected in a central location, when the day's work was done.

Later, I learned that over 8,000 villages had been identified for this 'honor' thus preparing the way for 500 agricultural-industrial centers, which would, in time, displace over 10 million people but gain 348,000 hectares of arable land. In this venture hundreds of churches were also to be demolished, yet the Metropolitan of Oltenia, Nestor Vornicescu, had the arrogance to speak out on behalf of the scheme:

"Despite the defamations coming from certain ill-willed circles abroad, traditionally hostile to the Romanian people, we wholeheartedly support the current modernization of commues and villages in our country... We support the drive in words and deeds, knowing that it brings not only a modernization of all aspects of life but also the preservation of all past achievements in the arts and architecture (including monuments of religious art) of our entire cultural heritage."

The Times of London rightly condemned this statement by classifying it as "one of the most shameful instances of dereliction of duty in the history of Orthodox Christianity."

Hearing these accounts and seeing first hand the destruction of my beautiful country, I was heart-broken and contrary to all my natural instincts, I was happy to be leaving soon with Louise and returning to America.

Before our departure from beautiful Bucovina, my family planned to have a reunion. They came from far and wide and in a lovely valley not far from Radauti they prepared a sumptious picnic. It was a glorious setting amid surrounding luscious growth. Everything was in full bloom, rhododendrons, apple, cherry and pear trees. The birds were busy with their nest building and chirruped happily as they went about their chores. The air fresh and perfumed with wild flowers gave new life to my joyful heart.

Gifts were presented to Louise during the meal - a traditional costume, complete with skirt, blouse, and jacket, beautifully embroidered and all done by hand. She was overcome with emotion. How could she think of taking such a precious gift! But there was no refusing this time, nor were any excuses accepted. The picnic ended with a dance indoors. Everyone had a great time and we parted reluctantly, late into the evening. Some, we would see again briefly, others, my dear sister, Veronica included, I would see no more in this life. Veronica died suddenly shortly after we returned to the United States. This was a great sorrow and shock to me especially since she was the sister nearest in age and was several years younger than I.

The trip home was more leisurely. We motored through the northern part of the country taking time to enjoy the extraordinary beauty of the Carpathian mountains. This time Louise appreciated how cautious I had been on our incoming journey, particularly since it was at night. The roads were so narrow though sturdily built, she marveled that I had managed so well.

Vatra Dornei was quite a quaint little town by daylight. The impression Louise had initially received was quickly dispelled when we arrived there about noon.

"There is one thing that never fails and never changes about these towns," Louise said, "the streets are consistantly full of pot-holes. What a shame they don't do something about them. Even the capital, Bucharest, is a complete mess. How can this country ever expect to attract tourists if it doesn't fix up its roads."

We did stop at Dracula's Castle not far from Bistrita. Built high in the hills it looked a formidable place from the valley below. When we reached the top it seemed even more sinister especially to Louise, who knew what all Westerners know, that Dracula was an impaler among other things. Bran Castle, as it is called was built in 1377 by the Teutonic Knights, guards one end of a narrow pass through the Carpathian mountains, a strategic route between Transylvania and Wallachia. Castle Dracula near Curtea-de-Arges was actually Dracula's stronghold, and is situated at the other end of the pass in Wallachia.

Apart from seeing the means by which Dracula tortured his victims, there was little else that the castle had to offer, but in defense of this man, whose name was Vlad - Voevod of Wallachea (1456-1462), I have to say that he certainly kept law and order. A story is told of how he left a gold goblet at a well one evening and it was there when he sent his servant for it the next day. Actually, Vlad wasn't much worse than any of his contemporaries. He had a kingdom to

325

protect against the constant incursions of the Turks and in order to deter these barbarian hoards, he devised every conceivable method of torture to disuade them from advancing beyond his border.

As a child he had suffered much having been given as a hostage to the Turks by his own father. He spent four years locked up in a castle high in the hills of western Turkey until at the age of eighteen, he escaped.

Upon returning home he immediately took up arms and wiped out all opposition - Romanian and Turkish alike. It appears that Vlad-Dracula got tired of hearing about the starving, the sick, and the crippled in his land. He invited all to a huge banquet near his castle. When they had eaten and drunk well, he excused himself for a moment, went out of the building and had it set on fire. "Now we won't have anymore poor, hungry people," he joyfully remarked.

We crossed the Romanian border late in the evening and although this time was not as lengthy and as strenuous as our entry, yet, it was rather ridiculous. The Romanian customs officers wanted to know if we were taking any national treasures with us. When they were assured that we didn't have Queen Marie's jewels or such like, they allowed us to exit.

We spent the night in Szolinok not too far from the Romanian border, in a very nice, clean zimmer. The husband and wife who kept the place were extremely polite and served us fine meals that evening and the next morning.

The Hungarian countryside did not evoke any wild exclamations. Flat, flat, and more flat, it was a real let-down after Romania. We decided we had to see Budapest, so we headed for the city. As I had been there before and know some Hungarian, I felt confident that we would have no trouble.

We arrived fairly early in the heart of the city. I parked and tried to get directions but either I had forgotten the language, or the Hungarians are not very polite for I never got a direct answer or any help whatsoever from anyone I spoke to.

Undaunted, we got back in the car and started off again in the general direction of Buda across the Danube. I wanted Louise to see the city as well as the Cathedral from that point.

It was a rainy day, not a pleasant one for sightseers. The traffic was heavy and we had decided to spend, at least, one night somewhere in Austria. Vienna should have been our choice, of course, but Louise thought we should avoid the hustle and bustle of more traffic. Besides, by this time we were both getting tired of the road and longed for a good rest, and somewhere to stretch our legs.

Journeying through Austria, our first impression, having so recently left eastern Europe, was how well the roads were maintained. At the foot of the Alps, this is a beautiful land, green, well cultivated, clean, the picturesque towns and villages scattered at regular intervals among the valleys and on the hillsides.

We stopped at a small town called Melk, just off the highway. We were attracted by its mighty Baroque Abbey. Originally a 10th-century fortress and the seat of the Babenberg family who preceeded the Halisburgs, it was eventually given to the Benedictines in the early 12th century. The present Baroque buildings were built in the 18th century. The library is one of the finest, housing 80,000 volumes and 1,850 manuscripts dating as far back as the 9th century. This huge building full of art treasures is also an important and integral part of the history of Austria. When we were there, there was a massive restoration program being carried out and unfortunately, we were not able to see many parts of the building but what we did see was magnificient.

Below the abbey, the town nestles in a small valley. It was so beautiful, especially at night with the lights of the Abbey glistening above, that we thought it would be a wonderful place to spend a night. We parked the car and as Louise was dying for some good pastries we entered a small cafe. Everything was delicious. Then we took a stroll into the center of the town - so picturesque, so quiet, no traffic - it wasn't allowed. The place was peaceful, serene, people walking, chatting quietly; some sipping coffee on the sidewalks or cool beer, coke, wine. Everyone seemed so relaxed. It was heaven. Surely, it was a fairyland - a story-book village of which one only dreams.

We checked in at a hotel, were shown where we might park our car and then led to our room - a large, clean, and very comfortable room at the extraordinarily reasonable price - $50 a night.

Later, after dinner, we went for another walk in the cool of the evening. The air was perfumed with roses, lilies and a host of other flowers. There were flowers everywhere and Louise remarked: "The Austrians know how to live."

We slept well and very reluctantly left the next morning. It was a place and an experience we would never forget.

I was sorely tempted to leave the beaten track we had decided upon, and head south to Salzburg, but Louise had a pain in her lower back which made travelling very uncomfortable, so I had to resign myself to getting to Stuttgart that evening, if possible.

Travelling in Austria was both pleasant and easy. The highways are excellent, and there isn't much traffic. However, Germany is another story. Although the roads are very good, the traffic is heavy, and, as in America, traffic never stops day or night.

Back in Stuttgart, we were again received with open arms by 'Hitler' and Virginica, wined and dined for several

328

more days before it was time to leave for home. It had been a most memorable holiday.

After a few days rest, Louise, who had fallen in love with Romania and its people started to do some research in the local schools where she discovered that there was absolutely nothing about Romania available for the children to read. She set to work, immediately to remedy that situation and the result of her efforts was *Escape from Romania*, a book about the adventures and trials of a young boy, named Mihai, as he and his mother escape from Romania during the Ceausescu years. This book was nominated for the Oregon Book Award for 1997. In 1999 it won the First Prize, The Constantin Badersca Literary Award, offered by the Province of Bucovina, Romania.

Louise had been writing stories and poems from an early age but did not publish. After she had finished *Escape from Romania*, I encouraged her to try to publish a novel she had been working on, for at least ten years - *Magheen*. This novel set in Ireland in the time of Henry VIII was published by E.M. Press of Manassas, Virginia in 1997. Anyone who reads it falls in love with it. From an English-critique the following lines tell more than I can say: "Magheen is a tender, carefully drawn story in the genre of prose romance, using the Bildungsroman pattern to follow the personal development of the heroine as she pursues her destiny...Ms. Gherasim's prose is measured and controlled, though also capable of sweeping lyrical description (her ability to parallel internal and external landscapes is particularly impressive) an incisive but humane analysis. The sixteenth-century setting of the text is conjured with a loving, almost painterly eye for detail, so that the reader derives a strong visual impression of the scenes through which Magheen moves."

Following upon these two books, Louise published another novel entitled: *In Endless Strife* which also received excellent review notes from Minerva Press, London. "The marvelous and figurative landscapes, and attention to the sound and song of the language communicate themselves throughout *In Endless Strife*, so as to give to us something of the soft lilt of the Irish language. This rhythm carries forth like the power of story-telling as it spans the generations…

"The story is eye-catching in detail and in the magnitude of the telling. This is the nature of the particularity of style invested in it. I believe it shows signs that place it in a long and honoured tradition of writing: it takes to itself the attributes of epic and family saga recalling Fielding and even into the later compelling what-happened-nextism of Walter Scott. This is an exciting, dramatic saga."

Grainne, for children was released in July of '98 and was again given an outstanding review: "*Grainne*, written by Louise Gherasim, is an accomplished and well-polished piece of work, with a taut, coherent plot and a writing style that is engaging and accessible to the age range at which the book is directed. I'm sure many girls will delight in this tale of ages old, which is in a rather more palatable form than a history book." (Jane Evans-Minerva Press)

Louise has written eleven books to date, and has helped me compile and translate this work. I'm very proud of her abilities and wish to make her name known in this country and in Romania.

My life is peaceful and tranquil for the first time since I left my little village of Granicesti over fifty years ago. Never, in my adult years, have I been so happy. I have my bees - a hobby of mine since childhood, my books, my writing - for I continue to submit articles for publication in various Romanian papers. I walk regularly in the country areas that surround our beautiful home and, of course, I have our garden - a job which never ends but which is worth it, it's so lovely. But most of all, I have Louise. We go everywhere together, and I especially like to invite her to a local coffee shop where we, like children, play the game of make-believe. Each time we pretend we are visiting a different city in Europe - Paris, Milan, Rome, etc. We imagine the setting and the ambience and thoroughly enjoy the moments we spend in our dream world.

Chapter 22

Love's Young Dream

Above your house are lit as then
The same bright stars of old.
That shone those summer evenings when
My passion's tale I told.

Mihae Eminescu
- When Memory

Michael was hired as a mechanical engineer, by one of the fishing companies doing business in the Alaskan waters. After four months of that harsh life-style and having risked his life in the icy waters of the North Pacific in order to save a man who had got caught in some netting, Michael returned home with his savings. He spent a day or two shopping for his bride-to-be, and then purchased his return ticket to Romania. He had the crazy notion that things would be better in the new Republic. It, might take time but things just had to get better he told himself.

Before Michael left, he expressed the desire to start a business but he needed capital. Louise was willing to help with a loan. With youthful eagerness and driven by the fires and passions of "love's young dream," he returned to Romania thinking to change his circumstances and standard of living for the better. He would work hard. He would make it; nothing could stop him. So full of optimism, so head-over-heels in love - what could I do.

Letters came fairly regularly after he got married in September '92. He had started a taxi service which he felt

333

was badly needed. He hired four men, friends, and bought four new cars from Budapest and a large van which he intended to drive himself. For a short time things went well, but about a year later it seemed everyone else in Bucharest was bitten by the same bug as Michael. Almost overnight, anyone who had a car was in the taxi business. There was no control on the numbers which took to the streets. All too soon Michael's dreams were shattered and by the time I again visited Romania in 1994, he had lost everything - his cars, to the wear and tear of Bucharest's pot-holes, and the lack of spare parts; his employees, because of theft, or bad work habits; his profits, to the new government, galloping inflation, rising gas prices, repair costs, and the devaluation of the lei.

I wanted to tell him, I told you so, but I declined and instead gave him some money to help him pay off the exorbitant taxes he owed the government for his failed business.

Like so many exiled Romanians, I also wanted to help the Motherland and would have exulted had Michael succeeded in his business endeavor but, given the Iliescu regime, inherited from his predecessor - Ceausescu, and the run-away inflation, it was impossible for anyone to succeed.

I cite another incident within my own family. My brother's daughter, an intelligent, hardworking and enthusiastic young woman, an engineer by profession, together with three other capable young women having built a structure of considerable proportions at great expense, decided to open a clothing business. Like Michael, they did well the first year but when they went to refurbish their stock everything had inflated to three times the price of the previous year. Thus their year's profit was instantly eaten-up. And though they struggled for a few more years, they eventually had to give up their business and start looking for work in the government owned enterprises.

It made me weep to see such energy, intelligence and hardwork wasted. What are the youth of Romania to do under such adverse conditions. Emigrate! Their fathers suffered injustice and suppression of their gifts and talents under the ignorant, Nicolae Ceausescu – "The Mad Man" as the American Ambassador to Romania in the 80's Mr. David Funderburk, called him. Now in the 90's initiative and ambition were being squelched by no less inept government policies. Michael would never succeed under such conditions.

I asked myself over and over again, why is it that a country so rich in natural resources, so blessed with acres of some of the most fertile land in Europe, with a population of energetic, hardworking, intelligent people cannot manage to raise the standard of living conditions for the vast majority of its inhabitants? And always the answer was the same - until a free democratic society with incentives for the entrepreneur and the hard working majority, is again firmly entrenched in Romania, it will never rise to its rightful place among the nations of Europe.

Romanians have never taken lightly to oppression and have exhibited an independent spirit as far back as Decebal and the Dacians. And as Mr. Funderburg pointed out in his book, *Pinstripes and Reds*: "From the beginnings of Soviet-imposed Communism in Romania there was significant opposition to the drastic, nontraditional, transformation of society by the atheistic and materialistic Marxist - Leninist." The author goes on to point out that, "some of the strongest resistance came from the peasants who resolutely fought against the collectivization of agriculture. Massive killings and arrests resulted from peasant opposition. It was not some minority of chiaburi (so-called Romanian kulaks or better-off peasants) but the masses of

335

middle peasantry who strenuously objected to the loss of land and the take-over of farms by the state.

"Nor was resistance and opposition confined to the peasant population. Factory workers and intellectuals have voiced their outrage over low wages, long working hours, and poor unsafe working conditions." Mr. Funderburg, who was in residence in Romania during the 80's, pointed out that "sabotage and strikes have occured more frequently than has been reported in the outside world. Most such actions have only led to greater repression by the security forces and to the arrests and jailing of the most active resistance leaders." But that did not stop the defiant attitude of those who remained. Mr. Funderburger continues: "I have heard many Romanians say that a deliberate practice exists in many factories of 'making things not work' as a form of protest against the hated system. There is no question of the extraordinary loss of productivity in factories being at least partially due to the dissatisfaction felt by workers."

Over the years other voices have been heard. Brave men and women have cried out against Communist oppression, among them Ana Blandiana whose poem Amfiteatru in 1984 caused much consternation. In another "Eu Cred" ("I think"), she expresses frustration at the apparent lack of revolutionary fervor, saying:

"I think we are a vegetal people,
From where, otherwise, the calm
In which we await our leaflessness?
From where the courage
To leave ourselves on the slide into sleep
Almost up to death
With an assurance
That we will be in a state
To be born again?
I think we are a vegetal people.

Whoever saw

A tree in revolt?"

For her daring and outspoken attitude, Ana was placed under house arrest. She was considered lucky to have escaped with her life.

In July 1978, Lieutenant General Ion Mihai Pacepa, the highest ranking defector ever from the Eastern bloc, secretly left West Germany in a United States Air Force plane. Tired of the lies, the corruption, and the abuse of power, he had much to tell the world in his book *Red Horizons* which he published in 1987.

To the Western mind and in particular the people of the United States it seems incomprehensible that one man, Ceausescu, could have such power. From demanding that handwriting samples for the whole Romanian population, starting with the first grade children, be obtained within three months from the day in which he issued his demand, to obtaining handwritten autobiographies from every employee's personnel files, Ceausescu would control all. In fact every aspect and facet of Romanian life was under the scrutiny of the Ceausescus. "After 13 years in power," Mr. Pacepa wrote: "Ceausescu looked upon Romania as something that he and his family literally owned. His wife, Elena, was on the rise, and nobody in the whole country was now being appointed to a high or middle-level position without her blessing. Ceausescu's brothers, Ilie, Nicolae, and Ion, controlled the armed forces, the DIE, and agriculture. Elena's brother ran the General Union of Trade Unions, which had control over all the working population of Romania. Their son, Nicu, was the head of the Union of Communist youth. And this was just the beginning. There is no system of government more susceptible to nepotism than the Communist one."

Even the population growth was dictated by Elena. When inspecting an exhibit set up by the General

Directorate of Technical Operations - DGTO, Elena asked the Commander, Lieutenant General Ovidiu Diaconescu, how many children he had. When he answered, "One, Comrade Elena. One soldier for the Party." Elena quickly responded: "That's why our population isn't growing. You should have at least four soldiers for the Party, dear comrade."

General Pacepa fastidiously recounts the conversations of the Ceausesus at the presentation of the 'new' technology which only Romania had invented 'an electronic monitoring center for use in Romanian embassies, along with passive systems, lasers, and encoded ultra-high-frequency transmitters for installation in such targets in the West as governments, institutions, military units and private homes.'

"How many people will we be able to monitor simultaneously by the end of our next five-year plan?" Ceausescu asked.

"I can only report, Comrade Supreme Commander and Esteemed Comrade Elena," said Diaconescu, "that, if our proposals are approved today, then as of January 1, 1984, we will be able to monitor ten million microphones simultaneously."

To this Ceausescu responded. "We are now building a beautiful life for the Romanian people, comrades. A new and independent life, which our people deserve, after two thousand and fifty years of struggle and humiliation. For the past decade, each year has marked something new in our Communist history. Let us make 1984 another cornerstone. Let us again be unique in the Warsaw Pact. Let us be the first in the entire world, comrades. In a very short time we will be the only country on earth able to know what every single one of its citizens is thinking. Five years is all that separates us today from a new, much more scientific form of government." Ceausescu paused, looked at his audience and then continued: "Why is American imperialism so unpopular? Because it does not know what its people think, because it is not scientific. What you are doing here, comrades, is the real science of government. It is a true public opinion survey. The Communist system, we are creating together is the most scientific ever, I repeat, Comrades, ever to be put at the service of mankind."

After loud applause, Ceausescu raised his arms asking for silence. "It is too bad we cannot tell our working people how the Communist Party is looking out for them, comrades. Wouldn't the miners go out and dig more coal, if they could just be sure that the Party knew what their wives were doing every single instant? They would, comrades, but we cannot talk about our system today. The Western press might accuse us of being a police state. That's imperialist propaganda, comrades. We do not have a police state, and we will never have a police state. We are a proletarian dictatorship preserving our ideological purity. Communism is the only real democracy, and history will attest to that for generations to come."

He concluded: "But someday we will be able to talk about what we are doing here, Someday, when our proletarian world revolution defeats the capitalist hydra, and our red flag is flying everwhere on earth!"

It was now 1994 and still the tactics and ideologies of the Ceausescu regime persisted. The government of Mr. Iliescu was Communism with a 'human face'. Nothing had really changed.

With such policies and control the youth of Romania were doomed to failure. After 50 years of terror, outlandish demands and slavish obeisance the morale, the determination, and optimism that should have existed, and sparked into life after the Revolution, was barely flickering in 1994. I can only conclude that it will take a long time, perhaps many decades for Romania to shake off the yolk of a government to which it has become accustomed and which has hindered its progress for so long.

Having visited my mother and the family for about a week, I returned to Bucharest. There Michael and Carmen were waiting to ask me to help them. They wanted to go to America. There was no future for them in Romania no matter how hard they worked.

The following morning the three of us went to the American Embassy. After I had spoken at length with the Consul explaining that Michael was my son, that I was an American citizen and wished to unify the family, she produced his files and informed me that he had already been granted a visa several years before - 1991.

"Why did he return to Romania?" she asked perplexed.

"Come and I will show you," I answered. I led her to a window which overlooked the courtyard where Michael and Carmen awaited me. "Love, that's the reason he came back."

The Consul looked at me, hardly believing what I said.

"Do you mean to tell me that young man gave up the United States because he was in love?"

"Yes," I responded.

"I have to meet such a man," she answered. "There are very few left who would do so."

She concluded by handing me the necessary forms which I immediately filled out.

We left the Embassy with the assurance that the case would be taken under consideration, but with no promises as to when Michael and Carmen would be able to emigrate.

My heart was heavy when I had to return to the U.S. without them. But there was nothing else I could do.

I called Michael regularly over the next two years. I telephoned Washington, D.C. Several times I made calls to the U.S. Immigration Dept. and invariably I checked and rechecked the Romanian Embassy in Los Angeles and

Bucharest to get information regarding Michael's status. The months slipped away. I had been told his number was under consideration one time, but the next time I called everything had changed. They were now processing about 2,000 persons every two months. Then, for apparently no reason at all, the Embassy closed down and all was at a stand-still. Meanwhile, Michael was working twelve to fourteen hours a day, six days a week and barely able to support himself and his wife. Carmen could not get work, although she was a willing and able young woman.

I could do nothing more, except send a little money now and again to keep them from starvation.

Finally, on December 8, 1997, Michael and Carmen landed in Portland, tired, and numb from the long plane journey, but relieved to have made it to the 'Promised Land'.

Michael soon found work, bought himself a car and quickly adjusted to a new style of life. Carmen wasted no time either. She took driving lessons and started to attend P.C.C. (Portland Community College) where she intends to graduate and then continue in Portland State University for a C.P.A. certificate. As well as attending school, she also works as an accountant in a local office. Thus, in two years, they have gained more than they ever could have imagined or ever hoped to achieve in a life time of hard work in Romania and its socialist system.

I thank God each day that my son was given a second chance to come to America and make his home here. It is a land of opportunity - a land flowing with milk and honey for those who work hard, but unfortunately a land of many contradictions and injustices also.

Chapter 23

Bolts from the Blue

Throughout the length of time, different and still the same
Their yearnings and their hopes are of one kind composed,
And though of countless fashions does seem life's secret
flame,
All are alike deceived that call upon her name;
While infinite desire is in an atom closed.

Mihai Eminescu
- Emperor and Proletarian

Louise and I were so happy together. God had turned His Face to me. Both my sons were strong and healthy. Gabriel was attending Portland State University; he wanted to be a doctor: "I want to help people, Papa." he had said to me. He was working with the Northwest Medical Team, and assisting in the schools with the Drug programs. Gabriel seemed to be everywhere, involved with one thing or another. I was a happy man, things were going well for all of us.

In late May, 1995 Gabriel went to Romania with his girlfriend, Shelley. They had gone on a well-earned vacation but also used the opportunity to take medical supplies and equipment to poorly outfitted clinics and hospitals in the more remote areas of the country. In keeping with his character, Gabriel could not go back to his native land without bringing much needed help to those who were less fortunate than he.

343

June 27,1996, Louise got up and went downstairs for a drink of water. It was about five o'clock in the morning. She had not been feeling well during the night and had complained of indigestion pains - rather severe.

She poured herself a drink and then started up the stairs to return to bed when I heard her call me. From the sound of her voice, I knew there was something wrong, so I immediately jumped out of bed and ran to where she was standing holding on to the bannister. As I reached her, she fell into my arms. I laid her on the floor; she had fainted. A moment later, she came to and asked me to take her into the livingroom as she felt cold on the tiles in the hallway. Again, I lifted her and laid her on the carpet. She was coherent and told me to dial 911 as something was very wrong with her. It was the immediate response of the Tualatin medical crew as well as the Fire Department that saved her life. Louise had had a heart attack and soon became comatose. She remained in intensive care for three days. After that things seemed to stabilize and within a week she was home again but only for one night. The following morning the same thing happened, she felt weak; so once again 911 came to the rescue. This time she was not completely unconscious, but the decision was made in the hospital to perform an angioplasty.

My heart was empty. What would I do without her. The shock was so great that I developed a severe toothache and had to go to the dentist. She found I had an infection and immediately prescribed antibiotics. Still the pain persisted. I was beside myself with worry about Louise and suffered constantly from the toothache. It was two weeks I won't soon forget, but little did I know then that another tragic situation was developing, one that would devastate the whole family.

It was a beautiful July evening; Louise was beginning to feel a little better. We were spending a quiet time at home enjoying our garden, listening to the trickling of the stream and the cascading splashes of the waterfalls, when the phone rang. Gabriel's girlfriend, Shelley, didn't want to alarm us, but she had to tell us that Gabriel had been contacted by the police. The details were not quite clear, at that moment, but my heart-rate increased and I could feel the blood pounding in my head. The very mention of police gave me a sick feeling in the pit of my stomach. I had had enough of their tactics and underhand operations in Romania. But, ever optimistic, I gathered myself together and told myself I was now in America, things would be different. People were reasonable here. I didn't tell Louise then; she didn't need anymore stress.

July 12, 1996, was an evening which I'll never forget. Gabriel had returned from his trip to Romania about a week before. He had taken some photographs and video tapes of various scenes and wished to have them processed by a Romanian friend who lived in the Tualatin area. On his way home, he happened to see a distraught Mexican woman sitting under a tree by the side of the road. Having just returned from Romania, where no one would think of passing another human being in distress, he pulled to the side of the road and asked if she needed help. She spoke in Spanish, "Tigard, Tigard."

Gabriel offered to take her so she got into the car. It was at that juncture he noticed the woman was not wearing her pants but was holding them in her hands.

"If I'm to transport you, you'll have to put on your pants. I'll pull into a private area and allow you to dress," he said. A few yards down the road there was a driveway which seemed a good place, so Gabriel pulled in and parked his car. It was then that the woman turned on him and started beating him with her fists. Being of frail constitution and also very much aware that his transplanted kidney was in the front of his body, plus the fact that the fistula in his left arm was in danger of being hurt which, if that were to happen, would or could cause instant death, Gabriel tried to defend himself. He was driving his girl-friend's car at the time. They had purchased a knife, an Indian hunting knife, a short time before which she kept under the front seat for her protection. A friend of hers, and the mother of two children, had been accosted and taken from a parking lot not far from where Shelley, Gabriel's girlfriend, lived. She was killed near the Gorge, several miles outside of Portland and her body dumped on the side of the road. Shelley was terrified after that tragic occurance and so kept the blunt knife near her at all times. She was, at the time, a student in the university and often had to take night classes.

Gabriel thought of the knife and in order to protect himself against the blows now falling on him, he withdrew it and brandished it in self-defense without any intention of harming the woman.

Whether it was the sight of this weapon or some other reason, the woman jumped out of the car and ran towards a group of mobile homes that were close by.

Gabriel though shaken and not feeling well that whole day thought it best to go and get himself checked in the hospital. He gathered up the woman's clothes and placed them on the ground close to where he had stopped the car. Then he left the spot and instead of going to the hospital and forgetting the deranged woman, he stopped when he saw a policeman. He got out of his car and reported the incident to the officer, telling him that there was a woman running around half-naked in a parking area not far away. He handed the officer his card and told him if he needed anymore information to get in touch with him as he wasn't feeling well, himself, and was on his way to the hospital.

Gabriel checked in at Providence Hospital where he underwent several tests. He was suffering from hypertension, nausea, and dehydration.

Later, in the night, he received a call from the Tualatin Police Department seeking more information about the episode earlier that evening. At two o'clock in the morning, he received another call. So, apart from the fact that Gabriel was not feeling well, he didn't get a good night's sleep either. Then at 5:00 that same morning, another police officer called and stated that Gabriel was a suspect in a very serious crime. Eight days later, on July 21, two more officers came to his door at 7:00 a.m. to arrest him.

"But, I did nothing." Gabriel exclaimed completely taken by surprise.

"You can tell that to the Captain at the station," replied one of the officers, meanwhile you come with us."

They handcuffed him, despite the fact that he had a fistula in the left arm which if injured would cause his death. Gabriel was in shock. But he assured himself everything would be fine, after all, he was in America. When he explained himself to the authorities at the police station, they would understand, and he would be free to go.

The reality was far different, so much so that to this day Gabriel and everyone else who knows him are unable to understand how such a thing could happen. What have we, in this country and all around the world, been led to believe - that the American Justice System is the very best on the face of the planet; that there is freedom and justice for all; that there must be witnesses before a man or woman can be accused of a crime; that one is innocent until proven guilty! The next few months that ultimately grew into years were to teach us all a very different lesson. If it could happen to our family - every member of which has never deviated one iota from the letter of the law - it can happen to any other family in this, the United States of America.

347

I was told that Gabriel had been sent to Washington County jail and was accused of kidnapping, raping and abusing a woman, among other things. Were they mad? What were they talking about? My son, Gabriel, who had never hurt a fly, who released a flying moth trapped behind a restaurant curtain! There was something wrong, something really wrong. I had to tell Louise. She was very upset, but like me, at that time, she believed in the American Justice System.

"He'll be fine. They'll question him; get the facts and then everything will be O.K." was her reply.

I felt a bit better. She had lived in this country for at least thirty years; she should know how the system worked.

The hours passed. Then we were told that we had better get an Attorney for Gabriel - a criminal attorney! Where would we begin. Before I had a chance to think, Gabriel and Shelley had decided on a man who had been recommended as the best and most experienced lawyer in the State. There was only one problem - he was very expensive, and he would have to be paid before he'd even consider the case.

What was happening to us. Was I experiencing a bad dream - a nightmare! Gabriel, the child I had given up home, family, country; the boy for whom I had worked so hard that I had caused myself to have a heart attack; the young man that I had literally saved from the jaws of death was now about to be apprehended as a common criminal. It was impossible. I had to hire a lawyer no matter what it cost, to defend a sick young man whom I knew was completely innocent of the crimes for which he was being detained. The only problem was where was I going to get the money.

Just when life's path had taken a turn for the best, when Louise was getting back on her feet, how could this be happening to me! to us!

The whole situation had to be settled fast, else Gabriel's frail health would surely suffer in the prison environment. The decision was taken based on the fact that the lawyer, in question, was certainly qualified, never having lost a case. A man of outstanding talents in his professional life.

We would take out a mortgage on our home. Louise was adamant that if Mr. X was all he was chalked up to be, we had to hire him. Gabriel's life was at stake.

He would be prosecuted under Oregon's new law - Measure XI, we soon found out. I had no peace night or day after that. Again, I cried to God. "Father, in heaven, how could this thing happen?"

The grand jury sent the case to trial. The ten days of trial which took place in Washington County May 14th - 24th, 1996 were a confused jumble of words and explanations for me. I felt inadequate, useless, incompetent. I could not speak-up for my son. I could not open my mouth. It was even worse than Romania under the Communists. There, I could at least speak my mind when allowed to speak; here, in America, I was obliged to remain silent or merely answer the questions asked - Yes or No, with no explanations, even when such would make all the difference in the world to the interpretation of the situation. I had studied Law for two years in the University of Bucharest. I knew the games the lawyers were playing - guilt or innocence didn't matter - this was a case to be lost or won by the lawyer who could make his/her arguements sound the most plausible. An onlooker in a tragic drama, where despite the obvious lies and make-believe stories of the Lawyer for the State who represented the Plaintiff - I was obliged to obey the orders of the Judge no matter what the outcome for my son. I had to be Silent.

But despite all the misgivings, Gabriel and I still clung to the belief that all would be well. America - the land of 'Justice for All' would not let us down. Truth would be on our side. The Jury would see the folly of the trumpted-up stories; they would surely study the inconsistencies and contradictions made by the police, the plaintiff, the D.A. and some of the witnesses called for the Plaintiff. There was, at the time, no doubt in my mind; no right-thinking people could, in conscience, convict my son. And, as I thought of his frail health and considered the conditions of a prisoner's existence, I refused to contemplate the possibility of a jail sentence - that would surely mean death for him.

Towards the end of the second week of trial, our lawyer wished to present a psychiatrist who having studied the plaintiff's symptoms was convinced she was suffering from Dissociative Amnesia. It was quite obvious, even to the layman, that her confused state of mind meant she was either traumatized or suffering from some mental disorder. She continually contradicted herself, reversing her accounts of what happened to her on July 12, 1996. But when the Judge was approached about this matter, he refused to allow the doctor to testify stating that it would place the plaintiff at an unfair disadvantage.

It was May 24th. The Jury had been out for several hours. Our Attorney was anxious. He didn't like a long debate. It was close to midnight. The long weekend was upon us. There was an air of tension, an atmosphere of urgency. The case must be wrapped-up before the holiday. To me, the whole situation was preposterous. What did it matter whether or not it took all night, or the entire weekend to come to a responsible and just conclusion - a fair and thorough examination of the case.

Shortly before midnight, we were told that the Jury had reached a consenses of opinion. Merciful Father in Heaven, I prayed, you know he's Not Guilty. Let the truth speak.

A palpable silence in the courtroom. I looked at Louise when she squeezed my hand. She, too, was praying. All around us, our friends were anxious and tired but ever hopeful. Gabriel would surely be exonerated.

The Judge asked if the Jury had come to a decision. The answer came swift and sharp and cut, nay cleft, my heart with its keen edge.

"Guilty on all counts."

Was I hearing correctly? I moved my head closer to Louise. I didn't have to ask. Her face told all — the horror, the disbelief. I was crushed, bent, broken. This was a travesty of Justice! My whole soul revolted. Surely, I was not in America! It just couldn't be. American Justice - the whole world clammered for the system known as American Justice. Now I experienced it first hand and what had it offered me? Great God Almighty was there such a thing as Justice anywhere in this world!

I slumped back in the seat and did not hear another word of what followed. I was told afterward that the list of Gabriel's supposed crimes were read and each one carefully innumerated. The process was long and tedious. I thought only of Gabriel. My heart was heavy; my mind numb. This farce, this mockery of a fair trial, how could it possibly have taken place in this the country of my dreams.

I looked at my son flanked by two armed guards - burley fellows with a no-nonsense attitude, and thought of Christ before Pilate. What had gone wrong? How could the jurors, if they had an ounce of intelligence between them, have believed the lies, the trumped-up charges? Weren't there enough inconsistencies, contradictions, and uncertainties to cast doubts in the minds of those twelve men and women as to the guilt of my son.

My troubled brain recounted the obvious - was it logical for a criminal, a guilty man to turn his name, address, and phone number over to the police at the very first opportunity? Why did the police lose the medical test results? Did the declaration of the medical doctor that there

351

was no signs of abuse, no marks, etc. count for nothing? Why did they, the authorities, not require a lab-test on the woman's clothes? Why did one of the police officer's make the mistake of classifying my son as an Arab? And there were so many more questions which my troubled brain would not allow me to overlook and kept repeating. But why had these obviously tantalizing arguments not occured to so many members of the Jury. Only one man, a physicist, held out against all of his fellow jurors and declared Gabriel - not guilty. For that small voice, alone, I was grateful.

I could see, from Gabriel's expression that he was in shock. Having lived through a like ordeal, I knew the feelings, the conflicting emotions - the utter despair, the frustration of not being able to respond, to fight back, to explain, to enlighten. It was a paralyzing, utterly incomprehensible situation. No one who has not experienced it can possibly understand.

The Judge spoke after the jurors had, each in turn, made known his/her verdict. Gabriel was to be kept in the Washington County Jail until he would be sentenced on July 2nd. He was then led away. I was not allowed to speak to him. Not allowed to give a word of encouragement, nor show any sign of compassion. Nothing remained for us to do but leave the courtroom. In silence, and in semi-darkness we traversed the long passage ways. I listened to the hollow sounds on the stone steps and as we emerged into the eerie darkness of the deserted empty street, my whole being reverberated to this awful moment - empty was my soul, darkness took possession of my mind, and a hammer beat against the resonating chambers of my tormented brain. I sat on a cold hard cement seat and, burying my face in my hands, gave vent to my pent-up agonies in a cry that rent the still air. I had no tears to shed; that would have been a relief - America! America! I wanted to shout the words - America what have you done to us!

America, the land for which I longed ever since I was a small boy. America, the country of my dreams, where have you gone wrong?

For another half-an-hour or so, my friends waited, not knowing what to do. Words had no meaning anymore, for were they uttered they would surely sound hollow. There was nothing anyone could say or do and that only added to the utter despair and desolation of the moment. We did not see the jurors leave; we did not know when the lawyers departed. We waited hoping, for some small word of compassion - perhaps, some sign that things, even at that late hour, would somehow not be as bad as they now appeared. But no one came. No one cared... Judge, lawyers, jurors. All these people who had the life of my frail son in their hands just walked away into the night.

Finally, Louise took matters into her hands, as she is wont to do in like circumstances, and knowing that the inevitable had to be faced, suggested we all go home and try to get some sleep. We would need our strength and wits about us for the days to come. She invited Shelley, to stay in our home, and since she was overwrought, her sister accompanied her.

Gabriel was sentenced to 90 months in the State Prison, the minimum sentence under the new ruling. At first, we weren't sure where he might be housed. It could be as far away as Texas, as there were programs set up between the different states to relieve the overflow of prisoners in one state or another. Finally, we thanked God that he was, on account of his medical condition, placed in Salem. This would allow us to see him at least once a week and for that we were truly grateful.

The next few months were a veritable 'hell' for every one of us outside the prison but only God alone knows what Gabriel, himself, went through. His health was grievously affected. He lost a lot of weight. He was unable to eat much of the food served in prison and we were not allowed to bring him any filtered water - a requisite in his case. It was impossible for him to exist in cells where prisoners in close proximity passed along all their infectious diseases. He caught every cold that was going around. He became sick from contaminated foods. The list of maladies was endless. So he had to endure a continuous battle within the prison itself, while all the while I agonized outside the walls and would gladly have exchanged places with him. How long could he resist under such conditions? Were all my sacrifices on his behalf for naught - home, family and country, my career, my long years of perseverance and hard work to obtain my doctorate. I was no longer a young man and I knew if I lost Gabriel, my own life would be at an end.

However, I found out after about three months, that Gabriel was made of a sturdier mettle than I had realized. His body although frail and delicate housed a mature mind and a will of iron. He had no intention of allowing the System, or any other force, to break him. By sheer will-power he overcame obstacle after obstacle. He, eventually, persuaded the prison authorities to place him in a single cell. Alone, he could avoid a lot of trouble and keep himself free from infection. For a while he did seem to improve under these relatively better conditions.

A year passed and his case, which had been sent to the Appeals Court, was due for a hearing. Friends and family, for by this time Michael and his wife, Carmen had arrived from Romania, were present as three judges who had reviewed the case gave their opinions. The decision for Gabriel's release pending a new trial was unanimous. We were overjoyed. At last!

During the ensuing months, I had convinced myself, and this conviction alone kept me going, that when the case would be reviewed by those who were conversant with the law, the decisions and convictions of his trial would most certainly be overturned. Again, I cried - At last!

We left the courthouse and rushed over to the prison to give Gabriel the news. Louise told him to pack his bags; he'd probably be home in a few days at most. We were euphoric, hardly able to contain ourselves. Our joy, however, lasted only a few days and again, my patience was tried. I felt like Job - how long my God, how long can I endure?

Gabriel's disappointment was not so obvious. He had steeled himself. Knowing the mentality and aggressiveness with which the Washington County D.A. had pursued her case, he was not too surprised when the news came that she would not accept the decision of the Appellate Court and had remanded the case to the Supreme Court.

"How long would that take?" I asked and was told at least a year, maybe two.

Another year! If we were lucky. Another period of waiting and hoping that Gabriel's health could withstand the strain, the environmental conditions and the poor medical attention. Despite his heroic struggle, it was clear to all that Gabriel was a sick man. Again his weight which was normally 155 lbs., bearing in mind that he is six-foot two, now dropped to 138 lbs. He was skin and bone. "Who will pay the million dollars necessary for another kidney" I asked, "when this one fails?"

What I most feared had happened. We were alerted one morning to the fact that Gabriel was in the hospital. His kidney had failed. March 4, 1998 - his 30th birthday - he was sick, severely sick and rushed to the hospital. The conditions under which he was forced to live were not bad enough, it seemed, so the doctor at the prison had to add to his troubles by denying him his anti-rejection medication for twenty-nine days. Such gross and flagrant conduct forced Gabriel, after his time in the hospital, to be permanently on dialysis. Three times a week he had to be transported to a clinic outside the jail accompanied by armed guards.

As the months passed, I saw Gabriel's physical condition deteriorate to the point that I was revolted each time I even thought of visiting him. He had now lost so much weight, although he was extremely thin even before he went to prison, that I feared he would not be able to resist too much longer. I was aware of the tell-tale signs - his grey coloring, the puffy cheeks; he was retaining too much fluid despite the dialysis and this condition, were it to persist, could cause great damage to other organs of his body.

Gabriel's lawyer during the Appellate and later The Supreme Court hearings, was a young man of great integrity, Mr. Jesse Barton. A hardworking, forthright individual who believed in Gabriel's innocence and was committed to doing all in his power to obtaining his release.

A panel of 5 judges heard Mr. Barton's arguments on January 28, 1999. The atmosphere in the assembly hall of Wilsonville High School, contrary to our expectations, was anything but favorable to our case, we thought. The judges were stoic in demeanor and even hostile to some of Mr. Barton's remarks and arguments. I and those who were there to support Gabriel left the session deflated, depressed, and with a sense that things were not going well for Gabriel. There was nothing left for us to do but wait and pray.

On my knees at all hours of the day and night, I besought heaven on behalf of my sick son. How long more could he endure prison conditions? - difficult for those who are guilty but doubly so for the innocent. If the Supreme Court reversed the decision of the Appellate Court, then there was nothing left for us. The Federal Court could take years and that I knew Gabriel didn't have.

So I had brought my boy to the 'Land of the Free' only to have him die in prison because through the kindness of his heart he had stopped one evening to help a woman in distress. What kind of a country was I now living in, I asked myself - for a good deed a man is imprisoned and then the irony of the statement made me laugh. What had I done to deserve four years in the dungeons of Romania - exactly the same thing as Gabriel; I tried to help those less fortunate than myself.

I must try to contact Amnesty International again. We were known to the organization; perhaps I could get help from that quarter once more. I had heard that some of the prisons in the United States were, at the time, being investigated. Time, itself was running out for Gabriel. He was visibly becoming more frail and continually losing weight. I couldn't stand idly by and allow the incompetent medical personnel in the prison system to jeopardize his life. I was, by now, totally disillusioned. America, for all its idealistic notions, the propaganda regarding justice for all, equal treatment under the law, individual rights, was in my mind, no better than the Communist system, and the injustice from which I had fled when given the opportunity.

While awaiting the decision of the Supreme Court, Gabriel brought an action against the prison doctor for his neglect. The case was heard in a Salem court and the Judge presiding seemed concerned, but nothing came of it even though the doctor became enraged and stormed out of the court. Some, it seems, are more 'equal' than others when it comes to the rules and regulations of the Court.

In January after the Supreme Court hearing,which unanimously upheld the Appellate Court's decision stating that Gabriel did not have a fair trial and therefore should be given another, Mr. Jesse Barton wasted no time in securing Gabriel's release despite the protestations of the D.A. and the advice of our first lawyer. Great was our joy, indeed, when we were told the time and date that he would once more be a 'free' man. God had turned His Face to me and I sank to my knees in a prayer of Thanksgiving.

This tragic and devastating experience was a rude awakening for me. The idyllic world I had built for myself in the 'Land of the Free' evaporated and I began to observe and take note of what was really happening in America. I was reminded, as I became more observant, of the Roman Empire which had ruled the then known world for twelve centuries. Why did it fall? Of course I knew the theories from Augustine, Petrarch, Machiavelli to Gibbon - who have "defined the limits of all later interpretation: Rome fell because of inner weakness, either social or spiritual; or Rome fell because of outer pressure - the barbarian hordes. What we can say with confidence is that Rome fell gradually and that Romans for many decades scarcely noticed what was happening." Although America has not existed as a mighty power for a thousand years or even half that time, yet it has achieved a position of prosperity and affluence in the eyes of the modern world - considered the 'Land of Freedom'; the 'Land of Opportunity'; A 'Land of Peace and Justice for all'. People from every country under the sun have risked life and limb, left literally everything they had known to be a part of this magnificient adventure in Democracy - this Uthopia of the West. And for a time America seemed to be the answer to, first, Europe's oppressed and down-trodden and in later years to peoples of the Far East, Asia and Latin America and even the Black race of Africa whom it dispised for so long. But then the sixties came and with those troubled times, a change. Beginning with the education system - my wife, Louise, had been a teacher for thirty-five years and witnessed first-hand the rapid decline in academic standards; the collapse of moral and ethical codes; the neglect of the practice of civilities; lack of respect for staff and peers alike. Upon the spurious excuse that there, no longer, was enough money to support the arts, programs in art, music, and foreign language were eliminated from the curriculum. As a consequence the educators soon found that "the man who hath not music in himself, and is not moved with concord of sweet sounds, is fit for treason, stratagems, and spoils; let no man trust him." The schools were producing a generation of ill-mannered, ill-bred and unlettered ingrates whose only ambition was to quit the classroom as quickly as possible and join the herds of slaves working at whatever they could find that paid the most for doing nothing, or they would follow their parents and swell the ranks of those who lived on Welfare. So much for the equalizing and lowering of the standards to encompass all. Everyone was discontented - the teacher who could not teach what had been handed down for countless generations as being the finest of man's accomplishments and therefore stimulating to the impoverished minds and souls of the masses; the students - especially the brightest, for there was nothing of consequence to stimulate their active minds; those of lesser capabilities who were often times incapable of acquiring even the minimum despite the acrobatics of the instructors and the constant battle to hold their attention. Nothing was grasped by these students because they needed one to one attention and a curriculum tailored to their abilities. Is it any wonder, then, that the education field lost thousands of its best teachers, while those who might be drawn to enter the 'hallowed halls' of academia were early discouraged having witnessed what went on in the classrooms in general, as they were growing up.

Along with the decline in learning came the break-up of family life. Broken homes became the norm and this added to the lack of enthusiasm for learning on the part of the child. Even those parents who were relatively good parents, who unselfishly devoted themselves to the well-being of their children, could give them nothing in the way of a vision of a bright future; they were unable to hold up a model or hero for them to emulate. The standards of right and wrong, good and bad were no longer relevant and there was no compass to guide either the parents or the children when a fundamental religious education disappeared. Discipline among the youth became a major problem and now we have arrived at the sorry stage where the schools have to be patrolled by police.

"Never was there an art form directed so exclusively to children," thus has Allan Bloom spoken on the subject of music, rock music in modern America. He continues to deplore its existence saying: "it has one appeal only, a barbaric appeal, to sexual desire - not love, not eros, but sexual desire undeveloped and untutored. It acknowledges the first emanations of children's emerging sensuality and addresses them seriously electing them and legitimating them, not as little sprouts that must be carefully tended in order to grow into gorgeous flowers, but as the real thing. Rock gives children, on a silver platter, with all the public authority of the entertainment industry, everything their parents always used to tell them they had to wait for until they grew up and would understand later." Again he states: "Young people know that Rock has the beat of sexual intercourse. That is why Ravel's Bolero is the one piece of classical music that is commonly known and liked by them. In alliance with some real art and a lot of pseudo-art, an enormous industry cultivates the taste for the orgiastic state of feeling connected with sex, providing a constant flood of fresh material for voracious appetites."

Having quoted Mr. Bloom with whom I completely agree, I now venture to appeal to Plato who declared that "in order to take the spiritual temperature of an individual or a society, one must "mark the music." And to him, "the history of music is a series of attempts to give form and

360

beauty to the dark, chaotic, premonitory forms in the soul - to make them serve a higher purpose, an ideal, to give man's duties a fullness."

And again in the words of Allan Bloom: "Bach's religious intentions and Beethoven's revolutionary and humane ones are clear enough examples. Such cultivation of the soul uses the passions and satisfies them while sublimating them and giving them an artistic unity. A man whose noblest activities are accompanied by a music that expresses them while providing a pleasure extending from the lowest bodily to the highest spiritual, is whole, and there is no tension in him between the pleasant and the good. By contrast a man whose business-life is prosaic and unmusical and whose leisure is made up of course, intense entertainments, is divided, and each side of his existence is undermined by the other."

Professor Bloom concludes his remarks on Rock music by saying that his concern is not with the moral effects of this music - "whether it leads to sex, violence or drugs. The issue is its effects on education, and I believe it ruins the imagination of young people and makes it very difficult for them to have a passionate relationship to the art and thought that are the substance of liberal education. The first sensuous experiences are decisive in determining the taste for the whole of life, and they are the link between the animal and spiritual in us. The period of nascent sensuality has always been used for sublimation, in the sense of making sublime, for attaching youthful inclinations and longings to music, pictures and stories that provide the transition of the fulfillment of the human duties and the enjoyment of the human pleasures." Lessing, speaking of Greek sculpture, said "beautiful men made beautiful statues and the city had beautiful statues in part to thank for beautiful citizens." This formula encapsulates the fundamental principle of the esthetic education of man.

"Young men and women were attracted by the beauty of heroes whose very bodies expressed their nobility."

As I further studied and analysed the environment and the 'culture' which had by circumstances and desire become my home and that of my sons, I could not condemn but only pity those who, for all their material wealth and affluence, were so poor in their spiritual values. With Christ I prayed "Father forgive them for they know not what they do."

For I considered what had happened to Gabriel to be the result of a lack of sensitivity on the part of the jurors - a hardening of heart, so to speak - which clouded their minds to the very possibility that someone might be motivated by kindness rather than illicit pleasure or evil intent, and wish to render a service to a human being in distress rather than take advantage of another's weakness.

I, therefore, concluded that this Orwellian concept which obviously had become part of the American psyche - permitting goodness and generosity to be punished by long prison terms, placing men of integrity and unblemished character behind bars, while the unscrupulous and hardened criminals walk the streets, surely heralded the demise of America as a nation.

Chapter 24

Exonerated!   Vindicated!

How then when upspringing passion,
Wild emotions in one rise,
How should one find sober judgement?
How retain impassive eyes?
Ah, one feels that then in thunder
Round one's head the heavens roll;
How should man find true expression
To describe his teeming soul?
Critic, you of sterile blossom,
Where's the fire that in you stirred?
It is easy to write verses
Out of nothing but the word.

Mihai Eminescu
- My Critics

After Gabriel's release from prison in January '99, my only thought was to devote myself to rebuilding his physical strength and moral courage. He had fought a brave fight and had won despite all odds.

Of course, I hoped that the whole wretched affair might now be cleared up and that he would not have to go through the ordeal of another trial. But, even if such a thing were to happen, my old optimism had returned and I felt sure that Gabriel would be exonerated in a new court, a new judge, a new jury.

We took him to dialysis three times a week and slowly but surely with good food, fresh air and pleasant surroundings, I began to see an improvement in his physical appearance. Gabriel's spirits, outwardly at least, always seemed to soar. He had learned to rely solely on God and to eliminate all negative thoughts from his brain. I marvelled at his fortitude and strength of will.

Life for me assumed a more relaxed pace. I could now tend to the things I liked - my bees, my writing, my garden. Spring came into our garden and painted it in a variety of vivid colors. The air was sweet and soft and the sunbeams danced on the dew in the grass and the cascading waterfall. Gabriel was happy. "This is heaven," he said, as he sat on the deck in the warm sunshine. He enjoyed the birds as they splashed and preened in the stream outside our back door; he watched them build their nests and marvelled at the beauty of the fir trees. Everything was alive and wondrous to behold. Surely, it was a beautiful world in which to live.

In May, upon the insistence of Louise, I again paid a visit home. My mother was in good health and overjoyed to see me. However, I did note quite a change in her. She had slowed down considerably - unable to move as easily as she had been two years before. But her brain was active and as sharp as ever, fully aware of all that was going on and eager to have her opinion heard. We had a wonderful visit.

Having spent time with other family members and friends, I left with a happy heart, hoping to return with Louise the following spring. But God had other plans.

Upon my return home, summer had come; Gabriel was looking well. The warm weather and the beauty of our garden had done wonders for him. It was to be a time of special bounty and graciousness for everyone. The bees gave abundantly this year and my vegetable garden produced more than I could possibly use. Autumn brought long lazy days, warm and sun-filled and decided to stay right into November.

Gabriel's spirit took flight and he poured forth his joy of living and life in general in a new book of poems entitled: *Lands beyond the Forest*. I like to think that some of these poems were inspired by the many replicas of Brancusi I have erected in our garden.

When I married Louise our beautiful garden needed some TLC (tender loving care). While pruning, clipping, and edging, creating new paths and flower beds, I had the bright idea that a section might be devoted to a display of Romanian works of art. This would serve two purposes: one, to create a familiar environment for myself - a little home away from home, and secondly, a repository of Romanian art in Tigard where such works were unknown. Thus began my collection of Brancusi treasures which I lovingly brought back from Romania each time I visited my native land. They are all carved from wood and against the backdrop of fir trees, shrubs, and flowers have found a home, I'm sure, the great man would have approved.

The Romanian sculptor, Constantin Brancusi (1876 - 1957) was born in Pestisani in the province of Oltenia. In his childhood and youth he was a shepherd and it was this experience, perhaps more than any other factor in his life that influenced his art.

To the west of his small hamlet lay the Carpathian Mountains and the Danube; while in the east, his beloved Jiu, the river which played such an important part in his life. His birthplace was an obscure village where the local people were uneducated but steeped in the traditions and folklore that dated back to prehistoric times. It was a land of vast forests and abundant orchards and vineyards.

Brancusi grew up "in a remarkably harmonious cultural environment, and according to all appearances, it affected him deeply. When he was a child, modern times had not yet caught up with Wallachia, a region at the foot of the southern Carpathian Mountains where folk traditions had remained firmly entrenched for a thousand years." [19]

Before my brief discussion of Brancusi's contribution to the world of sculpture, I would like to quote a few lines from Mr. Hulten's introduction to the book entitled *Brancusi*.

"A work of sculpture was an object of a very special kind, according to the belief generally held at the beginning of the century. It still is, but meanwhile the context of that perception has changed considerably. Serious efforts have been made to establish what it is that sets sculpture apart, and during the process sculpture itself has changed. Clearly, Constantin Brancusi belonged to the heart of the struggle to clarify and redefine attitudes toward art, a struggle that transcends aesthetics as a momentous effort is apt to do in any field of endeavor. When a work of sculpture is of the representational sort, its distinguishing features are, in some respects, fairly easy to pinpoint. It is an object fashioned from one or more materials in such a way that it resembles some other three-dimensional forms. During the four centuries of the Renaissance tradition in Europe, the great majority of sculptures were objects representing the human figure. The key word in our discussion thus far is object: a work of sculpture is an object apart, isolated by its singularity, its difference from other objects, but it is still an object like any other, and its difference rests on a long succession of set ideas and cultural norms, some of them worn quite thin by the early twentieth century.

"Brancusi, with his visceral need for truth, started very early in his artistic development to probe the reality and truth of the sculptural work as a singular object. Central to the Renaissance tradition is the concept that sculpture should be isolated from its surroundings, and the base or pedestal served to obtain this isolation, just as a frame 'sets

366

off' a painting. At the outset of his career, Brancusi found his principal difficulty in the fact that a sculpture was an object as well.

"Parenthetically, this problem, which at the time was a general aesthetic dilemma, seems to have elicited the strongest reaction from artists reared within the cultural context of Eastern Orthodox worship. The special status accorded to icons in their religious milieu must have been a contributing factor. At any rate, it is stricking that such Eastern European artists as Brancusi, Malevich, and Tatlin fueled some of the most heated controveries about the problem of the aesthetic object, and devised the most radical solutions.

"A sculpture is a man-made object which must in one way or another stand out, and convey inescapable, emotional power. Once this assumption has been made, the traditional line of reasoning, that this object has special status because it represents something, begins to look timeworn. Brancusi defined sculpture as an object, then he concerned himself specifically with aspects other than representation. Early in his career, especially, when he lived in Bucharest, Brancusi's quest was rather a solitary one, but in Paris he met an entire generation of artists absorbed by the same issues, and came to know well the most doggedly innovative of the young French artists, Marcel Duchamp. Given the sharp differences in their upbringing and education, Brancusi and Duchamp did not arrive at the same conclusions. Duchamp ended up with 'ready-mades,' proclaiming that any man-made object could be considered a work of art if one so decided. Brancusi, whose past was in peasant traditions, took an unacademic approach to truth and decided that the strength of a work of sculpture must come from the form, from the configuration of the object itself."

The contribution of Brancusi to the world of art and sculpture, in particular, evolved and "came to fruition in a series of works in the form of heads, the *Newborn* series. The head was the most emotionally charged form imaginable, for within it lies that mysterious electrochemical apparatus known as the brain. And the head of a newborn child, like the egg, so fragile, yet the guardian of life, corresponded exactly to the idea of an object having a high-powered impact."

Mr. Hulten continues to explain: "Does this make the Newborn sculptures representations of heads? Not really. In any event, what matters far more is that from various materials the sculptor made objects whose outward forms contains an inner force, in this case the brain. Form is the materialization of meaning or content, in this case the most potent of messages, the life force itself.

"With one majestic gesture, and within a very brief time, Brancusi had brought sculpture into a golden age, turning an object into a sculpture by investing it with existential power. It could be said that Brancusi's sculptures had become sacred objects, but they are not connected with any religion. From the beginning, once they were made they rested on no cultural conventions or guidelines, they made themselves felt through their intrinsic strength, with no literary or religious explanations or other sorts of embellishment. The existential force had to radiate from the form of the objects as plainly as light radiates from the sun. They had to be man-made objects that summed up human power."

Brancusi's influence on American art was significant especially in the 1960's and 1970's. This was to be seen in a number of ways. "For Claes Oldenburg, Brancusi's sculptures served as a source of inspiration in both form and content, and in ways varied and complex. Oldenburg's *Colossal Clothespin* (1972) is a reference to the formal relations of Brancusi's *The Kiss*, as Friedrich Teja Bach has noted; with extensive reworking, Oldenburg transformed Brancusi's pair of human lovers into a world, a realm where objects have a mysterious power to affect us and ultimately become recognizable as part of the generally enigmatic world that is our daily environment."

My insertion of the name Brancusi and the brief account of some of his work in this chapter of my book are merely to whet the appetite for a more profound study of the great man, not only by those who love art but by those who value knowledge.

My collection to date includes: *The Kiss, The First Cry, Yellow Bird* (Bird in Space), *Mademoiselle Pogany I, Narcissus fountain, Maiastra, Little French Girl, Endless Column, Princess X, Adam and Eve.*

* * * * *

On Friday, the 22nd October, 1999, I had a call from Romania with the news that my beloved mother had died suddenly the day before. The funeral services were arranged for Saturday. It was impossible for me to attend. There was no doubt in my mind or anyone else's in the family, but that she had gone straight to heaven.

"She's a saint if every there was one," were Louise's words.

Mother...

- Mihai Eminescu

O mother, darling mother, lost in time's formless haze
Amidst the leaves' sweet rustle you call my name always;
Amidst their fluttering murmur above your sacred grave
I hear you softly whisper where'er the branches wave;
While o'er your tomb the willows their autumn raiment
heap...
For ever wave the branches, and you for ever sleep.

On Friday Oct. 29, we were awakened by a phone call from O.H.S.U. (Oregon Health Science University). There was a kidney available and Gabriel should report right away.

By 1:00 p.m. Gabriel's tests showed that he was a good match and by 1:30 p.m. he was prepared for the operation. Four hours later he was in the Intensive Care unit with a new kidney which started to function almost immediately.

"Incredible!" I cried. "My God! how marvelous are the works of your hands." I was overcome with gratitude and emotion. Gabriel had received a second chance to live a normal life. I thought of my mother and knew she had a hand in this miracle.

The following days were critical but although he had his ups and downs, by and large his body adjusted well to his new kidney. The great gift has given him a whole new outlook as well - he's free to come and go as he likes; he wishes to return to school and complete his degree. And, as if all this weren't enough, he and Shelly have set the date for their wedding - January 8, 2000!

On December 19, I had a call from Bucharest. My friend, Aurel Iancu, was happy to tell me that, after 20 years, my Doctoral Dissertation had been reviewed and approved by the Minister of National Education, Bucharest. But even at this late date, there would be difficulties. My records had been destroyed. Nobody knew what had happened to all the academic files I had accumulated during the fifteen years hard work in the universities of Romania.

Eventually, after much deliberation, many long-distance phone calls and letters, it was decided that since there were several professors still teaching at the university who had known me as a candidate for the Doctoral Degree, a new set of documents would be compiled based on the original copy of my Dissertation and my published works over the years.

At this juncture, I would like to avail of the opportunity to sincerely thank Doctor Constantin Ionete, Director General of the National Institute of Economic Research and honorary member of the Romanian Academy of Bucharest as well as the other members of the examining board for all they have done to rectify the injustice done me twenty years ago.

Finally, I will receive my doctorate in Economics!

On January 5th 2000, I left for Bucharest a very happy man, indeed. My spirit soared; despite the long ordeal, and the persistent and cruel attempts of the Communist government of Ceausescu, I had the satisfaction of being the victor in the end.

"Nothing comes to pass but what God appoints. - Our fate is decreed, and things do not happen by chance, but every man's portion of joy or sorrow is predetermined." - Senecca

I arrived in the city of Bucharest to find the country was preparing frantically to celebrate the 150th anniversary of the poet, Mihai Eminescu's birth. This celebration would occur on January 15. I wept tears of joy - finally one of Romania's greatest treasures was receiving the recognition he deserved. The light of a new day was dawning in my beloved land - there was hope for the future of Romania! Perhaps now the truth would be told. Romania was not a backward uncultured nation whom the Russians sought to enlighten, but a country which had endured for several thousand years and was once "the vastest and most powerful empire in human history."

Chapter 25

God holds the Reins

Be stirring as the time, be fire with fire, threaten
the threatener, and outface the brow of bragging horror;
so shall inferior eyes, that borrow their behaviors from
the great, grow great by your example and put on the
dauntless spirit of resolution.

- Shakespeare

I have lived seventy years - a life of struggle, frustration, and continuous striving against what seemed, at times, insurmountable odds. Yet, I can say with all honesty that I never wavered in my quest for the truth. With God as my strength, I knew I would emerge victorious, that I would somehow achieve all my goals and that my spirit, guided by Him, would overcome all obstacles.

I set out to tell my story, the first part set against the backdrop of a Communist regime, while the latter part was and is being played out in the shadow of 'Lady Liberty'. My role on the stage of life has been a privileged one enabling me, despite my many obligations, to contemplate, at length, the Divine workings in the human spirit in a multitude of diverse ways.

In the Romanian dungeons of the Communist era, I lived side by side with the most heroic of human beings. Men, who despite their sick, tormented, dying bodies, and in the face of unspeakable tortures, cruelty, and starvation, never faltered in their faith, but trusted implicidly in God and their perception of what God meant - Truth, nobility, decency, all the higher attributes of the soul.

373

To these men and the hundreds of thousands like them, whom I never encountered, but who, nevertheless, endured equal oppression and cruelty, I pledged my word, that, were I to survive the 'Ordeals' of Jlava, Aiud, and Alba Iulia, I would, one day, tell the truth to the world. Men like Monsignor Ghica, General Arbore, Doctor Balmus, Cisek Oscar Luca, Ovidiu Cotrus, Professor Tudor Popescu and the Orthodox priest Ion Nichita incomparable individuals of the highest moral rectitude, intellectually gifted, educated in the best schools of Europe, refined, dignified, and culturally superior to any I've met since, though I've lived and worked in many parts of the world. All these men, without exception, gave up their immortal souls in the filth and degradation of those foul smelling 'grave yards' for one ideal, and one alone, - Truth.

In 1989, I was honored to meet the former Ambassador to Romania, Mr. David Funderburg - a man of integrity, courageous, and sophisticated. And, I might add, the only man who understood the subterfuge, intrigue, and cunning of Mr. Ceausescu. How did it happen that no one else in the State Department had his insight? How did it happen that no one cared to listen to him while he was in residence in Bucharest and was intelligent enough to know exactly what was going on in that capital? I can only conclude that it was not 'feasible,' not in the interest of America, at that time, to listen to this highly-principled man or to follow his advice. Eventually, Mr. Funderburg resigned his post and took that occasion and opportunity to speak his mind regarding the position of the U.S. toward the Romania of Mr. Ceaucescu. He quoted the words of a colleague who had been a former administrative officer at the embassy and who "had subsequently served in Manila, and periodically throughout mainland China as an inspector of the new consulates, saying - 'Conditions in Romania were worse than in the Soviet Union, China, and the Philippines.' From the perspective of the Foreign Service, he said 'that Romania should have the higher post differential as a hardship post of those countries mentioned.'" But, Mr. Funderburg continued: "The depressing stories from Romanians, the hardships of everyday life, the sadness and pessimism, all combined to make it grueling. Perhaps most disheartening, however, was the State Department policy which seemed to help perpetuate the misery. The regime in Bucharest remained the chief beneficiary of the U.S. policy."

Other remarks by the former Ambassador include: "One aspect of relief in departing (Romania) was to leave behind the polluted air in Bucharest and the generally unhealthful atmosphere. In my own case there was evidence of the embassy being radiated by waves sent out by the Romanians to several offices in the embassy complex... I did not mind leaving behind the tapped telephones, the electronic surveillance in hotels, restaurants, apartments, the semi-armored limousine chauffered by a Romanian driver who worked for the Securitate, and the official residence surrounded by walls and guarded twenty-four hours a day by Romanian soldiers carrying Russian machine guns."

From the lips of an educated and well-respected American these words give an eye-witness account of how successful the Roosevelt experiment in Communism for the Romanian people worked.

Why the United States, in the person of Mr. Franklin D. Roosevelt ever allowed Stalin to take over half of Europe when they met for discussions at Yalta, no one will ever know the true answer. But, it has been said that he did so as an experiment.

How would the more sophisticated people outside the Soviet Union adapt to such a system–to Communism?

But, I have often asked myself, to what purpose this experiment? Had Western man, in the person of Mr.

Roosevelt forgotten the age old principle that "the social order will only be stable and productive when it takes into consideration the personal interest and the interest of society as a whole. In fact, self-interest violently suppressed, is replaced by a loathsome system of bureaucratic or even dictatorial control which stamps out initiative and creativity in the human soul. When people think they possess the secret of a perfect social organization which makes evil impossible, they also think that they can use any means, including violence and deceit, in order to bring that organization into being. Politics then becomes a "secular religion" which operates under the illusion of creating paradise in this world. But no political society - which possesses its own autonomy and laws - can ever be confused with the kingdom of God." (Chapter 3 of Pope John Paul II's Encylical "Centisimus Annus.")

This is precisely what happened in Romania as a result of the Great Communist Experiment and today 50 years later, the Romanian people still suffer from these effects.

Like Martin Luther King, I also have a dream, a dream that one day my beloved country will take her place among the nations of the earth proud and prosperous. This can be accomplished by Romania's sons and daughters, if given the freedom to use their intelligence and initiative in a free and open market economy. That is the primary reason why Romania must be allowed to join the European Common Market as quickly as possible.

I have criticized the Communist regime of the East as well as the Materialist system of the West. We have all witnessed the demise of the former and the decline of the national standards in education, and morals in the West. However, the United States, I feel, being a young country and powerful, will by the force of its Spirit of independence and each individual's freedom of choice rectify, in time, these flaws in its character. With its stable economy, in which every man and woman has the security of a job and the assurance of a decent wage, thus affording a high standard of living conditions for the vast majority of its citizens, there will never be reason for revolt. America is undoubtedly, the strongest and most powerful nation in the world today and it will remain so as long as its people are free independent thinking human beings. This, alone, is America's strength and for this I'm grateful to be in this great country, despite its many faults.

For my native Romania, land of rivers, forests, lofty mountains, and fertile plains; land of music, poetry, and dance; land of an old and proud people, I wish only the best. I will not rest quietly in this life until I see my beautiful native country prosper and be counted among the independent states of a united Europe. To this end, do I devote my pen and my thoughts. Nor will I forget the promises I made to my companions in suffering, the dead heroes of the Communist prisons. I will continue to tell the Truth; I seek only the Truth. For, well, I know the Soviet bloc countries had their own rules for writing and rewriting history. That, I had learned, firsthand in the University of Bucharest in 1948-52 and has been attested to by many powerful and well-known personalities since. For example, we learn from the writings of Lieutenant General Ion Pacepa that in order to induce the Romanian born, Dr. George Palade, director of a microbiology institute in America and Nobel prize winner, to become a DIE member, Elena Ceausescu created a fictitious illegitimate child for him. This supposed fruit was the result of a love affair he had before his marriage, while he was a medical student in Romania. The invented son was registered in all the necessary public records and then given the identity of an illegal intelligence officer who had good credentials as an engineer. In order to force Palade to do their bidding, the Ceausescu's would, without any compunction, set up "a complicated operation to have Palade 'discover' his 'son,' who would be the illegal officer. The DIE was confident that the 'son's' romantic story and early photographs of his 'father,' together with his personal charm and professional competence, would induce Palade, once in contact with him, to do everything he could to get the 'son' an exit visa from Romania. Ceausescu had long since prepared himself for the meeting with Palade at which he would generously agree to this act of clemency."

I had long ago made up my mind, when given the opportunity, that I would, come what may, tell the Truth about Communist Romania. To this end, I have pledged my time and talents. I seek only that the Truth be known not only to the Romanian people but to the American, and all peoples of the world. The atrocities committed; the crimes and injustices perpetrated on innocent millions; the corruption, theft, bribery, and slavish exploitation that was the Communist regime must never again be tolerated in any part of the globe.

To my fellow countrymen I say:

"Let our objective be our country, our whole country, and nothing but our country. And, by the blessing of God, may that country itself become a vast and splendid monument not of oppression and terror, but of wisdom, of peace, and of liberty, upon which the world may gaze with admiration forever."

I quote the above words of Mr. Daniel Webster and would make them my own, for they portray more clearly than I can myself, the sincere, passionate love I have for my beloved land, Romania and all it once stood for. The long history of an independent spirit, the traditions, the customs, the music and poetry that distinguished it from all other countries of Europe and the world must be stimulated and preserved. For this generations of brave men and women have given their lives and endured countless years in the 'hell' holes beneath the earth, in the mines, and the Delta swamps.

"From deep within Rovine Vale,
O lady fair, we bid you hail,
Alas, by letter not by speech,
By sundering distance out of reach.
Yet am I fain to beg of thee
To send by messenger to me
What in your Valley fairest be:
The forest with its silver glade,
Thy eyes that long, curl'd lashes shade.
And I in turn will send to you
The proudest thing that here we view:
This mighty host with banner spread,
The forest, branching overhead,
My helmet with it feathery crest,
My eyes that 'neath their lashes rest.
I have both health and resting place,
Thanks be to Christ and to God's grace,
And now, dear love, I thee embrace."

Mihai Eminescu
Letter III

Michael & Gabriel
Portland, OR 1999

Louise, Rodica (friend) and Teodore, 1997

*Teodor &
Louise,
Portland,
1999*

*Gabriel &
Shelly
Portland,
2000*

*Michael &
Carmen,
Portland,
1998*

Footnotes

[1] Alecsandri, Vasile. Poezii. Bucuresti: Editura Ion Creanga 1985, pg. 222.

[2] Iacobescu, Mihai. Din Istoria Bucovinei. Bucuresti: Editura Academiei Romane, 1993, pg. 14.

[3] Eminescu, Mihai. Opere Complete. Iasi: 1914, pg. 62.

[4] Petrovici, Ion. Raite prin tara. Bucuresti: 1944, p. 107; Iacobescu, Mihai. Din istoria Bucovinei. Bucuresti: Editura Academiei Romane, 1993, pg. 11-21; 49-91; 93-304.

[5] Lupan, Nicolae. Instantanee fara Retus. Bucuresti: Editura Nistru Bruxelles 1995, pg. 230.

[6] Moisescu, C. Musicescu, M.A. Sirli, A.: Putna. Bucuresti: Meridiane Editura, 1982, pg. 66.

[7] Romanie - Eglises peintes de la Moldavie, UNESCO, New York, Paris, 1962, pg. 5.

[8] Dragut, Vasile. Romania, Pages of History. Bucharesti: 1987, pg. 250 - 255.

[9] Iacobescu, Mihai. Din Istoria Bucovinei. Bucuresti: Editura Academiei Romane 1993, pg. 274-284.

[10] During the rule of the Emperor Fanz Joseph II, these occupying peoples were allowed to live tax free and were relieved of military service for 50 years.

[11] Antonescu, Ion. Romanii. Bucuresti: Eclio, Editura. 1990, pg. 75.

[12] Idem, pg. 79.

[13] Eminescu, Mihai. Poems. English translation by Corneliu M. Popescu. Bucharesti: Editura Cartea Romaneasca 1989, pg. 117-118. This poem is censored in Northern Bucovina and Bassarabia to this day.

[14] Ion, Beldeanu. Bucovina care ne doare, Ed. Junimea. 1996, pg. 26-29.

[15] Ion, Beldeanu. Bucovina care ne doare, Editura Junimea. 1996, pg. 84-111, 1996.

[16] Ronnett, Alexander. Neam fara Noroc. Chicago: Centrul Cultural Roman. 1994, pg. 13.

[17] Ibid - Our Blameless Dead, pg. 124-127.

[18] Sgvanci, Stella, Camilian Demetrescu, Questo arderte desiderio del vero, Tema Editrice, 1988. Pg. 1.

[19] Hulten, Pontus. Brancusi. New York: Harry N. Abrams. Pg. 44, 1987.

Acknowledgement

Man supposes that he directs his life and governs
his actions, when his existence is irretrievably
under the
control of destiny.

-Goethe

I cannot close these the final pages of my book, without
a word for my beloved wife, Louise, without whom this
work would have been impossible. To her, I owe the best
and happiest years of my life. She literally plucked me
from an existence where my days were long and filled with
back-breaking toil only to gain a marginal standard of
living. I was unable to find a position in my field of
expertise because of my age and inadequate English skills.
She gave me everything! A beautiful home, a magnificient
garden, and a retirement in comfortable surroundings. I
can, henceforth, pursue my life-long interests - writing,
reading, and looking after my bees. For this and for all she
has done for me and my two sons, I'm eternally grateful.

I have spoken before of my great love for her. I never
cease to marvel at how completely suited we are to each
other. Despite the fact that she was born and raised in
western Europe, and I in the far-away corner of eastern
Romania, we both have the same respect and love for the
higher things of this life - music, art, books, and the
refinements of a culture we feel is of the past.

We are both occupied every hour of the day and sometimes the night. In fact, the days are not long enough to accomplish all we wish to do. I pray God will give us many years of health to fulfill the objectives we have set for ourselves. Louise has, at least three more books in mind and I have four.

The woods are lovely dark and deep
But I have promises to keep
And miles to go before I sleep
And miles to go before I sleep.
- Robert Frost

Published Works;
by
Teodor Gherasim M.Sc. Ph.D.

The following articles and books have been published in
Romania

1. Organizarea interioara a supermagazinului-Revista Comertul modern
   nr. 2/1968.

   Teodor Gherasim

2. Calcularea suprafetelor optime de expunere a marfurilor in
   supermagazine, Rivista Viata Economica nr. 43/1968.

   Teodor Gherasim

3. Studiu privind criterii de expunere si etalare si metode practice de
   determinare a suprafetelor ocupate cu marfuri in supermagazine-
   Editura Ministerului Comertului Interior, Bucuresti, 1968.

   Alfiri Gheorghe si Teodor Gherasim

4. Aspecte organizatorice ale Comertului din tarile socialiste. Editura
   Ministerului Comertului Interior, Bucuresti, 1968.

   Radu Paul si Teodor Gherasim

5. Organizarea activitatii de conducere a intrepriderilor. Revista
   Evidenta Contabila
   nr. 3/1969.

   Teodor Gherasim

6. Teoria Preturilor. Melode de modelare. Editura Academiei Romane,
   Bucuresti, 1970.

   A. Iancu si T.M. Gherasim

7. Modelarea tipurilor principale de preturi. Revista Finante si Credit
   nr. 11/1970.

   T.M. Gherasim

8. Modelarea tipurilor derivate de preturi. Revista Finante si Credit nr.
   12/1970.

   T.M. Gherasim

9. Corelarea preturilor cu ridicata la nivelul intreprinderilor si
   ramurilor, in cadrul BLR. Editura INID. Bucuresti, 1971.

   T.M. Gerasim

10. Prognoza si planificarea pe termen lung in activitateav de conducere a intreprinderirilor. Editura INID, Bucuresti, 1971.

ing. T.M. Gherasim ec. D. Cigusievici

11. Metode de fundamentare a preturilor prin parametrii tehnico-economici. Editura INID, Bucuresti, 1972.

T.M. Gherasim

12. Interdependenta, progresul tehnic si conducerea de perspectiva a intreprinderilor. Editura INID, Bucuresti, 1972.

T.M. Gherasim ec. D.Cigusievici

13. Factorii de influenta in previziunea preturilor. Editura Academiei RSR. Articol in volumul: Eficienta si cresterea economica. Bucuresti, 1972.

T.M.Gherasim

14. Probleme ale previzionarii preturilor. Editura Academiei RSR. Bucuresti, 1972.

T. Gherasim, Gh. Mosanu, C. Mihai, I. Marinescu s.a.

15. Productia mondiala de otel la scara deceniilor viitoare. Revista Viata Economica nr. 9/ 1973.

T.M. Gherasim

16. Metode de previziune tehnologica cu aplicabilitate la prognza nevoielor de energie in Romania. Editura INID, Bucuresti, 1973.

T.M. Gherasim

17. Prognoza costurilor de productie la oteluri. Editura Academiei RSR. Capitol in Biblioteca Economica, Bucuresti, 1976.

T.M. Gherasim

18. Prognoza productiei mondiale de otel (I). Principalele trasaturi ale actualei productii mondiale de otel. Revista Metalurgia nr. 4/1978.

Paul Petrescu, Gh. Varzan, T. Gherasim

19. Prognoza productiei mondiale de otel (II), Revista Mealurgica nr 5/1978.

Paul Petrescu, Gh. Varzan, T. Gherisim

20. Analiza valorii-o metoda moderna de conducere si crestere a eficientei economice a productiei. Revista Forum nr. 3/1979.

Paul Petrescu, Teodor Gherasim

21. Pentru o dezvoltare echilibrata a productiei de otel. Revista economica nr. 8/1978.

T.M. Gherasim

22. Aplicarea nomogramei in calculele consumului de energie in metalurgie. Revista de statistica nr. 1/1980.

Paul Petrescu si Teodor Gherasim

24. Aspecte energetice si ecomonice ale utilizarii peletelor prereduse in furnal. Revista metalurgica nr. 12/1980.

T.M. Gherasim

25. Aspecte energetice ale ansamblului furnale suflante. Revista metalurgica nr 8/1980.

Paul Petrescu si Teodor Gherasim

26. Prognoza industriei otelului. Editura Academiei RSR. Capitol in :Economia Mondiala orizont 2000, Bucuresti, 1980.

P. Petrescu si ing. T. Gherasim

27. Progresul tehnic si costurile de productie in metalurgie. Revista Tevi si trefilate nr. 2 din 1983.

T. Ghersasim

28. Prognoza productiei de otel pe plan mondial si in tara noastra. Revista Tevi si trefilate nr 3/1983.

T. Gherasim

29. Prognoza costurilor de productie la fonte, oteluri si tevi din otel. Revista Tevi si trefilate nr. 4/1983

30. Procedee moderne de fabricarea tevilor cu eficienta economica ridicata. Ed. Centrului de Perfectionare din Min. Metalurgiei, Bucuresti,

I. Moldovan si ing. T. Gherasim

31. Progresul tehnic si costurile in metalurgie. (teza de doctorat). Conducator stiintific Ion Rachmuth. Membru al Academiei Romane, Buc/ 1983.

Teodor Mardare Gherasim

The following articles and books have been published in Italy and America.

32. C'E un nuovo Ospedale che non ha muri, In Sabato 13-19 april 1985, p.11.

    Teodor Gherasim, Emilio Ronzoni

33. Transplant reusit la Milano. Revista Biserica Romaneasca. Publicationi Culturale dela Comunita Ortodossa Romena in Italia. Nr. 35/ian-mart./1985 p. 40.

    drd.ing.Teodor Gherasim

34. Romanian's fight ongoing in Portland (series). In the Oregonian, Aug.- Oct. /1987.

    Spenzer Heintz - Teodor Gherasim

35. The Art of Camilian Demetrescu, romanian Exil and the Paradox of the XXth Century, Simthsonian Muzeum, N.Y. 1988, p. 18.

    Teodor Gherasim

36. Bisericuta din livezi. In Rev. Bis. Ortodoxe Sf. Maria din Portland. Nr. 1/1991 p. 4

    Teodor Gherasim

37. Jurnalul intalnirii dela Gallese (serie). In ziarui Cuvantul Romanesc din Canada. Oct.- Dec. /1993; p. 9

    Teodor Gherasim

38. Sa cunoastem tinerele talente romanesti din Portland. In Columna/martie 1994. p. 1-2.

    Teodor Gherasim

39. Unirea Principatelor Romane. In Cuvantul Romanesc Canada. Ian. 1995, p. 16.

    Teodor Gherasim

40. Ucraina si Romania. In Columna/ april 1997, p. 16.

    drd.ing.Teodor Gherasim

41. In granitele ciuntite ale tarii (serie). In Nord press/mai-iunie-iulie/ 1995, p. 1-2.

    drd.ing.Teodor Gherasim

42. Arta trebuie sa fie ca un deget care-l arata pe Dumnezeu. Interviu cu artistul Alex.Costiuc in Luceafarul Romanesc, Canada, X. 1996, p. 17.

drd.ing.Teodor Gherasim

43. Sarbatoare la Kelowna. In Columna/ III. 1997, p. 2.

Teodor M. Gherasim

44. Dupa Insula Serpilor urmeaza Marea Neagra cu Axul Dunarii. In "America" (serie) /VIII/1997 p. 2, 4, 5.

Teodor M. Gherasim Ion Dumitreasa

45. Comunitatea Romana din Oregon. In Luceafarul Romanesc, Canada, /V. 1997. p. 14.

Teodor M. Gherasim

46. Obiceiuri romanesti de Craciun. In Origini/ XI-XII/1997, p. 3.

Teodor Gherasim

47. Un tratat rusinos. In Romanian Roots, /VII-VIII/din. 1997, p. 2.

Teodor Gherasim

48. Restaurantul Transilvania din Portland. In Columna/III/1997, p. 11.

Teodor Gherasim

49. Studiul de caz: Franklin Delano Roesevelt. In Romanian Roots. /V-VI. 1997, p. .

Teodor Gherasim

50. The Rights of Romanian Nation to The Northern Bucovina. In America-Chicago, p. 107-119/1997.

Teodor Gherasim & Louise Gherasim

51. Drepturile Natiunii Romane asupra Bucovinei de Nord. In Merdianul Romanesc, California, (serie) din 1.V.-8.V.-16.V. 1998.

Teodor Gherasim & Louise Gherasim

52. Perspectiva Unirii la Romani prin prisma generatiilor succesoare de la 1848. In Meridianul Romanesc, California./1an. 1998, p. 19.

Teodor Gherasim

53. De la Ana la Caiafa si asa mai departe!. In Meridianul Romanesc. /dec. 1998, p. 12.

Teodor Gherasim

54. Scrioare deschisa pentru Prim-ministru Radu Vasile Romanian Roots, Georgia, sep.-oct. 1998.

Teodor Gherasim

55. Timisoara Capitala Euroei de Sud-Est. In Origini/ XI-XII. 1998, p. 4.

Teodor Gherasim

56. Comunitatea Romaneasca din Portland a primit vizita Consulului General din Los Angeles (serie) In Meridianul Romanesc din California. /dec./1998.

Teodor Gherasim

57. Destin. In Meridianul Romanesc/ sep. 1998, p. 15.

Teodor Gherasim

58. Din rau in mai rau. In Origini/mai-lunie/1998, p. 9.

Teodor Gherasim

59. Interviu cu SS Pimen arhiepiscop al Sucevii si Radautilor. In Luceafarul Romanesc. Canada./martie 1998, p. 24.

Teodor Gherasim

60. Brancusi in America. In Origini/martie-april/ 1998, p. 16.

Teodor Gherasim

61. Camilian Demetrescu-portretul artistului exilat In Origini/iul-aug. 1998, p. 20.

Teodor Gherasim

62. Astride two Worlds. Carte autobiografica in lb. engleza. 400 p. In Criterion Publishing, Georgia/ iunie/ 1999.

Teodor Gherasim

63. Studiul de caz: Winston Churchill. In Romanian Roots./ian.-feb./ 1999, p. 22-23.

Teodor Gherasim

64, Dezvoltarea industriala a Romaniei in perioado interbelica. In Origini, /martie-aprilie 1999.

Teodor M. Gherasim

Books Publushed by Louise Gherasim

Magheen

In Endless Strife

Finola

With Proud Resolve

I'll Always Miss You

Hawaiian Holiday

For Young Readers

Domnica (Romanian & English)

Born to be Great

Grainne

Escape from Romania
(Romanian and English)
(First prize - Constantin Badersca
Literary Award, 1999 Romania)

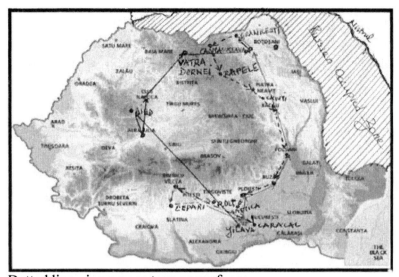

Dotted line - journey as teen-age refugee.
Continuous line - train journey home after prison release
Michael Gherasim